# THE CD ROCK & ROLL LIBRARY

30 Years of Rock & Roll
on Compact Disc

# THE CD ROCK & ROLL LIBRARY

## 30 Years of Rock & Roll on Compact Disc
By Bill Shapiro

Andrews and McMeel

A Universal Press Syndicate Company, Kansas City/New York

Library of Congress Cataloging-in-Publication Data

Shapiro, Bill.
   The CD rock & roll library: thirty years of rock & roll on
compact disc / by Bill Shapiro.
        p.      cm.
   Bibliography: p.
   Includes index.
   ISBN 0-8362-7947-6: $8.95
   1. Rock music—Discography.  2. Compact discs—Reviews.
I. Title. II. Title: CD rock and roll library.
ML156.4.R6S4    1988
016.7899'12454—dc19                     88-6261
                                        CIP
                                        MN

ATTENTION: SCHOOLS AND BUSINESSES

TO CARIN AND TONY
WITH LOVE

Rock & roll is a stance, an attitude—more so than a discernible musical form. Born out of the great schism of youth from their elders that began in the fifties and flowered unrepentantly in the sixties, it has had a profound impact on the nature of our world for the last thirty-plus years.

# CONTENTS

# INTRODUCTION

Obviously, there are no specific standards by which any art can be defined. Yet, I've often marveled at the fact that critics rarely provide defined criteria against which their conclusions can be measured. Perhaps this is because their readers take it as a given that criticism is ultimately wholly subjective. But it seems to me that readers deserve a bit more than that, if it can be provided.

The word "art" represents about as complex an abstraction as the human mind can perceive. For me, art is that which illuminates, that which enlarges my perception of the reality I know. Rock & roll has met that criterion in my life since Saturday, January 28, 1956, when I first saw and heard Elvis Presley on the Dorsey Brothers TV "Stage Show." For me, that moment still retains the etched vividness of defined time and space that the sixties' survivors all hold for that terrible moment when they heard that JFK was shot.

I like what to me sounds real—true—honest. I am keenly aware that rock & roll is the ultimate musical synthesis: Contained in its raucous joy are gospel, blues, R&B, country, western swing, reggae, afro, pop, folk, classical, funk, and experimental strains and influences. Yet I respond very poorly to that which appears derivative and lacking in originality of thought or feeling.

If you are a fan of heavy metal, Neil Diamond, the Doobie Brothers, Billy Joel, Steely Dan, or countless other "popular" artists, you might want to check out the willingness of your friendly bookseller to give you a refund. Like any fan, I have my own particular heroes and villains, and if an artist's work is omitted, I'm either ignorant of it or my dislike for the work is so great that I felt incapable of writing a "fair" review.

Finally, I think it's important in writing subjective opinions about the quality of sound that the reader be informed of the components on which that quality is judged. I have been a reader of record reviews for over thirty years and rarely, if ever, have I known whether the opinions on sound quality that I was reading were based upon the music coming from a standard issued Delco car radio or a quality component stereo system.

I have been an avid pop music fan since the mid-1940s, cutting my teeth on such classics as "Mairzy Doats" and, building my first "high fidelity" system from a mail-order Heath Kit in the mid-1950s (it didn't work until administered to by the local electronic repair shop). Over the years, my passions for both the music and its reproduction have grown correspondingly. Thus, as the years have added to the number of selections in my personal musical library, so have they added to the quality of the components by which I reproduce them. This is the system on which all discs covered in this volume were auditioned.

| | |
|---|---|
| CD Player | Accuphase DP-80 (player) |
| | Accuphase DC-81 (processor) |
| Pre-Amp | Mark Levinson ML7 |
| Amplifier | Mark Levinson ML3 |
| Speakers | Martin Logan Monoliths (full range electrostats with built in crossover and cone base) |

# THE CD ROCK & ROLL LIBRARY

30 Years of Rock & Roll
on Compact Disc

# THE
# MUSIC

The one cultural beachhead that the youth rebellion of the sixties took, and held, was in the realm of pop music. Before the onslaught of rock & roll, popular music was just another "adults only" province of what has come to be called popular culture.

The rock music that became the soundtrack for the madly turbulent sixties had its roots in the early/mid-fifties. It was then that the unlikely progenitors of the "devil's music" first stalked the AM airways, mounting a populist wave of rebellion against a staid, but ripe, society. A gay black dishwasher from Macon, Georgia; an enigmatic black hairdresser with a criminal record from St. Louis; and a white truck driver from Tupelo, Mississippi, who oozed defiance from every beautiful pore, merged the energy of hard-assed Saturday nights with the fervor of Gospel Sunday mornings to create the most exuberant art form of the century.

It is important to remember that before the world had heard the sounds of Little Richard, Chuck Berry, and Elvis, the pop music that emanated from the car radios and jukeboxes of post-war America was, for the most part, written by one or often two individuals (composer and lyricist) and performed by a totally unrelated singer or group. Thus, in the late forties and fifties it was not uncommon to have more than a dozen recordings of the same hit song covered by a dozen different artists. This music, which was primarily created on Broadway and Tin Pan Alley, was performed by artists whose roots were, for the most part, in

1

the big bands that brought the swing era to America in the thirties and forties.

The true revolution of rock & roll was the merger of the creator and the performer into a single artistic entity.

With that merger, popular music became an art with as much cultural legitimacy as film, fiction, or any other form of musical or poetic expression. In the process rock & roll attracted some of the brightest, weirdest, and most creative minds of a highly precocious generation as their preferred medium for expression.

It is equally important to remember the spark that ignited it all. That was: first, foremost, and always, rebellion against the status quo—whatever it might be or become, from time to time. To this day, one of the major elements that separates the real thing from the pale corporate-controlled imitations that smother our commercial airways is how effectively a given recording or performance captures that primal spirit of rebellion. It is when the music feeds on, as well as passes on, its dark swamp spirit that it has the power to truly shape the moment. And what moments they can be! There can be few people under fifty in the Western world who cannot recall some vivid time in their lives that wasn't partly shaped by the music of Elvis, the Beatles, the Stones, or Dylan.

In retrospect, it's obvious that the original energy that propelled rock & roll into nearly universal popular acceptance in the fifties and sixties also spawned its most enduring moments. The punk rebellion of the seventies was founded on a sound respect for the original scripture—kick out the jams! But the punk's demise was clearly self-inflicted. The casualties that were sustained by the originators of the fifties and sixties were too often the result of wounds inflicted by the other side. While Jim Morrison's death may have been the inevitable end result of self-indulgence to the extreme, those of Janis and Jimi could be traced, in part, to their association with an outcast form of expression. The critical blows dealt to the careers of Jerry Lee Lewis and Phil Spector were the results of conspiratorial attempts from within and without the music community to suppress the influence of the big beat and all that it stood for.

Americans who became teenagers in the early to mid-fifties were exposed to a shattering, completely novel experience that Saturday night in January of 1956 when an unknown kid out of Memphis, with the unlikely name of Elvis Presley, thrust his youthful sexuality and obvious disregard for prevailing social conventions into millions of living rooms across the country. Not that Elvis was some spontaneously generated mutant. His intellectual forebears were the Beats, who were fomenting a similar, but literary, spirit of rebellion against the staid prosperity of a nation whose global might and apparent supremacy had been established a scant decade before. He had popular counterparts suggested in certain screen portrayals of James Dean and Marlon Brando. Yet Elvis was different—more immediate somehow, more directly personal. Perhaps it was because he was the first to violate the sanctity of the home itself, through what was to become the most incursive technological icon of the postwar world—the medium of television. But more probably it was his choice of audience that established his vital role as the prime progenitor of the youth rebellion that quite literally defined many of the mores of the next decade. Here was a teenager expressing heretofore suppressed feelings of adolescent frustration with all the energy of youth to an audience strictly composed of his peers. An audience that was just beginning to find its private arena and one that then failed to perceive that its arena would soon be the biggest venue around. That didn't come until some years later when it was dubbed the baby boom generation. It was the confluence of their vast numbers combined with a general affluence not previously the province of the young that forged the stage on which rock & roll found its gloriously profane voice.

The teenagers of the fifties failed to immediately sense the full implications of the primally compelling new sounds that crept through their radios into the record stores. Hell, it just sounded great. It would take a few more years before youth came to accept and revel in their new potent role. But the institutions of the establishment sensed the challenge immediately, instinctively. It was decried as the voice of the devil from pulpits across the land. It was censured in the press and intimidated by governmental agencies at all levels. It was also inevitable and unstoppable. How long could a nation that had just severely bled for world freedom countenance the burning of records and general suppression of individual expression?

The opposition, of course, still has its agenda. In the mid-eighties, some thirty-plus years after the fact, there were still those in the Washington establishment who would attempt to suppress the music in the name of patently unconstitutional censorship. That the youth rebellion marching to rock's compelling beat has failed to eradicate this muddy thinking from the common consciousness is sad, but not unexpected. That the energy of rock in the eighties has been so drained of its original intent that it has not risen up out of its own grooves to smite down this latest manifestation of institutionalized ignorance may be the closest thing yet encountered to its true epitaph.

But within its relatively brief life span, this sometimes violent, often moving, frequently genuinely creative art form has both formed and reflected much of our recent history.

As the times have changed, so has the music. Yet it remains the most popularly accepted of all the arts—the rock artist speaks to the largest, most impressionable of all audiences.

Today's rock critics accurately bemoan the fact that it's been more than thirty years since Elvis, and almost twenty-five since the Beatles, literally changed the world—or, at least its popular culture. In part, that is the result of the fact that the surviving founders and their surviving audience have both grown into middle age. In part, it is the natural outgrowth of rock's phenomenal commercial acceptance with resultant economic success and excess. And, in large part, it is the result of the overall homogenization of Western culture brought to us largely by the same medium that helped spawn Elvis—television.

In the fertile fifties and sixties much of the energy that nurtured the creativity manifest in the best of rock & roll came from the clash of cultures and the music indigenous to those cultures. The seventies and eighties have brought us the golden arches and shopping malls with their inherent message of standardization. While diminishing our differences they have drained our vitality. But perhaps all is not lost, if the line between black and white (R&B and pop) in America has become indistinct, then the music may well find renewed vitality in the juxtaposition of world cultures, as evidenced by Paul Simon's *Graceland* in 1986.

The flame still burns, perhaps with less heat and noise, but burn it does. Thirty-plus years after Elvis jolted the pulpits of America, his spiritual descendants rock for Amnesty International and Africa's starving millions. Rock & roll . . .

Within its best lyrics is the poetry of our time.

Within its rhythms are roots to the inexplicably mystical powers of true voodoo.

Within its music are the sounds of all music—the synthesis of all our joyous noise!

# THE
# TECHNOLOGY

The moment the recording process begins, when the sound is first captured by the microphone, it is changed from a "live" experience, and that change is changed again in myriad ways in each step of the recording and reproduction process. For that matter, even the "live" listening experience changes from room to room, row to row. Thus, any form of sound reproduction is exactly that—a technological effort to re-create in the listener's home or car what the ear perceives to be an accurate restatement of a variable original source.

While the eighties have failed to deliver a revolution in pop music similar to those which occurred in the 1950s and 1960s, a revolution has occurred in the technology that delivers the recorded rock product to its audience.

It is probably coincidental that the formative years of rock & roll (the early 1950s) coincided with technological advances in the recording medium when the 45 rpm single and 33 1/3 rpm LP both became consumer products. There can be little doubt that a factor in the reinvigoration of the form in the mid 1980s is very much attributable to the advent of the compact disc. As the recent years have brought a wave of rock nostalgia, the amplitude of that wave has been magnified by the development and phenomenal consumer acceptance of CDs as the preferred form of listening.

In 1984, the first full year in which CDs were marketed, their

5

U.S. gross sales at retail totaled $113.4 million; in 1986, those sales had grown to $630.7 million.

Because it is easier to market the known or familiar (and because the rock artists of the fifties, sixties, and seventies generally had less restrictive contracts with their labels), CDs have brought forth new compilations of the work of those earlier artists who established or substantially enhanced rock & roll. Thus, while one of the major objections to the new medium has been the high cost of discs, the problem is now rapidly moving toward extinction. Value line releases of older material, greater market competition, and larger volume sales are all working toward price reduction. And it has always been the case that some compilation discs (providing upwards of an hour of music) could give the music collector a comprehensive package of major work for a very fair cost. Stated more simply, in 1985, fifteen dollars would have purchased the CD *Buddy Holly From the Original Master Tapes,* with twenty selections—everything most Holly fans would have wanted in their music library. In addition, the Holly selections are presented in sound quality unheard of before—arguably better than the original.

While this book is primarily about the music, it is about the music as packaged for and heard from the compact disc.

Many advantages of the disc format are obvious and appropriately heralded by the manufacturers, but other attributes are less well known to the listening public. What follows are some of the well-publicized features that account for the amazingly rapid public acceptance of compact discs as the preferred form of listening:

1. **Permanence.** Unlike its fragile predecessor, the LP, the sound of a CD is not readily affected by handling, although care always makes sense. Pops, clicks, and scratches, the bane of any serious audiophile, for all intents and purposes, have been totally eliminated. In addition, the LP was an inherently perishable medium; i.e., the quality of sound reproduction diminished, albeit infinitesimally, with each repeated playing; whereas, in theory, a CD should sound exactly the same on the first and one-thousandth listenings.

2. **Facility.** Most CD players utilize an elementary computer chip to perform simple, but rewarding, tasks. Specifically, these machines allow the user to program the order of selection of cuts to be heard, eliminating the undesired

and programming the remainder in any sequence. (Some units even "remember" the user's program on a predetermined number of CDs.) In an age when the record industry would have us believe that the threat to the well-being of society—second only to nuclear demolition—is home taping, this facility represents a major step forward in that banned activity, not to mention generally enhanced listening.

3. **Enhanced Sound.** CDs provide a dramatically increased dynamic range in sound reproduction. This term, usually found in manufacturers' specifications, defines the difference between the intensity of the loudest and softest sounds on a recording. Because the sounds from an LP are the result of the tracings by a stylus of a V-shaped groove that varies in surface and width, it is necessary, when converting the "live" sound to LP sound, to reduce the intensity of the loudest passages and, correspondingly, to increase the intensity of the softest to meet the physical limitations of the stylus. Since loud or intense sounds require more stylus movement, thus wider grooves, at some point the width of one groove can become so great that its walls affect the adjacent grooves. Very quiet passages, on the other hand, require minimal stylus movement, and at some point the groove becomes too small for the stylus to trace, so the engineer brings up the loudness to traceable levels. The end result of all this messing around is that the degree of difference between the loudest and softest sounds perceived by the listener is substantially greater in live performance than it is coming from an LP. The CD essentially eliminates this problem because the tracks that carry the sound, concurrent with its inherent mechanical limitations, are also eliminated, being replaced by billions of bits of digital information conveyed in numerical form. Thus, the sound from the CD is more lifelike. This lifelike quality is further enhanced by the medium's elimination of actual contact between the source of the musical information and the device which converts it into hearable sounds. In a CD player, that information is transferred from disc to sound system by a beam of laser light. No surface contact with the information source totally eliminates any surface

noise—when there is no sound coming from the disc,
there is no sound coming from the stereo system and
when music is heard, that is all that is heard.

It is principally for these reasons that a CD player has represented to the component stereo buyer the most sound-efficient
investment available in the last several years. The $100 it takes
today to purchase a reasonable compact disc player will provide
the component buyer with more pop for his sound dollar than
any other similarly priced addition to a home stereo system. And
the market has responded accordingly, making CD players the
most successful product ever introduced by the home electronics industry.

But there are other, less apparent, reasons why compact discs
have so rapidly caught the fancy of the listening audience. These
less obvious, but equally appealing attributes, arise out of the
nature of the actual technology utilized.

To understand that technology, think of a photograph, highly
magnified so that its component parts are visible to the naked
eye. As the magnification becomes greater, ultimately all that the
eye sees are series of dots of different intensity of light or dark.
Those dots are the representative expression of an instant of
light in time captured on photographic film, generally 1/60th to
1/125th of a second in duration. Now imagine, if you will, a
picture of sound taken at an interval of 1/44,000th of a second.
That is precisely the basis for compact disc technology. A computer bisects each second of a musical sound into 44,000 infini-
tesimal slices and makes a picture of each slice which is
recorded not in dots (like the photograph), but in a numerical
equation expressed in the binary language of computers. In
other words, each of the sound photographs is expressed as a
highly complex incredibly lengthy mathematical formula. The
amount of numerical information on a seventy-minute compact
disc, if converted to printed text, would produce 270,000 pages.
Thus, each compact disc is nothing more than a package of formulas handed to the disc player that turns those formulas into
44,000 sound pictures which are reproduced in the speakers
each second. Just as the eye blends the individual dots of a photograph to see a cohesive whole, so the ear blends these multiple
pictures into a continuous sound of music.

Since the information medium is a numeric formula, it is

totally variable. This is a key element in the unique quality of CD recorded sound that is sometimes overlooked by the public. The infinite variability of the numbers in the equation translates into total malleability in the nature of the sound which these equations describe. Therefore, a talented engineer working from strong basic equations (a first-quality original sound source) supported by a record company willing to spend the money for experimentation can quite literally produce a compact disc which sounds better than the original recording made one or more decades ago by simply manipulating the "numbers" in the formula.

To return to the analogy between a sound "picture" and a photograph, the digital mixing engineer is, in many ways, the equivalent of the photo lab technician who employs manipulative printing processes like "cropping," "dodging," or "burning in" to reframe the picture and heighten or lessen contrast, all intended to produce a final image with more impact that what was originally recorded on the film.

Unfortunately, not all discs are created equal, and not all engineers have the ears or financial support necessary to consistently provide top-quality conversion of original material into the digital format. One of the goals of this book is to provide a guide to some of the true gems that are to be found in the early catalog of compact disc releases and also to alert you to some of the real bummers that lurk out there.

Inevitably, this totally new concept in sound reproduction has bred misconceptions.

One is that "all CD players sound the same." At first glance, a theoretical argument can be made to support this invalid claim. After all, if we're talking about a device which simply reads numbers, then shouldn't all the answers come out the same and, thus, all the sounds be the same? If that were the whole story, then the claim would be true. However, just as in the recording process the engineer must convert the audio or sound information into numbers, so in the receiving process the CD player must convert those numbers back into sounds.

The methods and theories for dealing with this second conversion are as varied as the myriad minds that propel this technological era. Different engineering theories and different electronic components play a critically discernible role in the quality of sound reproduction. This is best evidenced by the fact that in the audio market of 1988, the consumer is faced with a selection of CD players which vary in price from under $100 to $8,000.

A second misconception which seems popular among both the media and the general public is that the technology that has brought us the compact discs will be rapidly outmoded by the next generation of electronic creativity. This is a questionable premise. The compact disc player represents the leading edge of today's technology applied to the reproduction of recorded sound. Its predecessor, the LP, provided the most cost-efficient form of home entertainment for over three-and-a-half decades. At the time of this writing, it is reasonable to assume that the LPs successor in the eighties will provide a listening life of substantial duration.

The final common misconception is that digital tape recordings (R-DAT) will replace CDs as the prevalent eighties musical reproduction technology. While this technology is commercially available outside the U.S., the American recording industry is seeking legislation to limit its utility, by requiring that R-DAT players sold in this country be hobbled by required electronics which will prevent direct digital taping from CDs. Thus, if the industry has its way, R-DAT will only provide digital recording from analog (LP, radio, or cassette) sources, thereby eliminating its greatest potential attribute—the ability of the home recordist to make up to two hours of a "perfect" digital reproduction of favorite CD material programmed solely to the recordist's discretion.

We may hope Congress will not succumb to the pressure to stupidly legislate against technological advance, but who knows what Washington will do next in any arena? If Congress succumbs, then the spirit of capitalism and the rampant wizardry of the computer era will surely lead to a new age of illegal "black boxes" which, for a price, will allow the music fan to express his or her derision for illogical legislative action by bypassing the restrictive circuitry to allow CD to R-DAT copies.

It seems painfully obvious and historically inevitable that the two technologies are complementary and should be allowed to coexist in the market without artificially legislated limitations. If that happens, then CDs will not disappear, but prosper. If it doesn't, then the economic future of the R-DAT, not the CD, is what will be jeopardized.

In reality, the disc is wonderfully designed to accommodate its users. Its portability makes it accessible to the "walkperson," and it has already made a strong inroad into the automobile audio market.

On average, in 75 percent to 80 percent of the conversions, the CD version of a recording is sonically superior to its LP or tape version, with the percentage being higher in the case of most newer material and lower in the case of original recordings made in the fifties and sixties. But when the sound engineering on a disc is right, the LP and cassette simply aren't in the same league. Unfortunately, particularly with older material, often the original sound source or the ear or competency of the person making the digital conversion is too limited to result in a disc that justifies its purchase price. In other instances, the digital remix may contain excessive tape hiss, muddy the mix, or overly emphasize the upper midrange to the point of harshness; not to mention pure audio glitches like drop out or shifting imaging, any one of which can result in a product inferior to its vinyl predecessor.

But the bottom line is that when the new medium's sonic benefits are maximized, digital has the clearly demonstrable ability to add a whole new vitality, an enhanced "lifelikeness," that establishes CDs as the preferred form of listening for those who seek the best form of sound reproduction.

# THE
# RATINGS

Because CDs represent a relatively new technology that, like all new audio technologies, was commercially midwifed by the audiophile community, many of the regular reviewers provide a dual rating approach; one for sound and a second for musical content. While the reviews that follow reference both attributes of the material, the discs are each assigned a single rating which considers both attributes. Thus, an "A"-rated CD is one which combines first-rate musical content with high-quality sound reproduction while a "D"-rated disc might contain quality music mutilated by poor sound quality or vice-versa. The ratings appear in bold face following the technical data listed for each disc reviewed. The ratings used are:

A— An essential recording
B— Generally first-rate material, perhaps less than ideally
    reproduced or containing a little too much filler
C— OK, but little of sustaining value
D— Either the engineer or the artist (or both) managed to
    screw things up
F— Unforgivable

It might also be noted that the reviews that follow are covered chronologically based upon the recording date of the material, rather than the date of issuance of the original recording or the

CD; e.g., Ray Charles, *Live* was released on LP in 1973, the CD in 1987; but the material was recorded at concerts in 1958, thus the disc is reviewed in the section on the fifties.

When an artist's career spans multiple decades, biographical information is included in the artist listing in the first decade in which his or her work was recorded; but reviews of specific recordings are included in the decade in which each recording was made or released. If all of this is simply too confusing, there is a listing of all CDs reviewed, alphabetically by artist, referencing all pages where the artist's work is specifically reviewed. This listing follows the section on the eighties.

# THE
# FIFTIES

". . . . Beware of change to a strange
form of music."

—Socrates

In a very real, physical sense, the war that this nation fought during the first half of the 1940s impacted upon Americans in ways that the electronic reproduction of the war this nation fought in the sixties simply could not replicate. The lives of the country's youth in the forties were directly affected by food and gas rationing and by the fact that Detroit was making no new automobiles. The lifestyle of this generation was partially measured by periodic paper and scrap drives generally conducted on school yards anchored by red, white, and blue grease boxes where drippings from Mom's kitchen were salvaged in tin cans to be returned to Uncle Sam for some sinister but, obviously, patriotic effort.

America's backyards were partitioned into victory gardens, where urban kids learned the tasks of weeding and harvesting and the satisfaction of fresh, hand-picked produce.

All across the nation, the young saw their fathers and brothers don uniforms and disappear to places far away, while their mothers left the primacy of home to fill the void in the work force created by Dad's departure. Thus, teenage self-involvement placed a distant second to the war that was pervasive. These were the children who first heard the words "Hiroshima" and "Nagasaki;" who first faced the inexplicable horror of the Bomb.

The fathers and brothers, some of them anyway, returned home around 1945; more sophisticated and anxious to build homes and raise families in the world to which they had given so dearly to make free. The products of these desires began to come of age in the mid-to-late 1950s and with them came the glorious roar of rock & roll.

The energy behind that roar was tindered by the friction inherent in the juxtaposition of divergent cultures within the boundaries of a "single" society. While America's black and white children, particularly in the South, generally attended separate schools (serving separate neighborhoods), their very separate forms of popular music could be heard on radio or record by anyone adventurous enough to simply "change the station."

From the blues to rhythm and blues, it was a relatively small step to rock & roll.

Because of the diversity of the music's "founding fathers" and pervasiveness of their varying influences, the exact moment of the birth of the music and place of its creation are impossible to specify. This much is clear: its home territory is the American South, historically, this country's richest cultural region, where the voodoo-rooted musical expressions of a black population hummed through tepid nights. It is also equally obvious that this was, at least initially, the music of the "have-nots" of America's polyglot society.

If one must seek a starting point, probably the Sun Studio in Memphis, Tennessee, in 1955 is as likely a candidate as any. It was here that Sam Phillips, one of many independent record producers operating outside pop music's bicoastal "establishment," supposedly tracked his legendary Bigfoot—a white man who could sing like a black. Phillips had been perceptive enough to realize that white kids, at least in the South, were naturally drawn to the rhythm and power inherent in black music—music which still belonged "at the back of the bus" as far as the mainstream white pop music industry was concerned. Known then as race music, it was separately charted by the trade press and was as alien to "The Hit Parade" as blacks in a Mississippi voting booth.

Of course, Phillips found his man or, if legends are true, Elvis Presley found Sam Phillips. And, in Elvis, Phillips found much more than just a white man who could sing like a black, he found a charismatic performer possessed of the style of youthful rebellion, gently interwoven with the straitlaced principles then common to white God-fearing southern youth.

For America's teenagers in the mid-fifties, Elvis Aaron Presley personified all that was unspoken and unspeakable between the worlds of youth and adult. He was the incarnation of the youth revolution, the barbarian to vault the barricades. In all probability, of the many attributes uniquely possessed by Presley which enabled him to ascend to the throne of rock & roll, the one that probably served him best was his unique sense of his time and place in American history. He not only saw the brass ring and grabbed it the first time around; he seemed to be totally aware of the act while it was taking place.

The rock critic, Greil Marcus, has said that with the exception of Presley's earliest "Sun sides" and perhaps the live footage done before an audience for the 1968 TV special, Presley always had the ability to stand outside of himself and not get caught up in the hysteria which he spawned. This attribute alone probably kept him sane for as long as he was able to manage survival in the absurd role in which he cast himself.

In retrospect, it is easy to see that Presley established many of the music's original attributes. The original Presley group, selected by Phillips and made up of Scottie Moore on guitar and Bill Black on bass (later augmented by drummer D.J. Fontana), laid down the basic rock or rockabilly sound that remains the authentic underpinning of much of what is still produced in the name of rock & roll today. Elvis also introduced rock & roll to the first visible specter of commerce, in the somewhat sinister form of former carny barker Colonel Tom Parker. The vast commercial potential of this pure teen product was first intuited and then exploited by this shadowy showman. It would only take five years or so before the full commercial potential of the music exploded with an impact not even Parker could have foreseen. It would only take another five to ten years before rock's commercial aspects became preeminent much to the detriment of the product itself.

But mostly, Presley brought the attitude—an attitude of rebellion combined with the belief that one could make music for an audience of youth and prosper in a world of adults.

As Marcus also aptly pointed out, perhaps the most intriguing and disturbing aspect of the phenomenon that was Elvis Presley is that he was the truest personification of the American dream. Born in nearly abject poverty, Presley achieved fame and fortune unprecedented in the history of pop culture. Yet, it all ended so badly. On August 16, 1977, the King died bloated, a sad personification of the "stature" to which his creation had fallen.

During those formative years, when Elvis was claiming his kingdom, there were others who defined the original parameters of the realm.

Chuck Berry survives to this day, a habitué of occasional oldies forays on television and a charter member of the 1980s' Rock & Roll Hall of Fame. If any single individual can validly be credited with being the architect of the musical form that expressed the voice of youth in the fifties and the decades to follow, that man is Chuck Berry. As a writer/performer, he was among the first, if not *the* first, to direct his lyrical messages specifically to the teenage audience. And, oh, what lyrics. More than one rock critic has compared the verse contained in Berry's lyrics to that of perhaps America's greatest poet, Walt Whitman, a comparison that can withstand scrutiny. To these words he added a vocabulary of basic rhythm guitar licks which loudly echo through the music to this very day and established the electric guitar as the music's primary musical voice. He combined all this with duck-walking showmanship that defined the rock musician's stage persona.

Perhaps the aspect of Berry's impact which is most impressive is that he popularized and established the role of the rock star as both creator and performer. Rock & roll thus became a medium of total expression, the performer/writer providing his or her audience with potentially a very singular and unique vision. True, this tradition is readily traceable to folk music; and, in a very real sense, rock & roll is the electronically amplified folk music of the technological age.

The concept of totality of individual expression in the rock format was greatly advanced by another of the fifties pioneers, Buddy Holly. Holly's fleetingly brief recording career left an indelible mark on what followed. Buddy took the idea of total artistic creativity further than any of his predecessors in that he realized that the recording process was as integral to the creative act as the writing or the playing. By his nerdy appearance he further proclaimed the everyman roots of the rock star; and, through his tours of Britain, spread those roots to where they would flower in the next decade.

And then, there was Little Richard!!!! The man who codified the music's first password: "awopbopaloobopawopbamboom."

Little Richard's music was the truest generational litmus test, i.e., one's reaction to his recordings quickly established which side the listener was on. More clearly than anyone else, Little Richard enunciated a basic truth of rock & roll—if the parents can't stand it, the kids are definitely going to buy it.

One of the elements which sets rock above mere aural wallpaper and makes the best of it sustain is its concern with the eternal confrontation between the forces of darkness and light. The voodoo power of the music's sound finds its heart in this conflict, as did much of the original (and continuing) reaction of society. The personification of this conflict survives in the form of "The Killer," Jerry Lee Lewis, the spirit of rock & roll incarnate. Lewis was called by his producer at Sun Studios the greatest natural talent he had ever seen. His life and career pulse with the energy that still fuels the best of the music.

Rock was more than a change in the sound of music; it was the first truly populist call to a change in the values of the listening society. It was rebellion pure and simple. As with all rebellions, the establishment rose up to resist it, and not without success. The Army took Elvis, the press took care of Jerry Lee, the penitentiary took Chuck Berry; and the church got Little Richard.

# THE FIFTIES
## on Compact Disc

"A white man, with black hips."
*New York Times*

## Hank Ballard

b. November 18, 1936—Detroit
Ballard, a Johnny Otis discovery, joined the vocal group the Midnighters as lead voice producing what has been referred to by some as "the first Motown sound." They garnered six Top Ten R&B hits between 1954 and 1956 and scored two pop hits with "Finger Popping Time" and "Let's Go, Let's Go, Let's Go" both in 1960. The Midnighters were originally known as the Royals and included in their first line-up Levi Stubbs (who ultimately gained fame with the Four Tops). Ballard scored his biggest success in 1954 by employing sexually explicit lyrics over a raw, traditional based gospel music ("Work With Me Annie").

### What You Get When the Gettin's Good

C.D. Charly 29 (41:42)    [C + ]
The sixteen selections on this disc cover most of the group's better known efforts and provide a good overview of the mid-fifties' black pop sound that attracted white listeners, opening the door to rock & roll. The sound quality varies all over the place, and some of it is pretty bad; but given the age of the masters, none of this is unexpected. You purchase this disc for its historical value and some good, but dated, party music, but it isn't one you're going to use to show off your CD player. Ballard, by the way, is the guy who wrote "The Twist," but it was Chubby Checker who scored with that song.

## Chuck Berry (Charles Edward Anderson)

b. October 18, 1926—St. Louis
In July of 1955, "Maybellene" took to the roads of America on car radios across the land and Berry, who at the time was trying to determine whether his career should be in hairdressing, photography, or music, found the light! Chuck had the audacity to identify and write for a youthful white audience, and to be embraced by that audience. For this mid-fifties heresy he paid his dues in a federal penitentiary (more than once). Aptly described by more than one critic as the Walt Whitman of rock & roll, this is the one pioneer whose contributions to the musical form simply cannot be overrated.

## Greatest Hits C.D.

Chess 21 (56:47)     **[A]**

In many senses, this is the original testament of rock & roll. Almost all the essential cuts are included among its twenty-three selections; unfortunately, the quality of the sound reproduced does not begin to equal the quality of the material which gives rise to that sound. But then, the audio fidelity of the 45s on which this material was originally released, was nothing to write home about either. Let's face it, the Chess Brothers who first gave Chuck studio time were just trying to make a buck, not history. As is often the case with compilation collections, the sound varies from recording to recording depending upon which sessions happened to produce each of these classics. While many of the selections are far from clean, let alone dynamically enhanced, the recording is generally clear and provides almost an hour of classic Berry on compact disc which makes it a must (just don't discard your old 45s or 33s).

## Rock'N'Roll Rarities

Chess CHD 92521 JVC-473 (52:00)     **[A–]**

The sound quality on this disc is generally better than on the above-referenced *Greatest Hits* recording. It provides a wonderful supplement to that disc, including alternate takes on some of the classic material ("Sweet Little Sixteen," "Little Queenie," and "Johnny B. Goode") which stand in quality with the original releases included on the *Greatest Hits* collection. In addition, this CD covers numerous "lesser," but nonetheless wonderful, selections in the Berry repertoire, e.g., the Christmas classic, "Run Rudolph Run."

## More Rock'N'Roll Rarities
## (From the Golden Era of Chess Records)

Chess MCA CHD-9190 (30:56)     **[B]**

These twelve cuts (recorded between 1956 and 1965) are mostly alternate takes of better known material, "Brown-eyed Handsome Man," stereo remixes, "I'm Talking About You," or demo recordings, "Sweet Little Sixteen." Since Berry's music is simplicity itself, these selections don't sound that different

from the more established versions, except that they lack that certain "finish" and spark which make Chuck's classic two-minute rock singles truly timeless. Berry's stature is such that there is legitimate interest in any recorded material available, but this is one for those whose interest goes beyond the casual—this is pretty esoterically primitive stuff. The sound is equivalent to a clean 78 (if you can imagine such a thing); respectable, but not particularly special and the liner notes are minimally factual.

## Two Dozen Berrys

Vogue VG 651 6000085 (60:07)     **[B + ]**

This French import provides the best sound quality of any of the CD collections currently available of Berry's work. Included are some interesting offbeat cuts as well as "other" or cover versions of some of the classic material. Certainly a valid addition to the library of anyone who seeks comprehensive coverage on this founding father; but the lesser musical quality of much of the material prevents it from being a first-rate offering.

## 20 Greatest Hits

Spectrum Stereo Speck 85004 (52:51)     **[F]**

God only knows where the "masters" for this French import came from, but it's a shame they were ever found. A rip-off.

## The Great 28

MCA CHD92500 (69:58)     **[A + ]**

Musically probably the best and most comprehensive of the Chuck Berry Chess collections. The sound quality varies substantially from cut to cut. Some of the better known material is pretty weak sonically. But on the whole, and once again considering the age of the masters, it's the best reproduction you're going to hear. Among the several Chuck Berry collections available in CD, this is the first choice. The breadth of the collection also provides insights into Berry's blues roots.

# James Brown

b. May 3, 1928—Macon, Georgia

Born into true southern black poverty of the Depression era, Brown literally picked cotton, danced in the streets, and eventually stole to survive in a less than hospitable world. His thefts resulted in his incarceration for three years; and, upon release, Brown tried his hand at prizefighting and baseball before returning to his gospel church roots with a group originally known as the Sewanees, which James rapidly converted into the Famous Blue Flames. He remains the single preeminent figure in black popular music of the last thirty years, the inventor of funk, the predecessor of rap, the godfather of soul.

**The CD Of JB**
**(Sex Machine and Other Soul Classics)**
Polydor 825714-2 (56:09)    **[A + ]**
These eighteen selections cover "Soul Brother No. 1's" pop output from his original "Please, Please, Please" to his mid-sixties hits. The sound quality is simply wonderful, making this historic collection of the roots of funk a must disc in any comprehensive collection of American popular music of the last thirty years.

# Ray Charles
# (Ray Charles Robinson)

b. September 23, 1930—Albany, Georgia

Ray, who has been blind since the age of six and who suffered the often traditional impoverished youth of many southern blacks of his generation, has been accurately called the creator of soul music. His combination of gospel forms with popular lyrics tinged with elements of jazz and blues was seminal in the formation of modern black popular music.

**Ray Charles Live**
Atlantic 781732-2 (72:02)    **[B–]**
A fascinating set of recordings particularly considering their 1958 vintage—Ray is a musical sponge, equally at home with jazz, R&B, soul, and gospel sounds. These record-

ings cover some of those divergent elements and illustrate how "The Genius" bound them all together to create soul music, God bless him! Unfortunately, these were live recordings done thirty years ago and while instrumentally the CD is an overall enhancement, on Ray's vocal mike, distortion reigns sadly supreme; and, as we all know, that's where it's at. Nonetheless, the driving, pulsing rhythmic energy behind these cuts still comes through, loud and clear.

# Eddie Cochran

b. October 3, 1938—Albert Lea, Minnesota
d. April 17, 1960

**The Best Of . . .**
EMI America CDP7 46580 2 (31:53)    **[B + ]**
Cochran possessed the true fever of rock & roll, but a blowout on a British road in 1960 brought an untimely end to a rockabilly career that had commenced three years earlier with "Sittin' in the Balcony." For those few years, Cochran's guitar burned and his raw voice howled. The sound on this musically comprehensive disc is bright and generally impressive, if a bit edgy in the upper midrange.

# Sam Cooke

b. January 22, 1935—Chicago
d. December 11, 1964

Like many of the great black soul and R&B singers of the 1950s and 1960s, Cooke's career began singing gospel in the black church (in his case, his father's). This is a man who was born to sing. He always made it sound so easy, so smooth, and, oh, so very sweet. While his roots and appeal were clearly established in the world of gospel, with the Soul Stirrers, his ultimate message proved to be more glandular than godly. Like another fifties giant, Jerry Lee Lewis, Cooke clearly embodied the essential rock/life conflict of good v. evil, but Sam carried it off with more style, right to the very end.

### Sam Cooke The Man and His Music
RCA PCD1-7127 (70:06)    [A + ]

A comprehensive twenty-eight song collection, most of which are outstanding, that runs the gamut from commercial pop to gospel fervor, and through it all soars one of the great pop voices ever heard. The sound quality varies, as expected, but overall, a vast improvement over any other recordings of this classic work. (As is the case with much of the RCA material covering fifties artists released on compact discs, the name Gregg Geller is reflected as A&R director. Geller, who has unfortunately left RCA, has been a major contributor to the disc recompilations of RCA's classic rock material, making an invaluable contribution to the recorded library of this roots music. Generally speaking, Geller's name reflected on a RCA pop disc is a good indication of quality material.)

### Gospel in My Soul
Suite Beat Records SBCD2011 (31:22)    [F]

This is gospel conceived and produced as bleached fifties pop songs. If that's not bad enough, the cover portrait and title notwithstanding, Cooke sings only on four of the twelve cuts included. The sound quality is as bad as the rest of it. (It does have some fine R.H. Harris true gospel efforts, but they aren't that good.)

### Live at the Harlem Square Club, 1963 One Night Stand
RCA PCD15181 (37:33)    [B]

The sound on this disc, particularly the first half, is pretty bad; but as bad as it is, the music comes through and just won't let go. A marvelous "window" into the real sounds of fifties American soul music on hot southern Saturday nights. This is Cooke at his roots-raucous best.

# Bobby Darin (Walden Robert Cassotto)
b. May 14, 1936—Bronx, New York
d. December 20, 1973

Darin, whose recording career commenced in 1958, represents a rather unique hybrid of pop/rock artist. While his major milieu really fell into the realm of popular, Broadway/Las Vegas music, his work was tinged with a freneticism that related to the essence of rock & roll.

### The Ultimate Bobby Darin
Warner Special Products 9-27606-2 (42:52)    [C + ]

The seventeen selections on this disc contain all of Darin's classic material: "Splish Splash," "Dream Lover," "Mack the Knife," "Bill Bailey," and "Beyond the Sea." It is a comprehensive package; however, its quality is diminished by the digital reproduction which, while generally clean, tends to be thin and often harsh in the vocals.

# Bo Diddley (Ellas Bates)
b. December 30, 1928—McComb, Mississippi

At an early age, Bo moved with his family from Mississippi to Chicago; there he picked up the nickname which he has made famous, originally using it as an amateur boxer. The proximity to the blues-saturated sounds of Chicago moved young Diddley to music, and the result was a grafting of a very personal syncopated form of rhythm on a basic blues form resulting in the "Bo Diddley beat" that echoes through rock to this very day. Irreverent, irrepressible, and underappreciated, Bo Diddley continues to embody the spirit of the music.

### Go Bo Diddley (Two On One)
MCA CHD5904 (63:54)    [B + ]

This disc covers Diddley's '55 through '58 recordings and, for the most part, crackles with the energy common to the fundamental releases that rocked 1955 into musical history as the year that the pop music world was turned upside down by the first insolent roar of rock & roll. His musical inventiveness (check out "The Clock Struck 12" or "Bo's Guitar") and eclecticism (marked by the use of unique instrumentation in the rock/blues form) is often overlooked as is the fact that he studied classical violin for twelve years. The sound quality of this recording, particularly on the first of the two first records included, is pretty awful, marred by distorted vocals and a non-existent bottom. But the second album on the disc is vastly superior and the music's compelling rhythm retains its attraction after thirty years.

## Dion (Dion DiMucci)

b. July 18, 1939—Bronx, New York
One of the great, multi-hit, white doowop groups of the late fifties, Dion and the Belmontes (named after Belmonte Avenue in the neighborhood where they were born), created an interesting blend of pop standards combined with driving rock originals that endure to this day.

**Dion and the Belmontes**
**Dion and Dion and the Belmontes**
Ace CDCH176 (46:01)      [B + ]
From saccharine fifties Hit Parade to white-power doowop, this disc provides late fifties sounds in a digital mix that should knock your ears off. There's some pretty wretched stuff here, but there are also some pure gems: "A Teenager in Love," "Run Around Sue," "The Wanderer," and "Lovers Who Wander."

## Fats Domino (Antoine Domino)

b. February 26, 1928—New Orleans
The self-anointed "Fat Man" was the artist who brought the New Orleans barrelhouse (i.e., boogie whorehouse piano) tradition into the pop mainstream and became a one-man musical industry in the process with hits like "Ain't That a Shame," "I'm Walkin'," and "Blueberry Hill."

**The Best of Fats Domino**
EMI America CDP7 465812 (32:39)     [B + ]
The first of many New Orleans-based rockers who drew upon a musical tradition uniquely rich among American cities. The essential element of the New Orleans sound, as it has evolved with rock & roll for the past three decades, has been its good time, party-down quality which the Fat Man pioneered nationally. The sound quality here, while generally good, is certainly flawed on occasion and varies appreciably from cut to cut; but all the early hits are included which means that the party is still going strong.

## The Everly Brothers

Don Everly, b. February 1, 1937—Brownie, Kentucky; Phil Everly, b. January 19, 1939, Chicago
The children of well-established country music artists Ike and Margaret Everly, Don and Phil brought country harmony, enhanced by their blood-relationship, to the formative years of rock & roll. It was their melodic contribution and truly gorgeous harmonies that distinguished and established this singing duo, who, after a long and sometimes troubled career, have come back in the 1980s with a renewed capacity to lend their special brand of singing to the world of rock & roll.

**Cadence Classics (Their 20 Greatest Hits)**
Rhino RNCD5258 (45:57)     [A]
Aptly titled, this is classic fifties rock by the Brothers Everly and that means that most of the selections included here will be familiar to any listener over the age of fifteen. Rhino, and its extraordinary digital producer, Bill Inglot, generally does a first-rate job with conversion from analog to digital material. This is no exception, providing bright, clean, and clear sound.

# Bill Haley and The Comets

This group formed about 1950, ultimately attained a stature in the pantheon of rock & roll not so much predicated on talent or musical contribution, but rather on the fortuitous fact that their work was chosen as the first rock movie soundtrack in a non-musical.

### Bill Haley and His Comets—From the Original Master Tapes

MCA MCAD5539 DIDX 202 (52:33)     **[B–]**
It may be cocktail rock, but since it was the soundtrack to *Blackboard Jungle* (one of the first "serious" movies about and aimed at the fifties youth audience), that's about all it took when the alternative was Mitch Miller. The CD is a sonic marvel—the stuff simply never sounded better.

# Buddy Holly (Charles Hardin Holley)

b. September 7, 1936—Lubbock, Texas
d. February 3, 1959
A major, often underrated influence, Holly initiated a number of what have become rock's fundamental traditions.

### From the Original Master Tapes

MCA MCAD5540 DIDX-203 (44:00)     **[A +]**
The musical reasons for Holly's somewhat subtle but pervasive influence are all here, h the original energy maintained intact. Due to the brevity of his career, this single disc can truly provide a comprehensive overview of his major contributions to rock's formative years. Sound-wise, this may represent the zenith of digital enhancement of older recordings. Clear, spacious, complete sound that is nothing short of phenomenal.

### For the Last Time Anywhere

MCA MCAD-3D48 (21:22)     **[D +]**
The material was originally released on LP in 1983 as "Lost Masters." There really aren't any true revelations on this brief package, and the sound, while generally clear, is largely harsh and edgy. "Bo Diddley" sounds like it came from a used edition of a bad 78. This is an interesting, bargain-priced CD for the compulsive fan only, although "That's My Desire" is a lot of fun.

# Jerry Lee Lewis

b. September 29, 1935—Ferriday, Louisiana
If one were to seek the story of thirty years of rock & roll as personified in the life and style of one human being, Jerry Lee Lewis probably stands as the single primal incarnation of the form. (Nick Toshes has captured this fact beautifully in his marvelous biography of the artist, *Hellfire*.) In his prime, Lewis and a piano were the only ingredients really necessary to ignite the inferno of rock & roll any time, anywhere. Trapped in the conflict between the good as exemplified by his church history and the bad, as exemplified by the Devil's music he played so urgently, Jerry Lee continues to act out this conflict with a power and a passion that is elemental to the best of the form.

### 18 Sun Greatest Hits

Rhino 5255 (39:54)     **[C–]**
Definitely not up to Rhino's usual high standards for compilation discs of early rockers. Its eighteen selections include all the essentials covered in the disc *Ferriday Fireball* as well as some offbeat others, but the sound quality is nothing special, and the Ferriday compilation is clearly the better value.

### Ferriday Fireball

Sun CD Charlie 1 (60:03)     **[A]**
Twenty-five of the historic original Sun recordings which comprehensively cover Lewis's initial rock & roll days, before bad PR drove him to country audiences. In other words, it's all here. The sound is good, given the age of the masters, but the dynamic range of the work is not greatly enhanced by the digital transfer.

### The Greatest Hits Volume II

IMP (Pickwick) PCD 840 (45:56)     **[D]**
Mostly second-rate renditions of second-rate material afforded third-rate production.

# Little Richard
# (Richard Wayne Penniman)

b. December 5, 1932—Macon, Georgia
While Little Richard stands alone in the annals of rock & roll, his history is not uncommon to that of many blacks who came to the music in the early to mid-1950s. As the third of fourteen children, he found himself dancing in the streets of Macon for nickels and dimes at the age of seven and was the lead singer in his church choir before he was fourteen years of age. Before his career as a pop performer got under way, he was working at the Greyhound bus station in Macon washing dishes. While Richard's recorded output is not extensive, the sheer intensity, exuberance, and irreverence (not to mention perceived lack of taste) embodied in those few releases added a coloration to the music which continues to this day.

### 18 Greatest Hits

Rhino RNCD 75899 (42:21)     [A + ]
This was music guaranteed to piss off Mom and Dad as maniacally performed by the self-styled bronze Liberace—it still sounds great. Nasty songs sung in a wildly, primally orgasmic voice pulsating to the rhythms of New Orleans voodoo music. (And all this at a time when Cole Porter's lyrics to "Love for Sale" were essentially banned from radio air play in America, for God's sake!) The sound is clean and outstanding given the age of the masters. This is rock & roll, the real thing! This disc contains music that seethes with energy and screams with rebellion. These sounds have truly left an indelible mark on all rock music that has followed.

# Rick Nelson
# (Eric Hilliard Nelson)

b. May 8, 1940—New Jersey (raised Los Angeles)
d. December 31, 1985
Riding the exposure of the famous "Ozzie & Harriet Show" radio and TV series, Rick brought his brand of Hollywood rockabilly into many American homes in the fifties, where otherwise rock & roll would have been totally unwelcome. Working with premier musicians, particularly James Burton on lead guitar, Rick Nelson ultimately proved to be sincerely committed to the simple, basic form of rockabilly which he presented with integrity and appeal.

### The Best of Rick Nelson

EMI America CDP-7 46558 2 (34:30)     [B + ]
Most, but not all, of Nelson's hits are included among the fifteen selections comprising this brief disc. The sound quality, while generally clear and spacious, is weak and often muddy in the low end, and on certain cuts reproduction is far from ideal. But considering the technology available when these recordings were made, the digital enhancement is still apparent. James Burton's guitar work alone is worth the price of admission.

# Carl Perkins

b. April 9, 1932—Jackson, Tennessee
Another of the originators whose first sounds emanated from the Sun Studios in Memphis, Tennessee, Perkins's role would have been assured by virtue of the fact that he wrote the rock anthem of the 1950s, "Blue Suede Shoes." In addition to that achievement, Perkins remains an extraordinary guitarist and continuing exponent of pure rockabilly sounds, with the emphasis on the country aspect of that form.

### Dixie Fried

Sun CD Charly 2 (59:56)     [B + ]
All of the key original Sun recordings are included. The sound quality varies from cut to cut, and the overall dynamic range is expectedly limited; however, the general clarity and mix are good. The musical content of this disc is great, including the obvious popular hits as well as some lesser known true gems like the title cut.

# The Platters

Formed Los Angeles, 1953
Perhaps the premier doowop group of the fifties. During their heyday the Platters provided some of the smoothest, most listenable hits available on fifties radio.

### Greatest Hits

Atoll Music ATO 8604 (32:26)      [C + ]
The contents live up to the title, although the group certainly provided much more in the way of fine doowop listening than is included on this relatively brief offering. The sound quality is generally clean but does not really provide a great deal of dynamic enhancement.

# Elvis Presley

b. January 8, 1935—Tupelo, Mississippi
d. August 16, 1977
In terms of record sales, and more importantly, influence, Elvis Presley is simply the greatest pop artist of all time. Elvis was the incarnation of America itself, from its crass commercialism to its brash vitality as well as its gross self-indulgence—beautifully obscene, irresistibly potent, he articulated our roots, perhaps more honestly than we ever imagined. He was and is the king simply because he was the first to claim the kingdom. The true American original, the total realization of the American dream, he ascended to the throne because he wanted it badly enough. But at a hideous price. By the time he had attained legal majority, his celebrity had reached a level which set him totally outside everyone else's "real world."

### The Sun Sessions CD

RCA 6414 2 R (72:33)      [A + ]

### Elvis Presley

RCA PCD 1-5199 (28:40)      [A + ]

### Elvis

RCA PCD 1-5198 (30:23)      [A + ]
Dave Marsh stated it as well as it can be stated: "Suffice it to say that these records,

more than any others, contain the seeds of everything rock & roll was, has been, and most likely what it may forseeably become." The chemistry and exuberance on the Sun Sessions are uniquely compelling—if you listen closely, you can almost feel the energy that infused these historic recordings. Soundwise, while the string reproductions are stunning, the vocals are sometimes a shade harsh (and occasionally badly distorted) but, this stuff *was* recorded over thirty years ago.

Bottom line: all the primal elements of rock & roll are here, generally reproduced with a sonic clarity heretofore unknown, 'nuff said? On the two orignal RCA compilation discs (*Elvis* and *Elvis Presley*), Elvis conveys the amazing breadth of his musical vision, which was pervasive; he could sing it all and make it all uniquely his own in the process. By making the digital remixes from the original mono tapes and retaining that format, RCA has done a marvelous job of sound reproduction (particularly vocal nuances). The fact that the clarity reveals all the blemishes is hardly a problem!

### Elvis Golden Records

RCA PCD1-5196 (33:40)      [A]
They're all here, the early monster RCA hits (fourteen of them, including "Hound Dog," "Heartbreak Hotel," "Love Me," and "Don't Be Cruel") "restored" to their original mono formats before digital conversion. Thus, the sound, while sometimes uneven, is generally first-rate for material of this vintage.

### Reconsider Baby

RCA PCD15418 (38:11)      [A]
This is music made for the sake of music, not material tailored and produced to capitalize on the myth. The musicianship, production, and sound quality are sometimes rough, but this is the blues, the rock & roll blues performed by the man who began it all in the first place with a blues song, "That's All Right, Mama." The material ranges from the earliest Sun sessions to 1971 (his killer version of Charlie Brown's "Merry Christmas, Baby"). If you like roots—this is roots, muddy, raw, and wonderful.

# The Shirelles

Formed 1958—Passaic, New Jersey

### Anthology (1959-1964)

Rhino RNCD 75897 (40:10)    **[A]**
The late fifties through the early sixties was
the time of Phil Spector and the great "girl
group" sounds (the Crystals, Ronettes, etc.),
but the Shirelles may have started it all and
were probably the best of the bunch, the
"wall of sound" notwithstanding. In addition
to their abilities as vocalists, the Shirelles
wrote much of their own material and, in
1963, the Beatles covered a couple of their
songs, "Baby It's You" and "Boys" on their
first English album. This almost comprehensive package, another sonic gem by Bill
Inglot, combines fine music with wondrous
production values to deliver digital magic in
its truest form.

# The Skyliners

Formed late 1950s—Pittsburgh, Pennsylvania

### Greatest Hits

Original Sound Entertainment OSCD 8873
(47:24)    **[C]**
"Since I Don't Have You" by the Skyliners is
one of prerock pop's more compelling ballads, enhanced by very sophisticated production for the era. On the whole, this late fifties,
early sixties quintet made predictable but appealing music—if you know and love it, this
disc is a must; if it is uncharted territory, stay
clear and look for the bigger hits on comprehensive oldies collections particularly from
the Original Sound Entertainment label. The
digital mix employed by Original Sound on
all their releases is specially enhanced (fds)
which results in a clear dynamic sound, albeit
very slightly overbright and mechanical.

# John "Guitar" Watson

b. 1935—Houston

### I Heard That!

Charly CD Charly 48 (44:15)    **[B–]**
Watson's recordings began when he was eighteen, in 1953, and continued at least into the
mid-seventies. The sixteen cuts cover his
work from 1953 to 1963. These are the urban
electrified blues sounds that have found a
steady audience in America since the forties,
and provided a nurturing ground for both the
music and the musicians who are elemental
to rock & roll. Watson has been credited as an
early Hendrix influence. What's for sure is
that he writes some fun blues material,
"Gangster of Love" and "Cuttin' In," being
two included here, and performs it with tight
aplomb. The sound is very clean, but compressed; certainly far superior to vinyl
versions.

# FIFTIES
# COLLECTIONS

"It's not music, it's a disease."
—Mitch Miller on R&R

### Atlantic Rhythm & Blues

Other than Motown, which literally created the form of music it recorded and so effectively marketed, no other American record company was more closely associated with a major segment of American popular music than was Atlantic Records in the R&B field from the end of World War II to the early seventies. Each of the CDs in this series essentially covers a double volume LP that constituted a seven-volume landmark release by this company in 1985. I have reviewed four of the releases here.

### Atlantic Rhythm & Blues

47-74 Volume I; 47-52 Atlantic 781293-2
(73:27)     [B + ]
We're talking prehistoric roots material here, but up the tempo and electrify the instrumentation and it wouldn't sound alien to any true rock fan. As has to be expected with material of this vintage, the sound, while unexpectedly clean, certainly reflects its age in its limited dynamic range. If you're interested in where it all began, this is a large part of the story.

### Atlantic Rhythm & Blues

47-74 Volume II; 52-55 Atlantic 781294-2
(73:37)     [A]
Rarities and classics by the artists and groups who were dominating black pop music when it was serving as an inspiration to those who would explode the musical world with rock & roll. Contains first-rate works by giants like Joe Turner, Laverne Baker, Clyde McPhatter, and Ray Charles, among others. The sound is generally clean and clear, but obviously compressed.

### Atlantic Rhythm & Blues

47-74 Volume III; 55-58 Atlantic 781295-2
(71:27)     [A–]
Black musical history just pours out of these compact discs. Included are the Coasters' influential classics (the masterworks of Leiber and Stoller, two of rock's largely unsung writing and production pioneers), along with Chuck Willis who receives merited attention along with later works by artists whose earlier efforts are chronicled on the preceding volume of this essential series. As this series moves forward in time, so does the dynamic range on these well-produced vintage efforts.

## Atlantic Rhythm & Blues

47-74 Volume IV; 56-62 (71:25)     [A+]

With this volume, Atlantic enters its golden decade. This was the vintage era for groups like the Coasters, whose musical vignettes remain among the most enduring and influential sounds of the times; and the Drifters; and their smooth soul lead, Ben E. King (whose "Young Boy Blues" is one of the many highlights on this recording). The sound, which has a few noticeable glitches, generally is done with quality and ever-improving dynamic enhancement.

## Rhythm & Blues House Party

Ace CDCH 179 (44:20)     [B]

If you ever wondered why the young Jerry Lee Lewis and other wilder southern pre-rockers of the fifties spent their Saturday nights in the "off limits" black clubs on the wrong side of town, give this disc a spin. The sounds are a little rough and harsh, but the energy and message are clear—this ain't no sockhop.

## The Sun Story

Rhino RNCD75884 (47:29)     [A+]

Combine the Sun Studios' soundtrack of hits (and classic near-misses) recorded between 1953 and 1959 by the likes of Elvis, Jerry Lee, Carl Perkins, and Johnny Cash, among others, with the digital artistry of Rhino's Bill Inglot, and the magic with which caring, meticulous digital reproduction can imbue historical material is little short of amazing. This disc is essential to any comprehensive rock & roll collection.

## The Original Rock'N'Roll Hits of the '50s Volume 1

Roulette RCD 58001 (40:49)     [B]

Included are the Crows, Orioles, Little Anthony and the Imperials, the Flamingos, and Frankie Lyman and the Teenagers—primarily one- or two-hit doowop wonders, who left a legacy of music based upon black street corner harmonies—simple and accessible. Perhaps it's pure nostalgia, yet these songs remain attractive to this day. Given that many

of these sixteen recordings were essentially one-shot efforts done on less than state-of-the-art equipment, this compilation's sound qualities are impressive, if subject to certain limitations.

## The Original Rock'N'Roll Hits of the '50s Volume 2

Roulette RCD 58002 (40:24)     [B+]

Doowop was an essential ingredient in the heady fifties musical mix that was distilled into rock & roll. This compilation features first-rate examples by some fine purveyors of those street corner harmonies that have proved so enduring. In addition, there are included some offbeat classics like Wilbur Harrison's "Kansas City." The sound, while frequently obviously compressed and occasionally flawed, is pretty good, given the original sources. The total value of this package would be enhanced with decent liner notes.

## Rock & Roll The Early Days

RCA PCD1-5463 (29:33)     [A+]

The quality of the production and the innate power, not to mention historic importance, of its musical contents overcome the embarrassingly short playing time (about 40 percent of the CD's capacity) of this essential disc. Real roots, presented as effectively as the medium and the source material will allow. These are the folks that flipped the switch and turned the lights on for everybody! (Another Greg Geller milestone.)

## Soundtrack—Stand By Me

Atlantic 781677-2 (23:36)     [C+]

Ten brief examples of classic fifties pop performed by Jerry Lee, Buddy Holly, the Del Vikings, Silhouettes, etc. The tunes are first-rate, the sound quality generally the same, but twenty-three minutes of music when the disc can deliver three times that amount simply amounts to a rip-off.

## 20 Rockabilly Classics

MCA 5935 (44:37)     [B]

Rockabilly, rock & roll's first form, is very pure, very simple music both in terms of its instrumentation and lyrical content. By adhering to a highly defined format, this music maintains its purity, but at the expense of its scope. This fascinating collection, which includes Dale Hawkin's "Suzie-Q," as well as work by Buddy Holly, Brenda Lee, Webb Pierce, Johnny Burnette, and Billy Lee Riley, is primarily made up of obscure offerings by unknowns whose fame was primarily regional, at best. But names or not, these artists all possess a naive intensity which infuses their music with an energy that endures a quarter of a century later. The sound is generally surprisingly clean and clear, without a great deal of dynamic or special enhancement. The notes, though brief, are factual and informative.

### The Best of Sun Rockabilly

CD Charly 16 (50:33)     [A]
Further proof of Sun Studios' claim as the birthplace of rock & roll. There is a sampling by the Studio's acknowledged giants, Jerry Lee Lewis, Carl Perkins, and Roy Orbison, but the contributions of such lesser knowns as Billy Riley, Warren Smith, the Miller Sisters, Onie Wheeler, and Malcolm Yelvington equal or exceed much of Sun's better known output. This was the music that didn't make it to New York or Los Angeles—you had to drop by a roadside tavern on a Saturday night for a couple of cold ones to really appreciate how much this music comprised an integral part of the fabric of the lives of small town America. If the sounds weren't enough, which they are, the liner notes are comprehensive, adding to the quality of the overall package. The sound does vary, as expected, among the cuts, but with two or three noticeable exceptions, the overall quality is extremely strong for material of this vintage.

### Hits From the Legendary Vee Jay Records

Motown MCD06215MD (68:04)     [B + ]
Probably a majority of record buyers pay scant attention to the "label" on which a recording is released—the only practical question being, is it readily available? If that

is an accurate assumption, it's regrettable, because the great independent record companies of the fifties and sixties were truly as responsible for the creation of rock & roll as the performers whose work they merchandised and popularized. Sun, Atlantic, Chess, Stax, Vee Jay—these names belong in the Rock & Roll Hall of Fame along with Presley, Berry, etc. Vee Jay lasted thirteen years from its founding in Gary, Indiana, in 1953 to its bankruptcy in 1966. Originally conceived as a black gospel label, it ultimately provided some of the fifties' best black doowop sounds, plus several name black artists (Jerry Butler and Betty Everett), not to mention blues greats John Lee Hooker and Jimmy Reed. All this fine material (exclusive of gospel recordings) is effectively sampled on this historic release. As usual, production values vary markedly from cut to cut, but, overall, these recordings are sonically the best renditions of this fine material available. The package is enhanced by strong liner information making this a wholly worthwhile compilation.

### Vintage Music Volumes I & II

MCA MCAD 5777 JVC509 (52:47)     [B + ]
From "Maybellene" to Pat Boone's "Love Letters in the Sand" this well-produced collection is an excellent sonic window on fifties rock radio—it's a little bit of doowop, some Buddy Holly, and other and sundry classics. While the admixture of selections is a bit random, the material covered generally highlights well-known hits from this era, and MCA's usual attention to the sound quality of its digital transfers makes this one of the better fifties rock & roll collections.

### Vintage Music Volumes III & IV

MCA MCAD5778 JVC510 (49:27)     [B–]
The above comments regarding the first disc in this series (Volumes I & II) are generally applicable here; except that the material included (aside from the Buddy Holly and Chuck Berry cuts, all available on an artist's collection) is generally weaker than that included on the first disc.

**The Vocal Group Collection (The Platters, The Penguins, Del Vikings, Dan Leers)**
Mercury 830283-2 M-1 (69:22)          **[D]**
Second-rate material from first-rate groups combined with the best work of second-best groups still adds up to a pretty boring outing. The sound quality, which varies, is generally clean, but compressed.

# THE SIXTIES

"—Seen at times thru dark sunglasses and other forms of psychic explosion, a song is anything that can walk by itself . . ."
—Bob Dylan. Liner notes from
*Bringing It All Back Home,*
Copyright 1985

JFK . . . Jack Paar . . . beatniks . . . Khrushchev's shoe . . . Casey Stengel . . . sit-ins . . . Gary Powers . . . The Wall . . . the twist . . . Peace Corps . . . Bay of Pigs . . . John Glenn . . . James Meredith . . . Cuban missile crisis . . . Lee Harvey Oswald/Jack Ruby . . . LBJ . . . Billy Sol Estes . . . Christine Keeler . . . *Hello, Dolly* . . . Tonkin Bay . . . discotheques . . . topless swimsuits . . . Vietnam . . . peace marches . . . peace symbols . . . Selma . . . Martin Luther King . . . Montgomery . . . Great Society . . . Watts . . . Black Power . . . big blackout . . . Richard Speck/Charles Whitman . . . Medicare . . . *Valley of the Dolls* . . . Miranda . . . miniskirts . . . hair . . . Twiggy . . . hippies . . . Haight-Ashbury . . . LSD . . . Timothy Leary/Owsley Stanley . . . Berkeley . . . Muhammed Ali . . . Dr. Spock . . . *Bonnie & Clyde* . . . Christiaan Barnard . . . Cape Kennedy . . . Robert Kennedy . . . Jackie Kennedy . . . Tiny Tim . . . U.S.S. *Pueblo* . . . Nehru jackets . . . airline hijackings . . . "Laugh-In" . . . Neil Armstrong . . . moon walk . . . Chappaquiddick . . . Broadway Joe . . . the Pill . . . Aquarian Age . . . My Lai . . . the sixties, pure rock & roll.

From grimy Liverpool to enlightened San Francisco, the pulse of this century's most tumultuous decade was rock & roll: the soundtrack for unique times. Times when everything was moving, changing, shining, and melting—usually all at once. Rock music defined style in an age when style was essential. Rock music defined rebellion in a time of immense social and political upheaval.

The musicians who created this soundtrack, in many instances, have become cultural icons, revered and influential beyond anyone's wildest dreams. Their involvements became the involvements of their fans to a degree that rock stars' endorsements were sought by the political establishment.

The Beatles, the truly transitional group that turned the fifties rock & roll into sixties rock, achieved a musical world union not experienced since. At one point in the sixties, eight of the top ten hits were Beatles' songs—eight of the top ten: a feat never approximated before and not repeated since. In June of 1967, the radios of the entire Western world became the *Sgt. Pepper's Lonely Hearts Club Band* chorale—the music was everywhere; the music mattered.

The yin to the Fab Four's yang, the Rolling Stones, carried forth the tradition of Jerry Lee Lewis on the sounds of Chuck Berry. One of the most complex, influential, and essential bands the music has yet to produce—their cynical view has proved to be sadly prophetic.

Meanwhile, back in the U.S.A., the Beach Boys, rock's only choir, created the most effective advertisement for a lifestyle and region yet witnessed in these commercially saturated times. What is the estimate for California's state population in 1990? Thirty-one million? In the process, they laundered the form to create an extraordinarily durable sound. The Beach Boys made rock & roll acceptable in venues previously deemed outside its influence; but then, how threatening is a tanned, smiling blond kid whose sole stated desire is to romp on the beach?

While the British were co-opting, repackaging, and selling America's pop musical heritage back to its homeland, San Francisco was announcing the dubious joys of modern (and ancient) chemistry to a newly potent, blindly optimistic generation; and psychedelia was added to the mix.

Across the continent in Greenwich Village coffeehouses, Bob Dylan, rock's towering intellect/poet, brought political currency to the medium. In terms of the form of the music, Dylan and Chuck Berry stand as rock & roll's two greatest individual contributors—it was Dylan who turned on the light so that everyone could see. During his conversion from folk hero to the creator of folk rock, Dylan's genius became incandescent and the classic recordings of that time not only still crackle with the energy of pure creativity, they stand with total authority several decades after the fact.

Then there was Detroit's other major contribution to the good times of the fun-seeking youth of the era: Motown.

In a very real sense, Motown, the most financially successful black business venture in American history, was a vindication—the full realization of the commercial potential of the black music that had been co-opted and exploited in white rock & roll. By mixing the joyous energy born of the black church gospel choir with lyrics aimed at the youth experience and serving it in brilliantly produced two to three minute doses, Berry Gordy found a formula that yielded some of the most perfect pop sounds yet experienced. The market, black and white, responded by acclamation—the Supremes alone had a dozen No. 1 hits between 1964 and the end of the decade, and Smokey Robinson and the Miracles, the Temptations, Marvin Gaye, the Four Tops, plus numerous other Motown acts were frequent contributors to the Top Ten.

But Motown was only a part of a black musical resurrection which, in its way, was every bit as potent and pervasive as that which was revolutionizing the bleached "Hit Parade." In the fifties, Ray Charles had begun to combine gospel and blues forms to create what has been dubbed "soul" music, which, in the sixties flowered through the efforts of an extraordinarily talented group of performers who were principally nurtured by Atlantic Records. Otis Redding, Aretha Franklin, Wilson Pickett, Ray Charles, the Coasters, and the Drifters were making music of broad enough appeal to escape the boundaries of color—music which combined with Motown's output insured that this was the golden decade for both black and white pop sounds.

This was also a time of maturation, and inevitable self-awareness—with attendant self-consciousness. It was the decade in which the rock press came into being. *Crawdaddy* and *Rolling Stone* in the U.S., and *Creem* in England, began to define and identify the music's community, ultimately an invaluable tool in its inevitable commercialization.

Obviously, a press is composed of words, and the authors of those words, at least the best of them, became an integral part of the rock establishment in the latter half of the decade. Critics like Greil Marcus, Robert Christgau, John Landau, Jonathan Cott, Peter Guralnick, Dave Marsh, Ed Ward, Nick Tosches, and Paul Williams created a body of commentary, not only covering the music itself, but also the milieu from which it arose. Their influence on their readers ultimately became an influence over the product itself. Today, Marcus has veered off in search of the fundamental attitude, an admirable but currently unrewarding venture; Marsh is either the wisest or dumbest man in the world, take your choice; and, John Landau saw "the future of rock & roll" and became a prophet in his own time.

This was the age of free-form radio, when the airwaves had personality and commitment to something more than the sale of another motorcycle or acne preparation, at least that was the case on the FM side of the dial. Until the sixties, AM radio was the dominant broadcast form in America and musically it was devoted to a "Top 40" or "Top 100" format, composed of frequently played hit singles, generally two to three minutes in duration.

FM, because of its better sound capabilities and, ultimately, its stereo broadcast capability, was reserved for classical music or simulcast of the "sister" station's AM programming. But in the sixties, the Federal Communications Commission intervened, requiring a majority of FM station owners who held both AM and FM licenses to provide different programming on each format. Thus, however unwittingly, Uncle Sam played a major role in the spread and development of rock music. With so many hours to fill of air time, and a predilection toward "popular music," it was inevitable that the FM stations in America would turn to populist rock & roll.

Since early FM radio was clearly the outcast form of broadcasting, various station managers employed disc jockeys to just fill the time, thus the birth of free-form radio; which programmed extended album cuts in lieu of heavily promoted singles. Ultimately, this meant the death knell for the standard two- to three-minute pop song because within the album format, rock musicians were extending the boundaries of their compositions to whatever length was appropriate to express an idea. Probably, Bob Dylan's "Like a Rolling Stone," which clocks in at six minutes playing time, was the song that broke through from FM programming to Top 40 radio, thereby shattering the time limitations along with countless other restrictions on pop songs forevermore.

This was the decade of the second, and to date, last, great cultural revolution fomented basically by teenagers with plugged-in guitars and personas.

It was the best of times. It couldn't last. It didn't. It left a heritage of gloriously moving sounds and a fair share of physical and emotional casualties. But there is always a price to be paid when the balance of power shifts—even slightly. The best rock music of this decade throbs with the energy of pure, innocent creativity; energy that still rejuvenates—still resonates.

It was a cornucopia of promises—it was a river of wretched excess; Woodstock and Altamont. Ultimately, the sixties proved to be times of involvement, times of community; and those were the richest of times.

# THE SIXTIES
## on Compact Disc

"For the reality of what is happening today in America, we must go to rock & roll to popular music."

—Ralph J. Gleason

## Joan Baez

b. January 9, 1941—Staten Island, New York

One of the antecedents of the flowering of rock & roll in the sixties was the concurrent folk music revival which gained its primary footing on the college campuses of America. Baez was the queen of this revival and its perfect symbol, embodying the achingly pure voice of the classic female balladeer with a social conscience directly traceable to the principles of Woody Guthrie.

### Any Day Now

Vanguard VCD 79306/7 (68:42)    [C + ]

Beautiful readings of classic songs, but the strength of Dylan (and these are all Dylan compositions) has to do with an edge of honesty, an intensity which Joan's interpretation sadly lacks—it's an empty package. She sounds so concerned with the music, she's ignored its meaning. The sound is like that of a perfectly surfaced LP and it beautifully showcases one of the finest female folk voices around; but, there is little detail or spatial enhancement from the CD version.

### Greatest Hits

Vanguard 811 667-2 (53:58)    [B + ]

These songs span a period from 1960 to the early 1970s, but a preponderance of the material is drawn from the sixties, which is the only time the folk queen was related at all to rock & roll, and that by virtue of the close Dylan association. She was very much a part of the turbulent sixties New York, Dylan-centered, creation of "folk rock," but Joan has remained true to her roots, sometimes treating rock lyrics like the folk material they very much are. This is a lovely collection that sounds bright, yet rarely harsh and clean, but thin.

## The Band

Formed 1967, Woodstock, New York

This five-man group (four of whom were Canadian) first gained notice working behind Ronnie Hawkins, and then achieved fame backing Bob Dylan. They captured, in rough, rustic, and real terms, America's rich southern-frontier cultural heritage better than any other group, and in the process, made enduring music.

41

**Music From Big Pink**

Capitol CDP7 46069 2 (42:05)    [A]

This, their first recording, was based upon Robbie Robertson's vision of American mythology as the foundation for the sixties rock & roll. At first listening it had the feel of "classic" about it and that has not diminished. The timelessness of its themes, honesty of its voicings, and artistic interplay of its instrumentation mark it as a recording of sustaining value. The CD's sound is clear, clean, and dynamic. Garth Hudson's imaginative organ work becomes even more impressive through the enhanced clarity of the digital mix.

**The Band**

Capitol CDP7 46493-2 (43:57)    [A + ]

Ralph J. Gleason called it "lean and dusty." *Rolling Stone* selected it nineteenth among the top 100 Rock albums of the 1967-1987 period and called it "a masterpiece of electric folklore." One basic element of the sixties youth "revolution" embodied a return to the simpler countrified values and truths of America's potent past history—its rural frontiersmen and agrarian pioneers. Many bands worked this rich vein as source material, but The Band truly represented its living incarnation. *The Band* was recorded in Sammy Davis, Jr.'s, pool house in Los Angeles, California, in the winter of 1968—and the somewhat boxy sound of that "studio" is retained on the CD—but it's part of it, this is the way it was meant to sound. It's clean and clear with a couple of glitches here and there, and the openings and closings of selections are clipped, but these are minor complaints. The digital conversion highlights the shadings in the plain vocals and harmonies which adds significantly to the listening experience.

# The Beach Boys

Formed 1961—Hawthorne, California

Building on Chuck Berry's foundations and Phil Spector's grandiose aural concepts, all enhanced by Brian Wilson's pure pop production genius, the Beach Boys were a uniquely innovative American rock group. It has been known for some time that relatives are able to sing better harmony than non-relatives and four of the five original members of this band (the brothers Wilson and cousin Mike Love) were related. This group has probably never been given its due in popularizing rock & roll with mainstream America, at least in the critical press.

**Made in the U.S.A.**

Capitol CDP7 46324 2 (64:17)    [A]

**Endless Summer**

Capitol CDP7 46467 2 (50:39)    [A + ]

The Beach Boys, or at least those who still survive, have been living off the music contained on these two discs for a over a quarter of a century, and hearing these CDs clearly explains why. The two contain forty-six cuts, thirty-six different songs. Buy both, and you've got 90 percent of a major sixties rock band's best work. The sound quality is generally good on both discs; however, there is some unevenness among the selections, as would be expected given the divergency of recorded source material.

# The Beatles

Formed 1959—Liverpool, England

The event that the compact disc world had been anticipating since the first CDs were released in 1983 finally occurred on February 26, 1987: Capitol Records released *Please, Please Me, With the Beatles, Beatles for Sale*, and *A Hard Day's Night* on compact discs. Over a million copies were originally shipped. The media covered this release as a major news story.

Was all this hype justified by the product? The answer is a resounding "Yes!" Not so much because of technological advances in the digital conversions (which are notable and positive), but because the availability of Beatles' material on disc caused music lovers to once again listen to what may be the one truly great group in the growing history of rock & roll.

The Beatles were the bridge between the music's somewhat primitive beginnings in the fifties and its ultimate flowering as a complex art form in the sixties. Their roots and experience began with the raw sounds and spirit of rock's first decade and, as a result, their product defined rock's second decade.

The amazing pervasiveness of Beatlemania, which encompassed vast numbers and cut through diverse age and social groups, created an international musical bond not duplicated since. If you lived through it, this music is probably an essential element in your personal history. If you didn't, it is still probably totally familiar because its popularity has been unparalleled in the annals of the form.

In a sense, this was more than just rock music. It was the essence of its moment in time.

These releases, listed below, constitute the "official" Beatles recorded output and have been issued on CD in their original English configurations, which means that the selections (on the discs up to *Sgt. Pepper*) vary from their U.S. counterparts with which most U.S. listeners will be familiar. It should also be noted that the first four recordings were released in mono, much to the chagrin of many critics, but this is really a bit of a tempest in a teapot—the CDs simply sound better than the stereo versions of the LPs. In fact, the fifth and following releases in the series, which are in stereo, tend to suffer somewhat from the extremity of the separation employed.

### Please, Please Me
Parlophone CDP7 46435 2 (32:48)    **[A + ]**
The first album statement—simply indispensable.

### With the Beatles
Parlophone CDP7 46436 2 (33:26)    **[A + ]**
Released the same year as *Please, Please Me*, it's essentially more of the wonderful same, with a couple more original Lennon/McCartney compositions and perhaps their single strongest rock & roll statement—John Lennon's reading of "Money."

### A Hard Day's Night
Parlophone CDP7 46437 2 (30:32)    **[A + ]**
The first recording made up of exclusively Lennon/McCartney compositions, not to mention its relevance to a certain film of the same name. Probably the best sounding of the first seven Beatles "original" releases.

### Beatles for Sale
Parlophone CDP7 46438 2 (34:15)    **[A]**
Released in 1964, this recording shows the Beatles moving somewhat away from their original roots material (and recorded cover versions thereof) and Lennon/McCartney's expansion of the actual form of pop song. A little of the influence of Bob Dylan is clearly felt in the content of the lyrics as well as the nuances of the lead vocals.

*Help, Rubber Soul,* and *Revolver* are three of the most important recordings in the history of rock & roll. Originally recorded and released in 1965 and 1966, this was the material that established Beatlemania, and forever changed the shape of the pop music that followed. It was within these grooves that the Beatles' amazing eclecticism, their non-pareil melodic power, and complete reshuffling of the conventions that had previously constricted rock music, were given free rein.

### Help
Parlophone CDP7 46439 2 (34:23)    **[A + ]**
Another soundtrack, but this may well be the best soundtrack recording ever released.

### Rubber Soul
Parlophone CDP7 46440 (35:50)    **[A + ]**
While the argument about which is the best album of this seminal group's ten-year record-

ing career will probably last as long as the music is heard, *Rubber Soul* is clearly a strong candidate for that designation.

### Revolver

Parlophone CDP7 46441 (35:01)    [A + ]
Psychedelia meets Beatlemania, and the world of pop music unalterably changed again. In retrospect, this recording, released in 1966, sounds the most dated of any of this group's work to that time, but it's still essential.

### Sgt. Pepper's Lonely Hearts Club Band

Parlophone CDP7 46442 (39:52)    [A + ]
On June 1, 1987, twenty years to the day of the original English release, *Sgt. Pepper's Lonely Hearts Club Band* made its digital debut. According to a consensus of rock critics assembled by Paul Gambaccini for his "Critic's Choice—The Top 100 Rock & Roll Albums of All Time," *Sgt. Pepper* is the greatest rock recording. *Rolling Stone* in its August 27, 1987, issue devoted to "The 100 Best Albums of the Last Twenty Years (1967-1987)" accords it the same distinction. Whether that is musically the case or not is difficult to pinpoint; however, it changed the rules of the game, and that's hard to do. It is rare when a single release so clearly and specifically is the cause of so much change. This classic responds to digital reproduction awesomely. Sure, you can hear the tape hiss. But the boys and George Martin (their producer, sometimes referred to as the fifth Beatle) created this madness by overdubbing with only three-track capacity recording equipment (sixty-four tracks or more are commonplace in the modern studio). The clarity of CD allows you to hear more of how it was all put together in the first place for better or worse. The spatial and dynamic potential of the disc gives the sound a punch which adds a whole new level to the listening experience. From the breadth of its lyrical subject matter to the sophistication of that sound, *Sgt. Pepper* declared rock & roll to be the equal of any contemporary venue of artistic expression.

### Magical Mystery Tour

Parlophone CDP 7 48062-2 (36:52)    [A]
The Beatles released two albums in 1967, the first being *Sgt. Pepper,* generally conceded to be rock's single most important release, and *Magical Mystery Tour,* generally undervalued because the film for which it provided the soundtrack was probably the Fab Four's first commercial disappointment (and justifiably so). *Rolling Stone's* review of this release in 1967 simply took the form of the following quote from John Lennon: "There are only about a hundred people in the world who understand our music." Viewed from the perspective of twenty years, *Magical Mystery Tour* (which is the brief soundtrack plus an assembly of excellent Beatles' singles) is very much of a piece with its illustrious predecessor, evidencing the same contagious, bizarre studio antics and showcasing more great pop songs: "The Fool on the Hill," "I Am the Walrus," "Hello, Goodbye," "Strawberry Fields Forever," "Penny Lane," "Baby, You're a Rich Man," and "All You Need Is Love." 'Nuff said? The sound is clean, crisp, clear, and open. However, its compression betrays analog sources, and it evidences a slight tendency to thin overbrightness.

### The Beatles (The White Album)

Parlophone CDP7464432 (Disc 1) CDP7464442 (Disc 2) (93:40)    [A + ]
It was 1968, the movement and the music had peaked in '67 (the Summer of Love), and while the "high" was still stratospheric, the signs of decline were perceptible. *The Beatles* is, historically, the group's most fascinating and naked recording. The individual personas begin to eclipse the group—the obvious first harbingers of the end which would come within the next couple of years. The tensions, however, energized much of the music, making this one of their stellar releases; although it doesn't require particularly close listening to perceive the fractionalization within the group. The sound is bright and punchy yet afflicted with telltale traces of its era; tape hiss is occasionally audible and while the spatial attributes and detailing are

both noticeably enhanced, there often remains an overall awareness of compression. On balance, the CD's sound is an improvement over that of the original LPs.

### Abbey Road
Parlophone CDP7464462 (47:26)    **[A + ]**
If you only own one rock CD, this should be the one. From the magical opening chords of John Lennon's "Come Together" (which *Rolling Stone* aptly described as his "word salad song") to the momentous summation of it all (the Beatles, the sixties—you name it) "The End," this is the essential Beatles' album—thus, the essential rock album. Occasional tape hiss notwithstanding, the digital conversion materially expands what was always an endless vision. It highlights McCartney's virtuoso bass work throughout and his soaring vocal on "Darling!," as well as, Lennon's perfectly acid guitar. A triumph!

### Live in Hamburg '62
K-Tel CD1473 (46:30)    **[C + ]**
Yeah, it sounds like the master tape was made on a cheapie portable recorder by someone wandering aimlessly through the audience with a low-grade, hand-held mike—but have you heard the LP version? As an historic icon of the rough early roots of the most remarkable group in pop history, this recording ties the band and their music to the American counterparts which inspired it. Generally the poor sound quality and miserable mix overwhelm the material, but every now and again the Beatles uniqueness and their compelling energy slip through the noise level and the future seems inevitable.

# Big Brother and the Holding Company
Formed 1965—California
This is the band which, in 1967, at the Monterey Pop Festival, brought the pride of Port Arthur, Texas, Janis Joplin, to the attention of a national audience.

### Cheap Thrills
Columbia CK9700 (37:13)    **[A]**
This is a rough, raw, blues-drenched live outing that remains easily the best recorded work Janis Joplin ever put down. For reasons that in retrospect seem highly suspect, after this release Janis abandoned Big Brother and the Holding Company (her "advisors" said that she was the real talent in the group and the band was holding her back) and never found as compatible a backup during the remainder of her sadly brief career. The sound is definitely "live," and somewhat limited, but it is a marked improvement over its LP predecessor.

# The Box Tops
Formed 1966—Memphis

### Ultimate Box Tops
Warner Special Products 9-27611-2 (51:10)    **[B + ]**
One of the many sixties high school bands that managed to crack the national charts; in the Box Tops' case, they succeeded more than once and quite effectively with "The Letter" (8/12/67) and "Cry Like a Baby" (3/2/68). What set this band apart was its lead singer, Alex Chilton, who has one of those raw, rough voices that seems almost indigenous to rock & roll and which was perfect for the blue-eyed soul that was the Box Tops' stock and trade. There is a quality to this music, limited though it might be, which has held a core group of fans for twenty years. The compilation covers all the charted hits plus some obscure, but strong cover versions of other groups' contemporary material. The sound on this CD is a pleasant revelation—the masters must have been pristine, because the digital transfer cuts the original recordings by a wide margin—a fine sounding collection.

# James Brown

### James Brown Live at the Apollo

Polygram 823 001-2 (73:34)      **[A]**

First off, this isn't the classic *Live at the Apollo* recording done in October of 1962. This recording was made in 1967 and while it lacks the pure animal fury that makes the '62 concert a legitimate candidate for the best live recording of all time, it is still Soul Brother No. 1, it's still the Famous Flames, it's still the Apollo, and it still pulsates as only the man can. The sound is sharp and generally clean. James Brown is a live performer first and foremost, and this is as close as you can get at the current time to his live work on CD. While there may have been more energy five years earlier, he still laid down a legitimate claim to being "the hardest working man in show business."

# The Byrds

Formed 1964—Los Angeles

### The Byrds Collection

Casle CCSCD151 (52:58)      **[C + ]**

The Byrds popularized Bob Dylan and laid down the foundations of what became country rock with their seminal *Sweetheart Of The Rodeo,* and included a brief sojourn as space cowboys in the middle of it all. This compilation covers all aspects of the band's relatively brief, but very influential, career. Their chiming guitar trademark sound has been resuscitated by many young eighties bands, most notably REM. Thus, it's surprising that this appears to be the only compilation of the their material currently available on CD which is too bad, because on it, their fine music is shackled with muddy, thick sound highlighted by too edgy highs. It's listenable, but certainly nothing to write home about.

# Ray Charles

### The Legend Lives

Arcade ADEH/CD/780 (62:06)      **[A]**

A rather strange German compilation that contains a few of the gospel-inflected "shouts" ("Hit the Road Jack" and "What'd I Say") which provide the basis for Ray's claim as the creator of soul music. However, a majority of the selections come from the *New Directions in Country Music* era, when the genius exposed the kinship of country and his soulful blues-based sound. Called by some the finest vocalist in contemporary music, this CD enhances the exemplary subtlety of his singing. While the source material utilized is somewhat obscure (the liner notes are virtually non-existent), the sound, while dated, is generally of consistently high quality.

# The Coasters

Formed 1955—Los Angeles

### The Ultimate Coasters

Warner Special Products 927604-2 (51:58)      **[D–]**

Working with Jerry Lieber and Mike Stoller, two of rock's most fascinating and talented "behind-the-scenes" pioneers, the Coasters created musical vignettes that were current, complete, often humorous, and consistently innovative in their production values. Unfortunately, Warner Brothers' digital conversion of this wonderful material is a crime—muddy, constrained, and distorted, so much so that some cuts ("Searchin'," "Youngblood," and "Along Came Jones") are literally painful to hear. The first time around much of this genuinely wonderful music never found the ear of the majority white audience; now that it's all here in a single package, it is the final injustice that slovenly engineering totally masks its true worth.

# Joe Cocker
# (John Robert Cocker)

b. May 20, 1944—Sheffield, England
This frenetic former steamfitter was one of
the few genuine sixties rock "stars" who
reached celebrity status by performing material principally written by others. Virtually un-
trained, but possessed of an emotionally
charged roughhouse voice, a voice that
launched a thousand parties, his expressive
powers place him among rock's premier vocal
interpreters.

### With a Little Help From My Friends

A&M CD3106 (40:43)     **[B]**
The first album release by the man who may
be the music's least likely hero. Even working
with some of England's better known rock
artists (Jimmy Page, Chris Stainton, and Steve
Winwood among them), the musicianship is a
bit rough around the edges, but the intensity
of Cocker's vocals perseveres. The ten selections, including compositions by Bob Dylan
and Lennon/McCartney as well as some
penned by Cocker and Chris Stainton, have a
certain rough, jam session feel which is very
consistent with Cocker's general stage presence and vocal qualities. The sound is clean
and precise, but lacks the general spatial
ambiance which the best digital conversions
can impart.

### Joe Cocker!

A&M CD4224 (35:24)     **[A]**
If he had made only this, his second album,
Cocker's stature in the star-studded sixties
would have been assured—his sensitive yet
raucous readings of songs written by some of
rock's best added new meaning and exposure
to very valid material.

# Creedence Clearwater Revival

Formed 1959—El Cerrito, California
Simply America's best singles rock & roll
band. While geographically aligned with the
psychedelic explosion that took place across
the bay in San Francisco, Creedence never
really was associated with the posturings or
prescriptions that colored so much of the
city's finery. In fact, because of their rockabilly
roots and bayou-sounding name, for years
many fans assumed that they were from the
South.

### The Best Of . . .

Fantasy VDP1024 (43:55)     **[B + ]**
Fourteen great singles which, while not a
comprehensive collection of CCR's greatest
hits, is fairly representative of their work. The
sound quality, with slight deviation, is first-
rate—clear, bright (albeit a little edgy in a few
vocals), and dynamic.

### Chronicle (20 Greatest Hits)

Fantasy FCD-623-CCR2 (68:13)     **[A + ]**
This disc contains six more selections and
about fifteen more minutes of music than the
*Best of* collection reviewed above; the addition of which ("Lodi," "Fortunate Son," "Run
Through the Jungle," "Commotion") make
this a truly comprehensive overview of this
wonderful band's most popular work as well
as a showcase for one of the truest and most
distinctive voices in the annals of rock & roll,
that of John Fogerty. The sound does vary
some ("Lodi" is unfortunately afflicted with
noticeable hiss), but overall a marked improvement over the LP.

### Chronicle Volume 2

Fantasy FCD-703-CCR3 (74:33)     **[C + ]**
Because Fogerty's voice and talent are such a
fundamental aspect of sixties American rock
& roll, it's hard to find fault with much of anything he does. But the twenty selections on
this CD weren't hits, because they just didn't
measure up to the twenty included on the
first volume of *Chronicle*. There are some
good numbers, but even the sound quality
isn't up to that of Volume 1.

**Greenriver**

Fantasy FCD-612-8393 (29:26)      **[A]**

Because Creedence was essentially a singles band (probably the best that rock & roll has yet produced), the compilation discs reviewed previously represent the best way to acquire their classic material. However, Fantasy has released most of the original albums on CD, which is not unexpected since this group has been that label's primary source of revenue for about two decades. This was the band's second recording, but the first that really defined its sound, and it's still a classic. The quality of the sound, while an improvement over the LP, is occasionally muffled, but it's generally clean and accurate, with some dynamic enhancement.

**Willie & the Poorboys**

Fantasy FCD-613-8397 (35:02)      **[A]**

Creedence provided the music you wanted to hear on the car radio when the top was down and the highway smooth. This is their other really great original album release that was geared for going. On the whole, the CD sound provides a noticeable enhancement over the LP version except for "The Midnight Special" and "Side O' the Road" which suffer from muddy, boxy sound.

# The Doors

Formed 1965—Los Angeles

Perhaps it is because Jim Morrison's screams of rebellion were as loud as any voiced in the sixties, or perhaps he was more successful than we imagined in conjuring up the darker spirits that he sought to invoke, but for whatever reason, the music of this highly influential group has managed to survive despite uneven, and frequently antagonistic, critical evaluation.

**The Doors**

Elektra 74007.2 (242 2012) (44:27)      **[A]**

Simply one of the strongest debut albums to come out in an era when giants came forth with unbelievable regularity. The sound is generally clean and dynamically enhanced with some weakness in the lows. Some of the mixes tend to make Morrison's vocal secondary to the instrumentation which is an improper shift of the focus of the group. But this is all nitpicking. A part of Jim Morrison's message was to conjure up the darker powers that in earlier times were the province of sorcerers and wizards—this recording is as close as he ever got. Truly a breakthrough release in that it expanded both the vocabulary and scope of the subject matter covered by rock & roll.

**The Best of the Doors**

Elektra 2CD 960345 (89:31)      **[A]**

This two-disc compilation opens with "Break on Through" and closes with "The End" and the seventeen selections in between make up most (but not all) of the band's best music. What sets this two-disc set apart is its sound. The Doors' longtime producer, Paul Rothchild, who has become a part-time keeper of the legend, has stated that these are the only CD releases of the group's material remastered from the original master tapes; listeners won't question that statement. The sound is wonderful (perhaps a bit bright on occasion) but clean, clear, spacious, and dynamic—it clearly conveys the magic of digital reproduction.

(Elektra plans to reissue all the original Doors' albums from the first generation master tapes which, apparently, were in Europe when the first CD compilations of that material was released. By the time of publication of this book, the CD recordings of original Doors' material should be of better quality than those which were reviewed above.)

# Bob Dylan
# (Robert Allen Zimmerman)

b. May 24, 1941—Duluth, Minnesota

Zimmerman begat Dylan and Dylan (along with the Beatles) begat a form of rock & roll that included an intellectual element to complement the visceral. He stands as the single individual whose persona and legend loom largest from this decade of rock's richest creativity. He gave the music relevance to the moment—he literally exploded the form—he created his own myth and with the anonymity it afforded, he was free to expose it all, the real and the surreal. His work from the sixties defines an astonishing, electrifying creativity, which has not since been equaled. Dylan's music, from folk to gospel, New York to Nashville, Jew to Gentile, comprises a contribution which ranks with the great cultural artifacts of any discipline in this century.

### Biograph

Columbia DK38831/C3K38330
(216:57—three discs)     [A + ]

Because of the permanence of CDs and their introduction almost thirty years after the history of rock & roll commenced, they offer a unique opportunity to package an artist's work in a form valuable to the permanent rock music collector. Columbia's pioneering efforts in this direction are evidenced in this three-disc release, meriting double commendation. The breadth of the material, fifty-three songs spanning twenty years (1961-81), includes crucial prior releases plus a modicum of fresh, but obscure, previously unreleased material or unreleased versions of familiar cuts (e.g., the surpassing live version of "Visions of Johanna") and makes this a remarkable collection. While Dylan is an artist famous for his casual, if not downright slovenly, attention to studio production values (and some of the masters utilized here were truly demo recordings), the sound quality evidences extreme care in the digital remastering. Obviously, the sound varies, given the vast diversity of sources, but only the most persnickety of listeners will be disappointed with either the sound or content of this

release. In addition to the music itself, the complete packaging provides insightful, enhancing printed material.

### Blonde On Blonde

Columbia CGK841 (71:73)     [A + ]

A lot of critics have stated that this is Dylan's best—some even say that it is the best rock record of all time. It is the consummate work by a man who may be rock's single most important creator. When one stops to realize what Dylan had already released in 1965 and 1966, *Bringing It All Back Home* and *Highway 61 Revisited,* if he had done nothing else, his stature would have been assured. But, *Blonde On Blonde* may be the most fully realized album in the annals of rock & roll. It is the work of an obvious genius at the height of his creativity. Soundwise, the worst of it sounds like a cleaner, slightly enhanced version of the LP; at its best, the dynamic and special enhancements added by digital conversion are wonderful. Unfortunately, Columbia has also shaved a few seconds off the music to get the recording on a single disc—better it should have been released on two CDs; classics are classics.

### Bringing It All Back Home

Columbia CK9128 (47:29)     [A + ]

The year was 1965, and the saviour of contemporary folk music was abandoning the purists by melding his lyrical topicality with the amplified beat at the heart of rock & roll. This obviously transitional recording (half recorded with rock instrumentation and half acoustic folk stylings) is the touchstone to yet another enlargement of the then burgeoning world of rock & roll. Dylan simply refused to be limited by prior conventions. His influence was pervasive, traceable in contemporary work of both the Stones and the Beatles as well as numerous other artists. The classics, "Subterranean Homesick Blues," "Maggie's Farm," "Mr. Tambourine Man," and "It's All Right Ma," as well as the clichés, began here. Soundwise, the low end lacks dynamics, but otherwise this is a very successful digital conversion.

## Highway 61 Revisited

Columbia CK9189 (51:40)    [A + ]

From the first resonant beat of "Like a Rolling Stone" (perhaps Dylan's finest song) to the piercing plaintive harmonica that closes "Desolation Row," this recording encompasses some of the best rock music ever made. The sound, while far from revelatory, is superior to the LP; it's clean and the detail enhancement is noticeable. This disc is essential.

## Greatest Hits

Columbia CK9463 (40:20)    [A + ]

With the exception of "Rainy Day Woman #12 and 35" the other nine classics included here are also available on *Biograph*. That aside, this is essential Dylan, with most of the early hits included. The sound quality is analogous to that on *Highway 61* reviewed above.

## John Wesley Harding

Columbia CK9604 (38:31)    [A + ]

In July 1966, Bob Dylan had a motorcycle accident that took him out of the maelstrom of his own creativity and the celebrity that attended it. During his recuperation in upstate New York (Woodstock), he privately explored his roots with Canada's great American roots group, The Band. This was summarized on *The Basement Tapes* not released officially until 1975. But the ambiance of this time was expressed in 1968 in *John Wesley Harding*. On it, Dylan turned away from rock's freneticism and returned to countrified folk roots. It remains an enduring recording, the first oblique expression of the devoutness that would overtake his output a decade later, as well as a direct precursor of the country sound that would overwhelm *Nashville Skyline*, which, like this album, was recorded in Nashville. The sound is certainly adequate, much like the other Dylan CD releases from this decade—clean, with some enhancement of detail, but not much dynamic or spatial improvement.

## Nashville Skyline

Columbia CK9825 (27:08)    [C + ]

Dylan's first really inferior release, 1969's *Nashville Skyline*, is not totally without merit. The commercially successful "Lay Lady Lay," and the re-recording with Johnny Cash of the lovely "Girl from the North Country," are quality material even by Dylan's high standards; but that's about it. The sound is a little better than that of the prior Dylan CD releases from this era, but it doesn't matter a whole bunch.

# The Four Tops

Formed 1953—Detroit

## 19 Greatest Hits

Motown MCD09042MD (58:46)    [A–]

The Temptations may have had more flash, but the Four Tops had Levi Stubbs, one of the great soul voices, and Holland-Dozier-Holland, the best of all the fine Motown production teams. The result was a justified string of hits, beginning with "Baby I Need Your Lovin'" (8/15/64) and running through "I Can't Help Myself" (5/15/65), and their all-time classic, "Reach Out, I'll Be There" (9/3/66). They're all included here—it's sixties Motown soul-style music at its best. You really don't need a whole lot more. The sound is clearly superior to the LPs, but that's easy given the quality of Motown's LPs. There is some dynamic enhancement and an increased instrumental clarity. Too often the lead vocals are plagued by minor, but irritating, distortion.

# Aretha Franklin

b. March 25, 1942—Memphis

The daughter of Detroit's well-known Baptist minister, Reverend C.L. Franklin who was also known nationally as a gospel preacher, Aretha defined female soul singing in the sixties; thus, her well-earned appellation, Lady Soul. Working with Jerry Wexler on the great R&B label of the era, Atlantic, Aretha has managed to score fifteen Top Ten hits since her recording career began in 1961. Her best work is infused with an energy and passion that sets it a cut above any of her peers.

## 30 Greatest Hits

Atlantic 81668-2 (99:31—two discs)     [A + ]
The music on this double-disc package defines soul singing. The material roughly spans the decade between 1964 and 1974, Aretha's most productive years under the sympathetic aegis of producer Jerry Wexler. Soul music is the bastard child of the unholy union of gospel and the blues—Aretha *is* Lady Soul, and there ain't nobody near second place. The testament to all that is right here: "I Never Loved a Man," "Respect," "Baby I Love You," "Dr. Feelgood," "Chain of Fools," "Think," "Spirit in the Dark," "Don't Play that Song," "Bridge Over Troubled Water," "Spanish Harlem," and nineteen other gems make this an essential sacrament of sixties sound. Obviously, the quality of that sound varies with the differing source material, the newer cuts sounding generally better than the earlier ones. On the whole, compared to prior vinyl versions, the sound is a genuine, discernible improvement. The liner notes (reproduced from the album) are excellent and informative, unfortunately, a high magnification microscope is required to read them.

# Marvin Gaye

b. April 2, 1939—Washington, D.C.
d. April 1, 1984
Gaye's history is almost archetypical of the black pop star—son of a preacher (in this case one of the most unusual to ever mount a pulpit), he began singing in church at three, then turned to doowop in the fifties; ultimately he became a part of the Motown "family" in the fullest sense. He married Berry Gordy's sister, Anna. He also worked as a drummer and backup singer behind numerous Motown acts. Even though he enjoyed great success with the company during the sixties, it wasn't until he broke free from its production-line approach (while remaining

on the label) in 1971 with the classic "What's Goin' On" that his unique talents were given free rein. A deeply troubled, albeit fascinating man, he died from gunshot wounds administered by his father.

## 15 Greatest Hits

Tamla TCD 06069 TD (58:51)     [B + ]
Most of the major hits are included, providing a representative overview of this important artist's career. As-expected, the sound quality varies markedly from cut to cut, and none of it is really outstanding. But considering the fact that Motown LPs often sounded as if they were pressed on used auto seat vinyl, just getting clean renditions is a major plus.

## Marvin Gaye and His Women—21 Classic Duets

Tamla TCD 06153 TD (57:45)     [B]
The duet was a staple of Gaye's recorded repertoire, and over the years he recorded with four talented women, Diana Ross, Mary Wells, Kim Weston, and Tammi Terrell. The highlights of those joint efforts are what make up this CD. Again, the disc, the sound of which varies from selection to selection, is a marked improvement over the inferior LP mixes and surfaces, yet, it is still far from what it might be. Specifically, the generally compressed sound stage on almost all selections and frequent harshness in the female vocals undermine what is conceptually a fine collection.

# Jimi Hendrix

b. November 27, 1942—Seattle
d. September 18, 1970—London
The self-appointed voodoo child of rock & roll, his voice was nothing to write home about (he was once quoted as saying that it was only after hearing Dylan that he had the courage to sing), but his playing was something completely different. The amplified guitar is the instrumental trademark of the rock sound and Hendrix was its greatest master; possessed of incredible dexterity with the instrument, he was simply nonpareil. It has been twenty-some years since Jimi first laid

down his fantastic left-handed licks on a right-handed guitar, and nobody has come close to approximating the magic that he could force out of those six metal strings. In his hands, the instrument literally contained all the sounds of the modern technological world and Hendrix was able to call upon them at will. Blues-based, psychedelically colored, and jazz-tinged, Jimi's classic material is indigenous to the music's greatest era.

### Are You Experienced?

Reprise 6261-2 (41:07)     [A + ]
Dave Marsh called it "probably the most stunning debut album of all time." Peppered with honest-to-God classics like "Purple Haze," "I Don't Live Today," "Hey Joe," "Fire," and "Manic Depression," it exploded on the scene in what may have been the music's greatest year, 1967, and was the equal of the best that came out. While Jimi's telecaster was always the star of the show, the Experience, Noel Redding and Mitch Mitchell, were a cohesive unit whose strength was underpinning as well as magnifying the greatest rock guitar player that we've known. While Jimi "grew" in subsequent releases, this is probably his most accessible work and contains all the elements that remained central to his unique musical vision. The sound is a significant improvement over its vinyl counterpart.

### Axis: Bold as Love

Reprise 6281-2 (39:30)     [A–]
Clearly a transition between *Are You Experienced?* and *Electric Ladyland, Axis* contains some of Jimi's prime ballad material, "Little Wing" and "Castles Made of Sand." Given the fact that so many of Hendrix's sounds were built on feedback and distortion (all precisely planned and executed), the sound on this CD is excellent, close to crystal-clear with more dynamics than are realistically expected from recordings of this era.

### Electric Ladyland

Reprise 6307-2 (75:36—two discs)     [A + ]
Jim was a space pilot, whose frontiers were sound. He bared his blues' soul from beneath psychedelic finery, but he was always true to that soul, cognizant of the dues paid and still due. Called genius, called wizard, he was a black light that burned like the sun at night. He was magic, mythic, and momentary. But the moment is partially captured here. Experience it. The sound easily surpasses the LP, but live cuts have noticeable mike hum and other minor glitches are apparent, although not extensive or intensive enough to affect a unique sonic statement.

### Jimi Plays Monterey

Polydor 827990-2 (41:17)     [A + ]
Woodstock and Altamont became sixties bywords, but the Monterey Pop Festival held in June of 1967 was clearly the musical event of the decade. In no small part this was because of Hendrix and the Experience, whose appearance marked a triumphant return from England. With this performance, Jimi introduced the American audience to another vocabulary for the rock guitar. On Sunday, June 18, in the clear coastal California night, Jimi's guitar burned—figuratively and literally. This historic moment has been captured with wonderful fidelity on the CD, particularly given its vintage and the fact that it is an outdoor concert recording.

### The Singles Album

Polydor 827 369-2 (90:00—two discs)     [A]
The twenty-three selections represent the A and B sides of all this important artist's important singles. The fact that Jimi's musical canvas covered a wide variety of styles, each somehow expressing his otherworldly persona, is amply illustrated on this fine compilation. The sound, while sometimes muddy in the bass and drums, still crackles with the electricity of Hendrix's genius. Distortion is supposed to sound distorted, but some cuts (e.g., "Gloria") sound very muffled. The liner notes, while brief, are factual and informative.

### Kiss the Sky

Polydor 823 704-2 (46:36)     [B + ]

This eleven-selection compilation includes work from various sources (albums, singles, and concerts) which is representative of the best of his ground-breaking contribution to the music in the 1960s. The sound quality varies all over the place, but compared to the LP counterparts of this material, it's a substantial improvement.

### The Jimi Hendrix Experience Live at Winterland

Rykodisc RCD 200338 (71:45)     [B + ]

This CD-only concert release recorded October 10-12, 1968, contains the only live versions of some of Hendrix's stronger material: "Manic Depression," "Sunshine of Your Love," "Spanish Castle Magic," and "Tax Free" probably making this a "must" recording for hardcore Hendrix fans. While Ryko has done an admirable job with the cleanness of the sound, it's still a concert recording (with mike hum, etc.) of a band for whom distortion was stock and trade. Given these limitations, it's a quality production right down to the packaging, which includes a reprint of the wonderful sixties psychedelic poster used by Bill Graham to promote the performance at which these recordings were made. This is a very good Hendrix concert release, but it lacks the fire that made *Live at Monterey* such an incendiary experience.

## The Hollies

Formed 1962—Manchester, England

This sweet singing quintet represented England's most successful sixties singles band, after, of course, the Beatles.

### The Hollies Greatest Hits

Epic CK 32061 (37:03)     [B + ]

Pop pastry elegantly served, but pastry nonetheless. This accurately titled twelve-selection disc should induce a little honest nostalgia for those who experienced these well-crafted confections firsthand in the mid- to late-1960s, and, whether one was there or not, "Long Cool Woman" still sounds great. The sound

quality varies among the cuts; overall it is more clear and spacious than expected, but the upper mid-range on the vocals tends to an edgy harshness too often.

## Tommy James and the Shondells

Formed 1960—Niles, Michigan

### The Best of Tommy James and the Shondells

Roulett RCD42040 (33:10)     [C]

In case you thought the sixties were a garden of Beatles and Stones, consider this: in a recording career of less than four years (the band broke up in 1970), Tommy James and the Shondells produced seven million-seller singles, including "Crimson & Clover" which, alone, sold five-and-a-half-million copies. But two decades after the fact, there isn't much to recommend here. It's not that it's bad, it just isn't that good.

## The Jefferson Airplane

Formed 1965—San Francisco

This group took folk rock to the land of chemistry (San Francisco was Owsley Stanley's home territory) and then were the first (by virtue of a national recording contract with RCA) to export the message around the world. While their earliest efforts were a bit rustic, the original lineup was made up of quality musicians whose work between 1967 and 1969 attained a richness and complexity sometimes overlooked. After that they caved in to the weirdness. The Airplane became a Starship, unfortunately, in name only.

### Surrealistic Pillow

RCA PCD13766 (34:55)     [C–]

What sounds so innocent today was revolutionary two decades ago. "White Rabbit," introduced here, became the first national anthem to the common drug experience. Musically, this is a fine release that is poorly served by the digital conversion. It sounds as if it was recorded at the end of a bowling alley. It is recommended you either save your LP or check out the Jefferson Airplane compilation recording, *2400 Fulton Street* (reviewed below), which covers the key selections on this otherwise fine release.

### 2400 Fulton Street (The CD Collection)

RCA 5724-2-RP1&P2 (133:13—two discs)     **[B + ]**
For all intents and purposes it's all here (maybe even a little more than you really want)—the major components of the psychedelic sound of San Francisco in the sixties. The sound quality obviously varies, but overall it's a bit muffled and boxy, though still better than the LP versions and much cleaner. During the Airplane's period of strongest creativity (1966-70), they moved from folk rock through psychedelic acid weirdness to political activism and science fiction babble. Their dense, often demented sound, still probably conjures up the Summer of Love more potently than any other band for most Americans. This is what the "heads" in the beads, sandals, and tie-dyes grooved on two decades past, and while it sounds a bit dated, it still sounds good.

# Ben E. King (Benjaman Earl Soloman)

b. September 28, 1938—Henderson, North Carolina

### The Ultimate Collection (Stand By Me)

Atlantic 7 80213-2 (56:33)     **[B + ]**
Working with the Drifters producers' Liber and Stoller (two of rock's least acknowledged, but most influential early architects) and Phil Spector, King was part of some of the most influential soul music cut in the early sixties. Perhaps because he was the lead voice on the reputed first soul hit to employ strings, "There Goes My Baby" (with the Drifters 6/1/59), his work has been too often smothered with overly sweet instrumental settings. In addition to being one of the premier male soul singers of the early sixties, King was a fine composer who had a hand in the writing of many of his hit recordings. As with all col-

lections assembled from recordings made at different times and places, it is difficult to generalize about the sound. Also, as is almost always the case with Atlantic, it is best described as sounding like a good LP; the CD does suffer from some vocal distortion and an overbright edge to some of the vocal tracks.

# Led Zeppelin

Formed 1968—England
Originally formed under the name the New Yardbirds, Led Zeppelin was the first exponent of the bombast that has mutated into the young white male phenomenon now known as "heavy metal," a subgenre which often seems like the indestructible cockroach of rock & roll. To ignore their instrumental talents and preconceived intent would be uninformed; to ascribe much meaning or importance to their extraordinarily popular output would be misguided.

### Led Zeppelin

Atlantic SD19126-2 (44:58)     **[B]**
The first explosion! To their blues-based madness—which Jimmy Page, their lead guitarist and the producer of this self-titled debut effort had developed during his stint with John Mayall's Bluesbreakers—they added a theatrical sense of dynamics which both heightened the bombast and sustained interest. Their form of rock was defined by *The Rolling Stone Encyclopedia of Rock & Roll,* "as sculptured noise." They were one of the earliest bands to understand and use the recording studio as another distinct element of their sound, and, with the excellent Glyn Johns providing engineering, the sound of their recordings is big and "bad." The CD sound, while free of hiss and powerful, remains compressed and muffled around the edges.

### Led Zeppelin II

Atlantic 19127-2 (41:40)     **[B–]**
Chosen by a panel of critics in the August 27, 1987, *Rolling Stone* magazine as one of the hundred best rock albums released between

1967 and 1987, it was described by the publication as "The Book of Revelation scored for an electric boogie quartet." It did codify the monster sound that rapidly became a noise heard around the world. This was rock's primal message of rebellion expressed in elemental form—almost pure deafening noise. And young male teen rockers understood it loud and clear, as have legions of heavy metal successors who have recombined Zeppelin's explosive sonic blast and occult preoccupations into a consistently successful commercialism. While not a concert recording, the album was cut in various locations during the band's initial touring phase, with resultant variation in its sound, which sometimes includes mike hum and tape hiss and often sounds dampened as if it were recorded in a padded cell; which, come to think of it . . .

# The Lovin' Spoonful

Formed 1965—New York City

### Greatest Hits

Deluxe CD1022 (23:20)     **[D–]**
This is a disc to avoid; abbreviated playing time with sound values roughly equivalent to a clean LP.

### The Very Best of the Lovin' Spoonful

Buddah BCD68002 (41:33)     **[B]**
This was East Coast folk rock at its friendliest. "Do You Believe in Magic," "Daydream," "Younger Girl," and "Summer in the City," you gotta love it. Not a lot of substance, but sure a lot of appeal. The sound wanders all over the place ranging from the merely pedestrian to a substantial improvement over prior LPs.

# The Mamas and The Papas

Formed 1965—New York City
The members of this fine singing group paid their dues in the Greenwich Village folk scene of the early to mid-sixties, but came together as a group in California. They employed their fine harmonies to extol the virtues of life in the golden state.

### 16 of Their Greatest Hits

MCA MCAD5701 (49:23)     **[B + ]**
In the early sixties the Beach Boys established southern California as the home of harmonious rock singles and this late sixties quartet, augmented by slick (but generally tasteful) Hollywood production, continued those traditions beautifully. The Mamas and The Papas were the perfect southern California sound during the Summer of Love; happy faces and peace signs. They were also instrumental in the creation of the 1967 Monterey Pop Festival. As usual, MCA has done a more than credible job of digital transfer—the sound is clean, clear, and appreciably more spacious than the LP. The beauty of the interplay of the individual voicings within these familiar harmonies is markedly enhanced.

# Martha (Reeves) and the Vandellas

Formed 1962—Detroit
This group represented the "blackest" of the Motown girl-group sounds in that Reeves's impassioned vocals were closer to her R&B roots than the pure pop product which Motown marketed so expertly.

### 24 Greatest Hits

Gordy GCD06170 GD (65:08)     **[B + ]**
Bright, brassy, and blues-based, Martha and the Vandellas showed more roots than any other female group to come off of Gordy's wondrous assembly line. This is get-down party music, Motown style, and a quarter of a century after it first fueled a Friday groove, it still performs. The sound is thin and over-bright, but as is usually the case with old

Motown vinyl, this disc is still an improvement over the LP.

# John Mayall's Bluesbreakers
Formed 1963—England

### Mayall's Bluesbreakers with Eric Clapton
London 800-086-2 (37:43)      **[B + ]**
Before rock & roll was commandeered by the
British in the early 1960s, there was an active
audience in that country for local interpreters
of American blues. This English musical tradition formed the launching pad for a number
of major rock figures. While Mayall is a respectable blues musician (particularly on
harmonica), his name is remembered more
for the musicians who played in the Bluesbreakers from time to time than for the music
actually made by that group. This disc features Eric Clapton and arguably includes his
finest recorded guitar work. The sound has a
slight "distance" to it (because of the subtle
reverberations that make it sound like it was
recorded in a small dive), but it's much
cleaner than any prior form of release, with a
slight, unobtrusive, brightness or edge to it.

# Van Morrison
# (George Ivan)
b. August 31, 1945—Belfast, Northern Ireland
The mystic Irish minstrel of rock & roll who,
after leaving Them (the band that first
brought him international acclaim) in 1966,
has pursued his private vision, on his own
terms, for two decades. In the process he has
created a legacy of unique music rooted in the
blues, jazz, and Celtic mysticism that maintains an enduring potency, perhaps unique in
the annals of rock & roll.

### T.B. Sheets
Bellaphone 288-07-001 (42:52)      **[B]**
Contains the fascinating transitional record-
ings done around 1967, between the end of
Them and the beginning of the Warner Broth-
ers solo career in 1968, which commenced

with the breathtaking *Astral Weeks*. From
"Madam George," which is included on both
recordings in markedly different readings, to
elements of other selections, this is the obvious precursor to Van's better known work. It
also contains the truly frightening title cut
and one of the two best rock singles of his
long recording career, "Brown-Eyed Girl" (the
other being "Gloria" from his Them period).
The disc has a clean but dated, hard-edged,
overbright sound, which suffers occasionally
from some nasty distortion.

### Astral Weeks
Warner Bros. 1768-2 (47:16)      **[A + ]**
Perhaps the single most enduring recording
in the history of rock & roll, and it probably
really isn't rock & roll at all, with its jazz
musicians and mystical vocal flights into
another "land on high." Recorded in about
forty-eight hours with little direction from
Morrison regarding the lyrical, musical structures which support the oblique, masterfully
sung poetry of its words. A recording for
those tranquil yet vibrant moments when
another reality seems to hover over the day
like the mists over Van's native Ireland. The
CD is very clean and clear, but adds little dynamic or spatial enhancement to its analog
predecessor. The most apparent difference is
an overall "brightening" of the sound, especially in the vocals, which, while short of the
edginess often criticized in digital sound, is
not necessarily an improvement.

# Wilson Pickett
b. March 18, 1941—Prattville, Alabama

### Greatest Hits
Atlantic 7813737-2 (71:18)      **[A]**
The wicked Mr. Pickett was one of the most
macho of the sixties soul giants who recorded
for Atlantic Records during the sixties, the
label's golden era. Beginning in gospel music,
Pickett moved to R&B with the Falcons and in
1962 scored his first hit with that group, "I
Found a Love" which is one of this collection's twenty-four selections, but one which is

terribly reproduced. Essentially, all of his raw, high-energy hits are included on this CD, the only exceptions being "Call My Name, I'll Be There" (5/18/71) and "Fire And Water" (12/25/67). "In the Midnight Hour," "Land of a Thousand Dances," "Mustang Sally," and "Funky Broadway," plus numerous other gems that never really moved out of the black market, make this an essential collection. Sound quality, not a forte of Atlantic, is a little above their average, but it is very uneven. Some cuts are plagued with hiss, others have vocal distortions, yet, the question is against what sonic standard are these twenty-year-old recordings to be measured. Compared to digitally recorded, mixed, and reproduced quality eighties music, they obviously fail to measure up. But compared to their vinyl counterparts, they are substantial audio improvements.

## Pink Floyd
Formed 1965—London
One of England's first psychedelic rock bands, their sixties output was a little more than imitative of the San Francisco acid-rock scene. However, with the seventies, and particularly the release of their enduring *Dark Side of the Moon,* Pink Floyd catapulted itself into a special role in the hearts of rock listeners.

### The Piper at the Gates of Dawn
EMI CDP7 463842 (41:58)    [C + ]
England's answer to the Jefferson Airplane, Pink Floyd persevered and prospered long after the Airplane crashed and burned. This, their original statement (recorded at London's Abbey Lane Studio at the same time the Beatles were recording *Sgt. Pepper* there), is revered by hardcore Floyd fans because it represents the vision of the band's founder and original prime mover, Syd Barrett, who shortly thereafter succumbed to a permanent drug-assisted psychedelia known more commonly as mental illness. As musical history, it's an interesting, but not really innovative, recording. However, the seeds of Pink Floyd's later

success clearly germinated in this wacky soil. The CD's sound is impressive.

## Gene Pitney
b. February 17, 1941—Hartford, Connecticut

### Anthology (1961-1968)
Rhino RNCD75896 (44:34)    [C + ]
If you happen to be one of the rare, surviving Pitney fans, you're gonna love this. Pitney, who at times sounded like a poor man's Roy Orbison, is a hard artist to pigeonhole. As a rock composer, he wrote or cowrote "Hello, Marylou" and "He's a Rebel," both clearly rock numbers. His own repertoire ran the gamut from rock to pop to country. All the essentials, plus some true rarities, are included among the disc's sixteen selections, all rendered in marvelous digital sound, thanks, once again, to Rhino's Bill Inglot.

## Elvis Presley

### The Memphis Record
RCA 6221-2-R (72:07)    [A + ]
In 1969, Elvis released one of his stronger recordings entitled *From Elvis in Memphis.* This disc contains that album in full, reproduced with marvelous digital enhancement which would make the CD, if nothing else were added, an outstanding addition to any rock library. However, fourteen uneven tracks have been added to the CD including some gems ("Rubberneckin'" and "I'm Movin' On"). All twenty-three tracks were cut in Memphis over roughly a two-week period when approximately thirty-five selections were produced. The ones that did not appear on the *From Elvis in Memphis* LP turned up later as singles or B sides on other recordings. In addition, some of this work appeared in the double album *Vegas to Memphis and Memphis to Vegas* which was abbreviated into a single album and sold for a period of time under the name *Back in Memphis.*

But this was the last time in the King's career that he appeared to really care about putting all that fierce talent on the line—it was early 1969, hard on the heels of the historic 1968 TV special that showed the sixties' upstarts once and for all why the King held the throne. This was, sadly, the final display of the essence of it all. Perhaps it was the return to home turf (it had been fourteen years since Elvis started it all at the old Sun Studios in Memphis), but as Peter Guralnick accurately observes in his liner notes to this release, on these sessions, Presley was infused with the gospel spirit that is at the heart of much of the music and clearly was a part of the heart of the man.

# The Rascals
Formed 1965—New York City

### The Ultimate Rascals
Warner Bros. 9-27605-2 (60:33)    **[D]**
The sixties white soul band that launched the career of Felix Cavaliere also scored some major chart success with "Good Lovin'," "Groovin'," and "People Got to Be Free," all included here. Unfortunately, the digital remastering of this material is pathetic; in short, it stinks.

# Otis Redding
b. September 9, 1941—Dawson, Georgia
d. December 10, 1967
One of the truly great male soul singers of the sixties, Redding's principle audience (at least prior to 1967 when he appeared at Monterey Pop) was the black community that supported soul music generally; however, his influence on numerous sixties rock stars is undeniable.

### The Ultimate Otis Redding
Warner Special Products 9-27608-2 (54:53)    **[C]**
In the golden age of great soul singers, Redding's raw, honest readings of classic material easily placed him near the top of the hierarchy. His influence on both white performers of the day, and on the youth audience that was just discovering the diversity of material upon which rock was formulated, was im-

mense. His performance was one of the highlights of the legendary Monterey Pop affair. The compilation covers essentially all of his important studio sides, but suffers from uneven, often weak, sound. The recording has an arid, almost sterile quality about it which is diametrically opposed to the gut-wrenching passion that fueled this major artist's best work. It's suggested that the buyer wait for disc versions of Redding's live material (*Live in Europe* or *At Monterey*) since this collection just doesn't make it.

# Smokey Robinson and the Miracles
Formed 1957—Detroit
After Berry Gordy, Robinson was the most important musical factor in the creation of the marvelous Motown sound.

### 18 Greatest Hits
Motown 6071-2 TD (58:34)    **[A]**
Smokey and the Miracles were primarily, if not exclusively, a singles band; thus, compilation albums were the norm for this group. "Shop Around" (12/12/60) was Motown's first hit record, the cut that put the company on the map. Throughout the sixties, Smokey and the Miracles were the musical pinnacle of Motown's gifted raft of artists, and the songs that proved that are all right here. In addition to Robinson's consummate sense of pop musicality, which shapes both the content and the form of the material, his soaring, silky voice is simply without peer. The sound is typical Motown, generally uneven, but, overall, an improvement over prior reproductions.

# The Rolling Stones
Formed July, 1962—London
After almost a quarter century of constant exposure, the Rolling Stones remain one of the most enigmatic bands in the history of rock & roll. Unlike a majority of their contemporaries who turned to the music to express their rebellion or as an avenue out of an un

desirable lifestyle, the Stones' approach always appeared somewhat more calculated.

As the self-appointed princes of darkness in the Beatles' magic kingdom of British sixties pop, their cynical, blues-postured stance enabled them to survive the death of the dream (Altamont) and to apparently effortlessly slide into supremacy with the advent of the self-indulgent, cynical seventies (the "world's greatest rock & roll band"). But their stature was obviously not only a matter of stance or attitude—musically these calculating ruffians brought a first-rate set of chops to the party—Wyman and Watts representing the best "bottom" ever; supporting Richards's classic, slashing Chuck Berry style primal guitar licks and Jones's enlightened, eclectic private madness.

They made seminal work in the seminal sixties and have continued a steady stream of material of widely varying quality for over twenty years. Their truly great contributions began with *Now* (1965) and ended with *Exile on Main Street* (1972). While the passing years have sapped the Stones' musical creativity, they have remained one of rock's cultural avatars for an impossibly long time. Until recently they seemed attuned to the cultural crosscurrents of their times more acutely than any of their peers.

### The Rolling Stones (England's Newest Hitmakers)

abco 73752 (31:12)    **[B + ]**
Obviously, a first album, one on which Jagger, most notably, was groping for his vocal persona, but, on some cuts ("I'm a King Bee") the most famous mouth in rock & roll was beginning to find his unique sound. If Jagger was groping, the rest of the boys had found their niche—hard-assed white R&B, and they performed it far better than any of the many who have sought that pulsing path to musical salvation. This is determinedly hard music, played as hard as they could. The sound on most of the abco Rolling Stones digital remasters is truly revelatory. The story at the time of their release was that great care had been taken to go back to the true master tapes and eliminate a lot of the "contouring" that had been done on the analog releases. Whatever technique was employed, it works. It must be remembered that on the earliest releases, this one being from 1964, there is still a primitive, compressed quality to the markedly improved sound.

### 12 X 5

abco 74022 (31:20)    **[B]**
Released in 1965, a clear successor to the '64 debut release *England's Newest Hitmakers,* this one bounces from the sublime "Time Is on My Side" to the ridiculous "Under the Board Walk." The rest of the heavily blues-oriented material is generally strong instrumentally, but somehow misses with Jagger's vocals. The sound is slightly more dynamic than that of the first recording, but is marred by occasional distortion.

### Now

abco 74202 (38:18)    **[A–]**
Also released in '65, but here Jagger has found his "voice," which insinuates through the thick aggressive blues-based rock that the band played better and better. The material is pretty much "of a piece" with its two predecessor album releases with "Mona" and "Everybody Needs Somebody to Love," clearly the class of the outing. The sound is more uneven than on the earlier releases, but while some muddy moments occur, it remains a real improvement over the LP.

### Out of Our Heads

abco 74292 (33:59)    **[B + ]**
Actually, one of their most uneven early efforts, a quality that frequently mars this great band's recorded output. Cuts like "The Last Time," "That's How Strong My Love Is," "Satisfaction" (for historical reasons), "The Under Assistant West Coast Production Man," and "Play With Fire" still hold their power after years of exposure, but much of the rest simply disappears. Too often the sound is murky, particularly the bass/drum track which is often distorted, but this wasn't supposed to be *Tubular Bells.* The garage band

syndrome is, by now, endemic to the form, but the sound could be better.

### December's Children (And Everybody's)

abco 74512 (29:52)     [C]

"Get Off of My Cloud" and "I'm Free" rank with the best Stones' singles of this period, but get them on a greatest hits collection, because the rest of this recording is lacking in both material and intensity. The sound, while generally an improvement over the record, is unlistenable on the live version of "Route 66" and varies from there.

### Big Hits (High Tides and Green Grass)

abco 8001-2 (36:14)     [A]

A powerful compilation that essentially, if not completely, sums up this legendary group's formative years, 1964-66. Not for the faint-hearted, but as honest a testimonial to the true spirit of rock & roll as any group bore during this golden period for the music. The sound varies, as expected, but this is a collection one would want in the permanent CD format.

### Aftermath

abco 74762 (43:46)     [A + ]

This is the landmark statement. With *Aftermath*, the Stones staked out their own territory, reflective of their sources, but dependent upon no one. Jagger's lascivious vocal style holds its center and the best rock band in the world begins to feel its awesome authority. The texture of their sound is enhanced by Brian Jones's use of offbeat instrumentation, and, while the lyrics seem a bit calculated, the end result is a clear and identifiable posture. The sound simply leaves the LP in the Dark Ages.

### Between the Buttons

abco 74992 (38:36)     [B + ]

Another change in the band's direction, marked by a quick, but inevitable withdrawal from the misogynistic lyrical posturing (and "down" sound) of *Aftermath*. It is not the musical equal of its predecessor, but contains some lesser known treasures, "Connection,"

"My Possession," "Complicated" as well as a couple of hits. The sound quality is more than satisfactory.

### Flowers

abco 75092 (37:49)     [B–]

At this point the band's album history gets somewhat confusing since most of the LP releases of the period were primarily singles compilations that included duplications. Thus, "Ruby Tuesday," "Let's Spend the Night Together," and "Lady Jane" appear on earlier albums. When these cuts, plus the filler items are eliminated, the only selections included here worthy of much attention are "Mother's Little Helper," "Right On, Baby," "Sittin' on a Fence," and "Have You Seen Your Mother Standin' in the Shadow" which are all strong sixties Stones' singles. The sound is noticeably different from cut to cut, but almost always preferable to the LP.

### Beggars Banquet

abco 75392 (40:37)     [A + ]

While most of the rest of the pop world was lovin' through the apocalypse, the Stones told it like it was (or soon would be), and it wasn't pretty—but, God, it's frighteningly strong. One of rock & roll's true masterpiece recordings, produced by a band whose mask was evil and whose reality wasn't far behind—only the Rolling Stones could have played Altamont. If you didn't know the dream was dead, or maybe never was, then you just weren't listening. Glyn Jones, the album's engineer, called it "the Stones coming of age." The CD chisels the sound in space with a clarity that enhances an already great album.

### Through the Past Darkly (Big Hits Vol. 2)

abco 80032 (39:31)     [C]

Here we go again with the overlapping inclusions on compilation releases. Everything here is on other album releases except "She's a Rainbow," "Jumpin' Jack Flash," and "Honky Tonk Women" (two of which reappear on *Hot Rocks*); even a sampling from *Their Satanic Majesties* which was the Stones' first travesty album. The sound varies, but is generally very acceptable.

### Let It Bleed

abco 80042 (43:00)      **[A]**

And the Stones adjust their stance yet again. But they were still working at the height of their dark powers and the end result is another enduring, if not a perfect, effort. While it lacks the consistency, and espoused brutality of its predecessor, it nonetheless achieves an equally sublime potency on a number of cuts. The sound, while far from crystalline, throbs with all the pelvic potency intended.

# Mitch Ryder and the Detroit Wheels

Formed 1965—Detroit

### Greatest Hits

Roulette RCD59020 (34:12)      **[B + ]**

Detroit has been a major contributor to American rock & roll, and one of its premier contributions was Mitch Ryder and the Detroit Wheels (among the music's true anthems, Ryder's "Devil With a Blue Dress/Good Golly Miss Molly" and "Jenny Take a Ride" still ring loud and clear). This is rock & roll. The sound varies all over the place, but overall it adds a dynamic punch and highlights the raucous noise which was Ryder's pure rock voice.

# Simon & Garfunkel

Formed 1957/1964—New York City

This immensely popular duo really was more folk or pop-oriented than true purveyors of pure rock & roll; however, their pioneering efforts, marked by Simon's eclectic musical craftsmanship and creativity, broadened the rock audience throughout their highly successful career.

### Parsley, Sage, Rosemary and Thyme

Columbia CK9363 (28:34)      **[B + ]**

The master of sardonic eclecticism in his collegiate folk phase, but Simon's sense of musicianship and compositional craft, combined with Garfunkel's truly lovely voice, has resulted in music of sustaining quality. Additionally, ever since producer Tom Wilson made the duo stars by investing their acoustic "Sounds of Silence" with some "after the fact" studio electric guitar magic, they always handled their production with meticulous care, thanks largely to the engineering precision of Roy Hallee. That care pays off on the digital conversion. The sound has a purity to it, particularly in the glorious harmonies.

### Bookends

Columbia CK9529 (29:49)      **[A + ]**

It was the year after *Sgt. Pepper*—it was the time of "concept albums." Most who undertook this format failed, either by comparison or by simple lack of talent. Simon & Garfunkel were the exception. *Bookends* is an essential musical picture of its time and place. "America" is one of the great pop/rock songs. You're gonna love how this CD sounds.

# Percy Sledge

b. 1941—Leighton, Alabama

### The Ultimate Collection (When a Man Loves a Woman)

Atlantic 780212-2 (57:59)      **[C + ]**

Soul for the soap opera set—Sledge sludged through some of the most tear-stained lyrics to be found in sixties soul music. He did it pretty well, often overblown productions, notwithstanding. His popularity reached its zenith in April of 1966 when his "When a Man Loves a Woman" reached the No. 1 position on the charts; it was his first release. As is too often the case with Atlantic's vintage material, the sound is comparable to a clean LP; not bad, but not what it might be.

# Sly and the Family Stone
Formed 1966/1967—San Francisco
Sly is one of the most underrated major contributors to the history of rock & roll. In addition to his innovative rock/funk sounds, Sly was the first to physically present a band reflective of the social ideals of his audience in that it included performers both male and female, black and white.

## Stand!
Epic EK26456 (41:31)     **[A]**
A positive, intelligent expression of the upheaval that energized the sixties, by a band that broke all the rules and produced some of the best and most innovatively exciting music of the time. This is music that seethes with vitality—it makes you happy—it speaks the vernacular of its day. The sound is strong and clean but, occasionally, a bit edgy.

# The Supremes
Formed 1960—Detroit

## Diana Ross and the Supremes 20 Greatest Hits
Motown MCD06073 MD (58:34)     **[A + ]**
The greatest creation of Berry Gordy, the man who finally, effectively marketed the great black pop product to the white audience—and market it, he did. In the case of the Supremes, all the way to the No. 1 on the pop chart twelve times, which is little short of amazing; particularly in the sixties, the richest musical decade ever known. One listen to this disc is all the explanation needed—it's still perfect pop music. The sound, which has its weak moments, is, overall, markedly superior to the low-end vinyl that originally conveyed this joyous product.

# The Temptations
Formed 1962—Detroit

## 17 Greatest Hits
Gordy GCD06125 GD (58:04)     **[B + ]**
For all of Berry Gordy's assembly-line precision, Motown remained a producer's studio and the Temptations' most inventive producer was Norman Whitfield (the man who brought us, "I Heard It through the Grapevine" by both Gladys Knight and Marvin Gaye). The original Temptations lineup, which featured two of the era's better soul lead voices, tenor Eddie Kendricks, and baritone David Ruffin, was a perfect vehicle for Whitfield's creativity which ultimately helped to open up and sustain the Motown magic as well as employ the medium for something more than just the financial rewards ("Poppa Was a Rolling Stone"). It's all here, and it all sounds better than you ever heard it before.

# Ike & Tina Turner
Formed 1957/58—St. Louis

## The Best Of
EMI America CDP7-46599-2 (46:08)     **[C + ]**
The music is great, the sound quality is, unfortunately, best described as abrasive, particularly on the classic early material (the disc covers work from the early 1960s through the early 1970s). This is primarily noticeable with Tina's voice which tends to stridency in the first place, a quality which CDs do not readily accommodate. But Ike ran one of the tightest, most explosive soul revues of the sixties, so the music is almost strong enough to overcome the sonic limitations, and the later cuts are less diminished by distortion. Unfortunately, it contains their most popular selections; earlier ones ("I Idolize You") sound the worst. Even at its best, the sound on this disc is thin.

## River Deep-Mountain High
A&M 393 179-2 (37:14)     **[B + ]**
One of the strangest pairings in rock history—Phil Spector's Wagnerian production with Ike and Tina's spare, hard-edged R&B attack. This is the recording that temporarily moved Tom Woolfe's "Tycoon of Teen" (Spector) out of the industry that he had conquered only a few years earlier. Apparently Phil's high-handed airs caused the industry to sabotage the marketing of the title selection,

which Spector had dubbed his consummate studio effort. Thus, while *River Deep* surged in Britain, it stiffed in the U.S. This album is a bit of a hodgepodge, veering between Phil's grandiose, echo-laden effects and Ike's reworking of earlier classic material, yet it remains fascinating, if flawed. The sound, while far from ideal, is a great improvement over the LP and substantially cleaner than that on the *Best Of* collection.

# The Turtles

Formed 1963—Inglewood, California

### 20 Greatest Hits

Rhino RNCD5160 (52:26)     [A–]
Properly conceived and packaged, the compact disc provides the current ideal for musical information. Rhino Records, which has carved out a profitable niche in the music market by realizing the value of preserving material from earlier eras, has extended their sensitivity to the CD format and Rhino's combination of vintage works on CD mesh like the proverbial "hand in glove." This disc is a prime example of how a little care and intelligence can result in an invaluable package. The Turtles, a mid-sixties L.A. "folk/rock" group (with appropriate New York roots), scored one No. 1 hit, "Happy Together" (2/11/67) and a number of other Top Ten singles that captured the innocent, joyous side of the sixties with precision. While not great innovators, they made very polished, very popular music through a five-year career (1965-70), and, basically, it's all here. Enhanced by informative liner notes and excellent production of twenty-year-old material, this is a disc that will sustain.

# The Velvet Underground

Formed 1965—New York City
One of the most succinctly accurate observations of rock criticisms ever made was, "The Velvet Underground didn't have a lot of fans, but every one of them formed their own rock band." The influence of this amazing group on the music of the seventies and eighties has been both pervasive and potent.

### The Velvet Underground & Nico

Verve 823 290-2 (48:26)     [A + ]
The testament to the Velvet's greatness is all right here. It's not pretty music. But it's real music, made at a time when the mass audience was less than beguiled with reality. *The Velvet Underground & Nico* is one of the most important recordings in the history of rock & roll. This is one of those rare records where it all cosmically came together, or, as John Cale later said of the experience, "We just started playing and held it to the wall." The sound is both intentionally and unintentionally scuzzy (the original recording costs for this album supposedly totaled $1,500). This CD brings you the scuzz with new clarity, which is perfect.

### White Light/White Heat

Verve 825 119-2 (40:01)     [B + ]
Dissonance, both lyrical and musical, was always a part of the Velvet's sound. Well, this is their paean to the electronically discordant. While it is not pleasant listening, it is serious music. The sound is more open than the LP, but it's far from clean—it wasn't recorded clean.

### The Velvet Underground

Verve 815 45402 (43:00)     [A]
This is as laid-back as this cruelly prophetic band got. The recording is very well crafted and listenable. Unfortunately, it followed *White Light/White Heat,* the dissonance of which alienated a substantial number of the band's already less than substantial following of fans. That's too bad. Hopefully this disc release will awaken more listeners to the edge of truth which echoes through these recordings. The sound, while far from perfect, is a discernible improvement over the LP, and adds a warm intimacy to the preponderance of valid material included.

# The Who

Formed 1964—London

### The Singles

Polydor 815 965-2 (58:17)      [B + ]
This disc covers sixteen cuts from 1966 to 1981 (some of the earliest in mono) and seven of them are from the group's sixties glory years. Ultimately, one of the era's more self-conscious concept bands, thanks to Townshend's intellectual pretensions, the enduring work they did, the songs treasured by their fans, are the garage-band singles comprehensively included here. Driven by Keith Moon, probably the finest drummer in the history of rock—the man was a veritable war back there—their great singles captured the teenage spirit of rebellion (which knows no decade) as well as any group around. It was their core strength, and when their music sought to be "more," it generally just overreached. The sound doesn't provide a lot of surprises; it varies markedly from cut to cut and decade to decade. But the early material particularly suffers from compressed reproduction and most of it is a bit on the harsh side. Still, probably a worthwhile addition to the comprehensive rock CD library.

# Jackie Wilson

b. June 9, 1934—Detroit
d. January 21, 1984

### The Jackie Wilson Story

Epic EGK38623 (64:46)      [B + ]
This collection was released in 1983, but covers material from Wilson's earliest recorded efforts (Berry Gordy's "Reet Petite" from 1957 and his first real hit "Lonely Tear Drops" in 1959) to his mediocre, limited seventies output. During the sixties, Wilson was a genuine star on the R&B circuit, combining a first-rate singing voice with an athlete's performing pyrotechnics. Too often, his material was sabotaged with overbearing arrangements and the artist's tendencies to show off his vocal prowess. It's all here on this extensive package: the good, the bad, and the ugly. This is one of those CDs which, thanks to thoughtful song selection and comprehensive, intelligent liner notes, provides a fine encapsulation of a total career. The sound, of course, varies from cut to cut and a few sound awful, but, all in all, it's clean and an improvement over the corresponding LPs.

# The Yardbirds

Formed 1963—London

### The Best of British Rock

Pair SPCD2-1151 (49:03)      [A]
The English link between American R&B and international heavy metal, the Yardbirds' mid-sixties music, covered on this sixteen-track release, has had an extensive and enduring influence on the rock music that followed. This arose out of the group's succession of lead guitarists, Eric Clapton, Jeff Beck, and Jimmy Page, each possessed with technical dexterity, emotive purity, and a feel for the blues. These three expanded the vocabulary of electric guitar with their use of fuzztones, feedback, and other innovative techniques to accommodate a creative fusion of their blues roots with the psychedelic posture of their times. Of course, the end result was Led Zeppelin, who opened the gates to the unwashed horde that followed. But that doesn't detract from the quality or innovation that was evidenced in the best of the Yardbirds' music. The selections on this CD were all recorded in 1964 and 1965 and included all their best known cuts, the lead guitars on all tracks being either Eric Clapton or Jeff Beck, and their licks are lively. The sound varies but is never anything real special; though still far superior to LP versions.

# Neil Young

b. November 12, 1945—Toronto, Canada
Rock's most sophisticated primitive. A loner, despite numerous career affiliations: Buffalo Springfield, Crazy Horse, and Crosby, Stills, Nash & Young. An artist whose oblique persona may be as much a factor in his

commercial success as his musical talent. Called a visionary by some, he has managed to sustain a sometimes brilliant, sometimes banal, but always interesting career for more than two decades.

### (With Crazy Horse) Everybody Knows This Is Nowhere

Reprise 2282-2 (40:31)    **[B]**
Young's star shone brightest in 1972 when *Harvest* became his all-time best-selling LP, though musically it was really little more than a mediocre effort. *Everybody Knows This Is Nowhere,* released in 1969, the first to include Crazy Horse, a first-rate California bar band, is superior to *Harvest* and includes a few of Young's better songs, notably "Cinnamon Girl" and the album's title cut. The sound is generally an improvement over the LP, but it's far from perfect—heavy hiss on "Down By the River," weak and often muddy bottom on many cuts, yet it also adds a greatly enhanced presence to much of the recording.

# Frank Zappa

b. December 21, 1940—Baltimore
Rock's reigning intellectual and in the eighties, perhaps its most eloquent spokesman. His absurdist, satiric, sophisticated work encompasses rock/jazz/symphonic aspirations as well as the crassest forms of apparent scatological pandering. He has created a body of work which stands unique in the annals of popular music and which has attracted and held a substantial hardcore audience for over two decades.

### We're Only in It for the Money/Lumpy Gravy

Rykodisc RCD40024 (70:54)    **[A–]**
A two-fer for the twisted. *We're Only in It for the Money,* Zappa's satirical response to *Sgt. Pepper,* the Summer of Love, San Francisco, and anything else that would stick to the ceiling. Sound/music/montage/collage—ultimately an homage to the art of tape editing. *Lumpy Gravy* (his first solo release) presents his weirdness leading the fifty-person Abnuceals Emuukha Electric Symphony Orchestra and Chorus—'nuff said? The sound is truly outstanding, crystal clear, beautifully spaced, and absolutely insane.

# SIXTIES
# COLLECTIONS

"I love Beethoven, especially the poems."
—Ringo Starr

**Atlantic Rhythm & Blues (1947-1974)**
**Vol. 5 (1962-1966)**

Atlantic 7 81297-2 (72:45)     **[A]**

Volume 5 of this essential series covers R&B hits of such well-known acts as the Drifters, Otis Redding, Sam & Dave, Percy Sledge, and Wilson Pickett, as well as gems by lesser-knowns Barbara Lewis, Chris Kenner, and Don Covay. It adds up to twenty-six classic selections representative of the best of this type of material from an era when it was a vibrant musical form. The sound, while varying, is generally clean, but is clearly reflective of the limitations inherent in masters of this age, including some too apparent hiss on certain cuts. Unfortunately, Atlantic did not extend the same concern for recording qualities as they did on artists and repertoire. It's still a wonderful package, superior soundwise to the LP counterparts.

**Atlantic Rhythm and Blues (1947-1974)**
**Vol. 6 (1966-1969)**

Atlantic 7 81298-2 (73:15)     **[A + ]**

The twenty-five selections provide a fair sampling of Aretha "Lady Soul" Franklin's most popular recordings, as well as hits by Sam & Dave, Wilson Pickett, Joe Tex, and Otis Redding, among others. This is the cream of the great soul music explosion of the late sixties.

The sound, which is similar to that described on Volume 5 of this series, is a bit more dynamic and spacious than that heard on the earlier volumes.

**Atlantic Soul Classics**

Warner Special Products 9-27601-2 (44:41)     **[A]**

A curious fifteen-selection sampling from the great Atlantic R&B catalog which is fairly comprehensively covered in the multi-volume *Atlantic Rhythm & Blues (1947-1974)* series reviewed earlier. You really can't complain about the selections which encompass many of the "greats": Aretha, Otis, Sam & Dave, the Coasters, the Drifters, Ray Charles, Wilson Pickett, and other less successful but nonetheless talented artists from what was once known as the chitlin' circuit. While care has been taken to clean up the sound, which varies with each cut, overall it does reflect the compression inherent in most analog source material from this era.

**The Big Chill Soundtrack**

Motown MCD06120 MD (43:40)     **[B + ]**

Obviously, this material, encompassing numerous Motown classics plus other familiar sixties hits, e.g., Three Dog Night's "Joy to the World" and Procol Harum's "Whiter Shade of Pale," is marvelously appealing. The

67

movie and its soundtrack are credited with much of the sixties musical revival that has ultimately resulted in classic rock formats on many FM stations in the eighties. The sound is not the equal of the music, and it varies from selection to selection. While some cuts are well recorded, others like Marvin Gaye's signature "I Heard It Through the Grapevine" are plagued by excessive hiss. Overall, the sound of the disc is thin and compressed, however, excessive distortion is generally avoided.

### Great Songs Written by Holland-Dozier-Holland
Motown MCD06138MD (60:08)      [A + ]
Motown has been as creative as any record company in the repackaging of their classic hits for the CD market (they pioneered the two-fer concept—two albums on one disc). The Composer Series, out of which this package arises, rightfully focuses on the men and women behind the scenes who had so much to do with the label's success. Holland-Dozier-Holland, working with the Supremes, the Four Tops, Marvin Gaye, and Martha Reeves, were the sonic architects of many of Motown's contributions to the sixties Hit Parade and these twenty cuts are representative of the best pop music of the times, highlighted by the big multi-instrumental productions for which this team was duly noted. The sound is pretty clean (especially for Motown) but has a tendency toward overbrightness, particularly on the female vocals.

### The Great Songs Written by Smokey Robinson (Various Artists)
Motown MCD06139-2MD (48:27)      [A–]
If there ever was any doubt why William "Smokey" Robinson was the No. 2 man at Motown, one listen to this compilation featuring sixteen of his more popular compositions will extinguish it forever. Supposedly, Bob Dylan has called him one of the great poets of contemporary pop music (and if he didn't, he should have). The sound varies—different artists, different recording dates, and it's far from perfect—but it still beats the vinyl versions all to hell. Included are Smokey's great hits for

the Miracles ("Tracks of My Tears," "Shop Around"), the Temptations ("My Girl"), Mary Wells ("My Guy"), and Marvin Gaye ("Ain't that Peculiar").

### Highs of the '60s
Warner Special Products 9-27607-2 (53:52)      [B]
With the advent of the sixties, the democratic roots of rock & roll resulted in the emergence of bands from all over the place—after all, this was everyman's music; so, theoretically, every man and woman could make it. All of this resulted in a number of regional acts that became "one-hit" wonders, often generically described as psychedelic garage-band music. This strange assemblage of material includes a number of genuine classics of the form by such enduring artists as the Kingsmen, Count Five, Shadows of Knight, Blue Cheer, and the Seeds. Actually, the "hits" by these groups were often classic rock & roll imbued with raw, driving energy, and many are included here. Strangely, also included are the Association, the Knickerbockers, the Beau Brummels, and surf music from the Marketts whose selections add nothing, and actually dilute the rough edge that gives the other cuts stature. The sound is not as bad as one might expect considering the primitive sources and this label's generally poor attention to digital conversions.

### Nuggets (A Classic Collection from the Psychedelic Sixties)
Rhino RNCD 75892 (50:20)      [A]
Call them "one-hit" wonders. Their music has been labeled trash rock, garage band, sixties psychedelia; but under any name, it's indispensable to rock's indispensable decade. When the music rose to supremacy in the sixties, it brought with it literally hordes of local bands affecting the image and lifestyle of the era's musical heroes. Some of them had their cosmic moments which is what this disc is all about. If the Troggs, the Seeds, "Psychotic Reaction," the Nazz, or "Journey to the Center of the Mind" strike any responsive chords, then this is a must CD; if all of the above sounds like a foreign tongue and you

want to check out some of the sixties' sleazier successes, climb aboard, it's a worthwhile trip. Again, Bill Inglot's meticulous production values result in a wondrous revitalization of original Chevy recordings. It all works— works because it's infused with the joyous spirit of rock & roll.

## Oldies But Goodies Volume 3

OSCD8853 (45:35)

## Volume 4

OSCD8854 (44:12)

## Volume 5

OSCD8855 (43:24)

## Volume 6

OSCD8856 (36:46)

## Volume 9

OSCD8859 (39:54)

## Volume 10

OSCD8860 (44:53)

## Volume 11

OSCD8861 (43:54)

## Volume 14

OSCD8864 (49:59)

## Volume 15

OSCD8865 (45:13)    **[B]**

This series almost defies description in terms of the crazy quilt admixture of selections, the sequencing of the same, and the issuing sequence of the volumes themselves ("Oldies But Goodies" have been available as LP compilations for years). The material covered runs the gamut from the fifties through the seventies, but since a majority of the work included is from the sixties, these compilations are included here on the theory that this is as good a place as any. The collection is the brainchild of Art Laboe, "a disc jockey from L.A. who shares your special memories," and maybe that's all the explanation required. Laboe does provide liner notes which include release dates of each cut and chart position attained, if the cut ever charted. But most of the material is familiar, at

least to those over thirty-five or forty. Other than idiosyncrasies evidenced in the juxtaposition of eras and artists, what sets this series apart is the sound. A part of the digital conversion process on this series involves a patented enhancement process dubbed "fds" that adds heightened dynamics to much of the material. Frequently, the versions of popular cuts included on the "Oldies But Goodies" CDs represent the best sonic examples of the material available from any CD source. It's difficult to compare the volumes. Suffice it to say that the material covered on any given disc is generally appealing, so if you like the included songs, you won't be disappointed with the recording.

## The Soul of New Orleans

Charly CD Charley 14 (61:15)    **[A + ]**
From Fats Domino to Little Richard, the musical heritage of the Crescent City (a heady mixture of African, Caribbean, and Cajun influences) has provided the source of some of this country's best pop music of the last thirty years. This excellent collection, which features some of the City's premier sixties local stars (Lee Dorsey, Robert Parker, Aron Neville, the Meters, the Dixie Cups, and Hughie "Piano" Smith, among others) is a wonderful summary of the upbeat, polyrhythmic sound clearly identifiable with New Orleans. This is music which inspired a lot of rock hits. While the age of the source material can still be heard on the CD, this is one of the better sixties compilations in terms of sound quality.

## Toga Rock

Dunhill DZ5029 (42:48)    **[A + ]**
Despite the insultingly silly title and cover, this turns out to be one of the better sixties compilation CDs (and it is all still great party music). A first-rate collection of elbow-bending, hip-shaking "standards" ("Louie, Louie," "Woolly Bully," "Mony, Mony," "Devil With A Blue Dress" . . . you get the idea) with high quality sound. Dunhill has been a company that has respected the permanent nature of the disc by taking the time to do careful digi-

tal conversions from the cleanest, least manipulated masters available, and the audio payoff comes through loud and clear.

## 20 Party Classics

Warner Special Products 9-27602-2 (49:26)    **[D]**
Whoever chose the twenty included selections deserves a pat on the back—whoever did the digital mastering deserves a kick in the ass. 'Nuff said.

## More Party Classics

Warner Special Products 9-27670-2 (43:20)    **[B + ]**
This time out the material is not as consistently strong. The sound quality is generally improved, although still far from what it might be. Overall, a slightly better package, but there are much better sixties collections.

## Wonderwomen (History of the Girl Group Sound)

Rhino RNCD 75891 (41:16)    **[B + ]**
During the early to mid-sixties, a strain of pop/rock was established that has garnered the tacky title "girl group sound." It is, however, descriptive. Probably founded by the Shirelles (included here), the form was popularized by Phil "Wall of Sound" Spector with his grandiose productions behind the likes of the Crystals and Ronettes (not included here). Actually, these sounds represent an interesting bridge between the more standard pop form that dominated the charts before the advent of rock & roll and the music of the sixties rock revolution. Like the standard pop, this was music usually created by committee, i.e., a writer, an artist, a producer, and an arranger. But, like rock, it was dominated by propulsive rhythms and a teenage lyrical stance. This compilation, especially the true

"girl group" cuts, is consistently first-rate. As is the usual case with Rhino, the sound, while reflecting its age from time to time, is a solid improvement over any other versions of hits made at a time when women vocalists enjoyed their greatest popular success. Excellent album notes complete a fine package.

## Woodstock/Woodstock II

Mobil Fidelity Sound MFCD41816
(226:09—four discs)    **[B]**
More aural history than concert recording. To say that it's all here would obviously be a literal overstatement—the festival ran for over three days (and these selections were drawn from seventy-two hours of recorded tape). But after listening to the three hours and forty-six minutes of music as well as the now infamous stage announcements, it's as close as one is going to get almost two decades after the fact. It's worthwhile to remember that the 400,000 who were a part of this event were representatives of the last real people's revolution this nation has experienced. Impossible as it now seems, they and countless others like them really did stop the war. Woodstock was the first great sixties event, the first mega-be-in and no one was prepared for the human outpouring to which it bore musical witness. Soundwise what you get is the magic moment with all its warts intact—the feedback and the hums, the flat performances and the faux pas that make this more concert verité than musical pinnacle— it was really a question of who was there and why rather than what they played or heard. This CD package captures that as well as it can now be done, but you won't play this one for its sound quality.

# THE
# SEVENTIES

"Everything all the time."

—Anonymous

Like the third month of each year, the third decade of rock & roll came in like the proverbial lion and left like the proverbial lamb.

The early seventies, for the most part, marked a continuation of the great musical creativity that had exploded from the mid-sixties forward. But all was far from perfect in paradise.

The very success of rock and its acceptance by vast numbers of the affluent culture of the western world began to nurture the seeds of destruction, or, at least, substantial diminution.

Popular acceptance in a commercially oriented world means material excess for the accepted. By the mid-seventies, the gross revenues from the sales of direct recorded products (LPs, 45s, and cassettes) were approximating $4 billion a year. In addition to those revenues, the industry was earning substantial amounts from the sale of concert tickets, T-shirts, and related memorabilia, as well as vast sums from the publishing rights that reflected the domination of rock music over national radio.

As was inevitable with the American economy, that kind of meteoric financial success attracted the business establishment, which, during the seventies, was marching to its own drummer: conglomeratization. The end result of this unholy alliance was a transfer of control over the creation, promotion, and distribution of the rock product from artists whose principal concern was the music, to executives and accountants whose principal concern was the bottom line.

To suggest that commercialization alone was responsible for

the decline in the quality of the music would be unfair. Both the adulation and the excess of success took their toll on the performers who had made the sixties a magic musical decade. The early seventies brought the drug-related deaths of many; and, in the case of too many of the survivors, it brought a preoccupation with the lifestyle as opposed to a continued commitment to art. This result was inevitable. For rock & roll to have retained its purity in the face of such massive monetary seduction would have been an event unique in the annals of human economic history.

It also must be remembered that these "rock stars" were generally young, in their late teens or early twenties, whose commitment to their music had often consumed their short lives. Usually the children of middle- to lower-middle-class backgrounds, these youthful phenoms had no preparation for stardom. How does someone who is an unknown in Port Arthur, Texas, or Los Angeles, for that matter, become a world-renowned celebrity showered with adulation and wealth almost overnight and remain unchanged by the experience? Would you?

Since artists generally draw upon their life experience as a fount for their creativity, when that life experience is exploded with the potency of stardom, it inevitably affects the creative process. This can be illustrated by comparing the quality of an artist's or group's first and second recordings. Generally, debut records are stronger than second releases. In part, this is because debut material is culled from the trial and error of the road and the dues that had to be paid to get to make the record in the first place, and frequently, in part, it is because the success which allowed the second recording to be made also severed the band from its original creative roots. Of course, sometimes the transitions themselves become stimuli for renewed creativity, but that's what frequently separates the stars from the lesser luminaries.

While the audience that had enshrined the sixties icons, who survived and continued to perform into the seventies, seemed content to age with its heroes, the youth (at least some of it) of this era accurately perceived that the torchbearers of yesterday held little relevance to their present. And thus, the mid-seventies brought youth's response, decorated with safety pins, rendings of flesh and fabric and accompanied by technologically abbetted abrasive "noise." Punk. It was, and it is, wonderful—

the wild essence of the music once again roaring its subversive call.

Perhaps because the audience was too comfortable or too emotionally spent from the dislocations of the mad sixties, whatever the reason, punk proved to be more theoretical than tangible in its ultimate impact. The failure of the new wave of seventies music to revolutionize the rock establishment was also attributable to its failure to produce any creative personalities with both the charisma and talent to attract a mass audience. But then, that may be just another case of the chicken/egg debate.

The Ramones in New York's then fertile lower village scene and, more potently, the Sex Pistols in Malcolm McLaren's London scene first sounded the clarion call of change. But the really sustaining artists to arise out of this short-lived movement were Talking Heads in New York and Elvis Costello in England—both performers who perceived and capitalized upon the intellectual nature of their respective enterprises. Both are fine artists whose work has been illuminating and sometimes challenging, but this wasn't any third revolution—that is yet to come.

Perhaps the biggest obstacle to continued real creativity (in the sense of originality) was the homogenization of the music's audience during the so-called "me" decade. Increased communication (McCluhan's "global village"), with its attendant commercialization, homogenized the audience, blunting the cultural edges which had previously sparked the artistic impulse.

Actually, the most interesting advent of the decade may have been the development of a world audience for the rhythm and revolution of Jamaica's principal cultural export to the modern world: reggae. A fascinating synthesis of New Orleans-based rock/soul sounds with Rastafarian ritual and belief overlaid on the same voodoo roots that started it all in the first place; it extended rock's central message to the Third World population most responsive to its siren call.

The seventies were the decade that saw the music's focus move from Dylan to disco while radio changed from free form to format and honesty of expression gave way to commercial complacency.

# THE SEVENTIES
## on Compact Disc

"You're too old and your hair's too long."
—Johnny Rotten

## Allman Brothers Band

Formed 1968—Macon, Georgia
The first and most successful of the Southern rock bands. Featuring the brothers, Duane and Gregg Allman, the band also included dual drummers and a raft of fine blues-oriented musicians. During the early seventies, they were one of the biggest draws on the rock circuit—they headlined the huge (600,000 persons) Watkins Glen Festival held July 28, 1973. The band seemed to have been subject to a cruel curse (Duane Allman and bass player Berry Oakley were both killed in motorcycle accidents; Greg turned state's evidence in the drug conviction of Scooter Herring, his manager). But before those problems hit, they reached the pinnacle of success. Subsequently, the group disbanded and reformed on several different occasions, unfortunately, always with diminishing quality.

### At the Fillmore East

Polydor 823 273-2 (78:36—two discs)     **[A]**
The band's forte, and its foundation for commercial success, was live performance and the extended instrumental jams that the freedom of such performance abetted. On this classic live release, it all works, each sound contributing to the intent behind the music. Duane's guitar work easily verifies his stature as one of rock's best-ever guitarists; and the rhythm section drives like a moonshiner on a moonless night. Given the fact that this was a live recording done over fifteen years ago, the CD sound is all that one can reasonably expect; in fact, it's pretty damn good.

### Brothers and Sisters

Polydor 825 092-2 (38:02)     **[D]**
Released in 1973, this recording contains Dickie Betts's "Ramblin' Man" and the then popular instrumental "Jessica." While Greg's vocals remain the high point, it's obvious that the band's fire had gone out several years before. The sound is, at best, adequate, like that of a clean LP.

# Gregg Allman

b. December 8, 1947—Nashville

### Laid Back

Polygram 831 941-2 Y-1 (35:45)      **[B]**
Wracked by tragedy and treachery, the
Allman Brothers Band disintegrated in the
early seventies. This was Gregg's first recording following that break-up. It's an excellent
southern rock/blues album, which rightfully
focuses on Allman's laid-back but affecting
vocals. While the overall quality of the material is pretty good, the standouts, "Midnight
Rider," Jackson Browne's "These Days," and
"Multi-Colored Lady" are exceptional. The
CD's sound is very clean, with nice vocal definition and placement, and is a clear improvement over the LP.

# Joan Armatrading

b. December 9, 1950—St. Kitts, West Indies (raised in
England)
One of the best female writers and performers
to debut in the seventies, her sensitive, intelligent, complex music which draws on a
number of sources has always enjoyed a better critical than audience response.

### Classics Vol. 21

A&M DC2519 (68:36)      **[B]**
Joan's sophisticated music is more pop than
rock and evidences a strong jazz/folk/funk/
reggae orientation. Possessed of a large, expressive voice and first-rate guitar technique,
Armatrading's performances extract max-
imum impact out of her compositions which
lack the musical hooks necessary to achieve
popularity. Her self-confessional lyrics are
never maudlin, rather, they reflect the tough-
ness expected of the post-feminist modern
woman. The eighteen cuts sample her
recorded output from 1973's "Whatever's For
Us," to 1985's "Temptation" with most of the
highlights in between adequately represented. Over her recording career, Joan has
consistently worked with name producers,
and the sound of this disc reflects their above
average production values; clean, bright, spacious, and appropriately punchy. The only
sonic criticism is a tendency to over-bright-
ness, which sometimes results in vocal
harshness.

# The Band

### Rock of Ages

Capitol CDP7 46617 2 (71:59)      **[B−]**
Released in 1972, this live double record
(slightly edited to fill one CD) covers sixteen
selections recorded at the New York Academy
of Music on New Year's Eve, 1971/72. Arguably, it is the group's last real quality release,
with a possible exception of its 1978 reprise,
*The Last Waltz*, which officially marked the
Band's final appearance. When you get right
down to it, there really isn't much new
involved here, three of the songs had never
been previously released, and the basic musical unit is augmented with a fine horn section
arranged by New Orleans resident musical
genius Allen Toussaint, which adds coloration, if not structure, to the material. The
musicianship is consistently first-rate, the end
result is appealing, but certainly nothing
extraordinary. The CD's sound is clear and
relatively clean for a live effort, but overall,
the lows are weak and the sound is excessively bright, sometimes bordering on
harshness.

# David Bowie
# (David Robert Jones)

b. January 8, 1947—London
A musical gadfly—the man of a thousand personas. An artist whose mastery of media
manipulation was as much an attribute of his
extraordinary popular success as his true
musical creativity. But Bowie has proved to
be an accurate mirror of his changing times
and has enjoyed immense popular success
throughout his multi-faced career.

### ChangesOneBowie

RCA PCD1-1732 (46:40)      **[C]**

## Fame and Fashion

RCA PCD1-4919 (55:03)    **[C]**

Within these two greatest hits collections are Bowie's best-known selections from 1972 forward. Like MTV without the video, this is music for faddish mass consumption, a triumph of form over substance, all surface surrounding an empty shell. The sound, while nothing extraordinary, is clean and serviceable, not much different from the LP versions.

# Jackson Browne

b. October 9, 1948—Heidelberg, West Germany

Very much a part of the commercially successful L.A. singer/songwriter coterie that achieved pop dominance in the early to mid-seventies, Browne's strength has been his writing—his singing voice being charitably described, at best, as serviceable. His early to mid-seventies work involved romantic insights into interpersonal relationships during the so-called "me" decade. With the passing of the years, he sustained personal tragedy (the suicide of his wife) and his vision broadened, resulting in a marked political stance in his eighties compositions.

## Saturate Before Using

Asylum SD50551-2 (41:15)    **[B +]**

One of the better lyricists of the last thirty years of pop, Browne's finely crafted words and occasionally inspired melodies reflect a serious artist who has consistently attempted to grapple with the current state of the human condition. There is an unevenness in both the content and performance on the ten selections which comprise this debut release, but, at its best—"A Song for Adam," "Doctor My Eyes," and "Rock Me on the Water"—it represents the benchmark by which other seventies singer/songwriters can be measured. The sound is clean and surprisingly spacious, although little detail enhancement is noticeable.

## For Everyman

Asylum SD 5067-2 (41:09)    **[B–]**

Browne was a premier member of the early seventies singer/songwriter school—in his case, the emphasis is on the songwriter side. *For Everyman* includes some fine examples of his lyrical skills: "These Days," "Redneck Friend," "Ready Or Not," and the title cut being the most notable examples. As usual, he is backed with sympathetic, professional arrangements, but the CD's sound is nothing special: it's murky, with limited dynamic enhancement and some tape hiss.

## The Pretender

Asylum 6E 107-2 (35:30)    **[A +]**

The perfect culmination of the first phase of Browne's career (1972-1976). Produced by Jon Landau, *The Pretender* is the artist's final statement on the role of everyman in contemporary society. In this instance, Browne's always outstanding lyrics are set to melodies and production values which provide a perfect accompaniment. Perhaps because of Landau's positive influence, this is more pure rock & roll than the pop/ballad form which had previously dominated Browne's work. The LP had first-rate sound when it was released, and the sound is enhanced with a greater spatial quality that fits the material to a tee.

## Running On Empty

Asylum 6E 11302 (42:30)    **[A +]**

Audio verité—one of the most conceptually fascinating recordings in the history of rock & roll. With *Running On Empty*, Browne attempted to capture the experience of a rock & roller's life on the road. To achieve the desired result, the selections (most of which were not written by Browne) were recorded both on and behind the stage, on the tour bus, and in motel rooms: the milieu of the rock tour. As must be expected with an undertaking of this type, there is variation in the quality of the recordings, but not as extreme as one might expect. The CD sound is full and open, consistent with the entire enterprise, even to the extent of providing background details inaudible in prior releases.

# James Brown

**In the Jungle Groove**

Polydor 829 624-2 (63:45)     [A-]
This compilation of late sixties to early seventies efforts by the Godfather of Soul and his famous funksters, the "J.B.s," includes some previously unissued material, some remixes and some classics, "Soul Power" and "Hot Pants (She Got to Use What She Got to Get What She Wants)." From start to finish the hardest working man in show business and the J.B.s cook. The sound varies, evidencing occasional hiss and some compression, but overall, it is amazingly clean, tight, and dynamic.

# Jimmy Buffett

b. December 25, 1946—Mobile, Alabama

**Songs You Know By Heart**
**(Jimmy Buffett's Greatest Hits)**

MCA MCAD 5633 (42:28)     [B-]
Caribbean country by the man who invented the form, and, as a result, has managed to live the life that he sings about. This is highly listenable music—party songs for the laid-back crowd. Included among the thirteen songs are some, but far from all, of Jimmy's better efforts: "A Pirate Looks at 40" and his *piéce de résistance*, "Margaritaville." Actually, Buffett, beach-bum persona notwithstanding, is an intelligent lyricist possessed of a genuine comic flair. It's too bad that this collection doesn't do a better job of underlining that fact. The sound varies with the divergent sources, but is generally clean, well-detailed (particularly in the lead vocals) with a nice openness, but occasionally it succumbs to an overly bright mid-range.

# J.J. Cale

b. December 5, 1938—Oklahoma City, Oklahoma

**Special Edition**

Mercury 818 633-2 (39:22)     [C + ]
The laconic, loping, blues-influenced Cale sound is fairly presented on this compilation disc. Since there is repetitive sameness to all of Cale's writing and performance, this probably represents as comprehensive an overview as any but the most ardent fan would desire. It does include his major claim to fame, the hit "Cocaine" (probably a triumph of timely subject matter over musical form) as well as some of his stronger, earlier compositions: "Magnolia," "After Midnight," "Lies," and "Crazy Momma." This is very listenable but also very limited music. Soundwise, there is some quality variation among the cuts, but overall the CD delivers more punch and detail than its LP counterparts.

# Rosanne Cash

b. May 24, 1955—Memphis, raised in southern
   California

**Right or Wrong**

Columbia CK36155 (38:07)     [B-]
Released in late 1979, this recording was called by Dave Marsh "the first real country album for the eighties." Rosanne's fine vocal attributes and intelligent manner with a lyric are admirably showcased by her husband Rodney Crowell's production and compositional contributions. A striking marriage of Nashville and L.A. country, *Right Or Wrong* was a strong debut recording which holds up over time. The CD sound, while a bit bright every now and again, is more dynamic and much cleaner that the LP.

# Eric Clapton

b. March 30; 1945—Ripley, England

During the late 1960s, as the featured guitarist with bands like the Bluesbreakers, the Yardbirds, and Cream, Clapton became the first great English guitar hero. He has never really appeared totally comfortable in the role of individual star or group leader, but has sustained a career that has been negatively impacted by some of the more corrosive attributes of the rock & roll lifestyle.

### Timepieces (The Best of Eric Clapton)

RSO 800 014-2 (44:58)    **[C + ]**

One of rock's great lead guitarists, his singing abilities are merely adequate, at best. Probably for this reason, the recordings which feature him as leader and vocalist have never attained the levels of intensity or importance accorded to his contributions as lead guitarist on other artists' albums. This collection of his seventies hits (originally released in 1982) certainly captures the highlights—"Layla," for one—as well as essentially all of his most popular cuts from the decade. The sound is equivalent to that of a very clean LP, with occasional, not overwhelming, distortion.

# The Clash

Formed 1976—London

Admittedly inspired by the Sex Pistols who sounded punk's late seventies revolutionary cry, it was the Clash who ultimately brought intelligence, supplemented by powerfully compatible sounds, that fleshed out the British punk testament.

### The Clash

Epic EK36060 (43:55)    **[A]**

This was music to make your heart beat once again—it was an assault, a violation—it was rock & roll the way God meant it to sound. You loved it/you hated it; at least you felt something about it. The fifteen politically inspired cuts that make up this forty-four-minute attack on the "revised" edition of this, the band's debut recording, present as concise, yet complete, a summary of the punk purview

available. Not necessarily pleasant listening, but, in sad fact, one of the last real rock & roll albums to be issued. The CD sound has a bit more spaciousness than the LP, but this music wasn't made with great regard for its audio-technical aspects (the album was recorded over three weekends), so don't expect any miracles. Still superior to the LP.

# Joe Cocker

### The Very Best Of/Greatest Hits

Fun FCD501 (58:02)    **[B + ]**

The sixteen selections are representative of Cocker's most popular and best recordings of his career to the date of this collection's release, originally 1977. This is first-rate music by one of rock's best vocal interpreters, and affords a decent one-disc overview of the singer's early career. Its sound quality varies as expected, and, while a few cuts are burdened with minor distortion, overall the sound is essentially equivalent to that of a clean LP.

### Mad Dogs and Englishmen (Music From the Original Soundtrack)

A&M 396002-2 (76:19—two discs)    **[B]**

The 1970 Mad Dogs & Englishmen tour featured a great, brass-enhanced driving band led by Leon Russell behind Cocker's frenzied vocal antics. It was one of the decade's more hysterical events—guaranteed excitement made pervasive by the successful motion picture diary of the tour, one of the first rock concert movies ever released. The sixteen selections are faultless picks (with the exception of Rita Coolidge's one contribution), but the fairly insistent high energy level, perhaps inevitable in this format, becomes somewhat wearing. The concert quality sound is also pretty consistent, and, while clean for its source, has a marked tendency to some overbrightness.

# Ry Cooder

b. March 15, 1947—Los Angeles
Rock's preeminent musical archivist, Cooder's
guitar prowess, among the best ever, has
been an important component of the recordings of countless major artists. His own
recordings provide a breathtaking overview
of the more esoteric, but nonetheless important, musical strains that have become a part
of contemporary American pop music.

### Paradise & Lunch

Reprise 2179-2 (37:24)      **[A]**
Of all the musical potpourris Cooder has con-
cocted over his almost twenty-year solo
career, this melange of historic "Ditty Wah
Ditty" to contemporary "Mexican Divorce,"
gospel to Salvation Army Band, marvelously
succeeds in blending the divergent musical
elements that can be found in American pop
song. This, of course, has been Ry's stated
direction since he emerged as one of the sixties premier session players. For all its diverse components, this recording showcases
American popular music and perhaps the
American musical experience as well as anything to come out of the rock era. The sound,
unfortunately, is not revelatory—it's equivalent to a good, clean LP.

### Jazz

Warner Bros. 3197-2 (38:31)      **[B]**
The music dates back to the turn of the century and before—the days of brass and string
jazz bands (before Louis Armstrong modern-
ized the form), where the bass line was often
provided by a tuba. The selections were composed by artists whose careers commenced in
the last century—Jellyroll Morton, the New
Orleans whorehouse pianist whose Creole-
influenced sound still remains influential,
and Bix Biederbecke, the first great white jazz
trumpet virtuoso. But it is the string playing
conducted by famed Bahamian Joseph
Spence that adds a distinctive quality to these
ragtime instrumentals. The sound is good,
not great, like that of a clean LP.

### Bop Til You Drop

Warner Bros. 003358-2 (40:15)      **[B + ]**
A landmark: the first pop all-digital recording
released in 1979. While its musical sources
touch on blues, jazz, and country sounds, the
general orientation is toward fifties/sixties
R&B. Featuring some of LA's best session
players and singers, among them Jim Keltner,
David Lindley, and Bobby King, plus Chaka
Khan vocals on a couple of tracks, this is classic material lovingly presented. It features
both the honest vision of Ry Cooder and his
virtuoso string playing as the central element
of it all. The sound is detailed and dynamic
with nice spatial attributes; although, a couple of cuts, "Little Sister" and "The Very Thing
That Makes You Rich," are marred by muddy
or extraneous sounds.

# Elvis Costello (Declan McManus)

b. 1955—Liverpool, England
The most important single artist to survive
England's seventies punk explosion. Costello,
the son of a dance band leader, began his
commercial life as a computer operator, but
was soon working as a roadie for the Brinsley
Schwarz Band. He first began releasing
records in 1977 and has since proven amazingly prolific. A thorny, difficult personality (a
natural adherent to the rude punk attitude),
Costello has been quoted as saying that his
artistic purpose was "revenge and guilt." This
modern Elvis has never followed the traditional avenues to stardom, preferring his
purposely obscure, often abrasive, public
image. But Costello's massive talents, evidenced by his wit and mastery of wordplay as
well as energetic commitment to musical
intensity and inventiveness, rank him among
the major artists in rock's thirty-year
pantheon.

### My Aim Is True

Columbia CK35037 (36:38)      **[B–]**
A truly stunning debut release. With it Costello announced his prickly presence to a
musical world generally gone flat and fat.

While it lacks the instrumental bite of later offerings, due, in part, to the fact that the backup musicians were the Clovers and not the later formed Attractions, who proved to be the glove to Elvis's hand, it does contain some of his most enduring music: "Less Than Zero," "Watching the Detectives," "The Angels Wanna Wear My Red Shoes," and the haunting "Alison." Sadly, this fine recording is very poorly served by the digital conversion which suffers from both too apparent hiss, distortion, and a severely compressed, dirty overall sound.

**This Year's Model**

Columbia CK35331 (33:24)      [B + ]

With this release, Costello had found the backup band suited to his jagged vision and on this recording they underpin him with a dense, driving rock & roll sound that adds to the intensity of the statements, but doesn't necessarily clarify or enhance the fascinating lyrical excursions. With the exception of "Radio," "Pump It Up," "Lip Service," and "No Action," none of the other individual tracks have achieved much recognition, but the overall lyrical involvement with sexual, personally oriented material is fascinating. The bite and acuteness of Costello's overview of male/female relations in the modern world remains compelling. The CD sound is not an appreciable improvement over the dense intensity of the original LP.

**(And the Attractions) Armed Forces**

Columbia CK35709 (36:50)      [A–]

Originally to be issued under the more de-scriptive title *Emotional Fascism, Armed Forces* is generally considered this artist's most successful recorded venture. The arrangements involve more variety and a far greater "pop" sensibility than were evident on earlier recordings, but remain driving, intense statements. Costello's lyrical preoc-cupation with sexual politics remains the keystone to the wordplay; however, here he had enlarged his expressionistic canvas to reflect political concerns in a broader sense. As usual, his talents spill out all over the

place, but the recording is highlighted by his classic "Oliver's Army" as well as "Accidents Will Happen" and "Green Shirt." The greater attention paid to production values is evident in the CD sound which has slightly enhanced dynamic and spatial qualities, but tends to excessive brightness.

**(And the Attractions) Get Happy!!**

Columbia CK36347 (48:20)      [B + ]

This is Costello and the Attractions' New Wave reworking of the soul sounds of the six-ties (including a frenetic cover of Sam and Dave's "I Can't Stand Up For Falling Down"). While it evidences a genuine feeling and affection for the roots reworked (particularly Steve "Naive" Nason's always outstanding keyboards), it is a bit of a hodgepodge. Twenty cuts totaling forty-eight minutes—bits and snippets, interspersed with some true gems (among them "Motel Matches" and "High Fidelity")—yet, as Costello himself has said of it: "It wasn't in control, it was very maniacal and emotional." Not necessarily negative elements in the context of rock & roll, but here, they served to undermine the overall quality of the effort. Soundwise, this is the class of the artist's seventies recordings, providing an openness and clarity missing from the earlier productions.

# Creedence Clearwater Revival

**Cosmos Factory**

Fantasy FCD 608 8402 (42:56)      [A–]

The last recording by the original band, shortly after its release, older brother Tom Fogerty wearied of John's dominance and left, which marked the beginning of the end. In-cluded are some of CCR's better known crea-tions, "Travelin' Band," "Lookin' Out My Back Door," "Run Through the Jungle," "Up Around the Bend," "Who'll Stop the Rain," and "I Heard It Through the Grapevine." The CD sounds like a clean LP, similar to the sound on *Willie & The Poorboys,* but overall less hampered by incidental distortion or hiss.

# Jim Croce

b. January 10, 1943—Philadelphia
d. September 20, 1973

### Photographs & Memories His Greatest Hits

21 Records 790467-2 (41:06)      **[B]**

The early seventies brought the singer/song-writer to the fore in pop music, and Croce, having begun his career in the Greenwich Village sixties coffeehouse scene, fit right in. While the pop productions afforded his folk-styled material probably had much to do with his primarily posthumous success, his serviceable melodies, unpretentious singing, and playing style—combined with an eye for lyrical detail and laced with an ironic sense of humor—all added up to a consistently and easily listenable experience. The fourteen selections fairly represent a comprehensive career overview. The sound does vary among the selections, but generally is acceptable, LP-like, but clean with some spatial improvement.

# Crosby, Stills, Nash (and Young)

Formed 1968—Los Angeles
Superstar folk rock. Their celebrity always outshone the limited quantity of their recorded output. Hell, Crosby's two-decade personal drug opera has been accorded more ink than was ever expended on critical reviews of their artistic output. But every now and again they had their musical moments, and when they did, they generally managed to resonate with some critical moments in a momentous era.

### Crosby, Stills & Nash

Atlantic 19119-2 (40:43)      **[C]**

They brought impeccable credentials to the party, but somehow it never quite managed to get off the ground. This, their debut recording, was as good as it ever got, and it wasn't that bad if you don't mind what David Marsh adroitly labeled "adult bubble gum." A slick-surfaced step to stardom. If you can bear the hiss, which is no worse than on the LP, the

sound is significantly more open and dynamic than on vinyl.

### So Far

Atlantic SD 19119-2 (43:19)      **[C–]**

This was music made for the market, not for the more personal expressive needs of its creators, and, it shows (occasional quality additions from Neil Young notwithstanding). But popular older music is often enduring for its nostalgic value, if nothing else, and this collection provides a fair overview of some very popular late sixties and early seventies material. The sound is a mixed bag, sometimes compressed, sometimes harshly bright, sometimes marred by loud hiss, but it still surpasses the LP's due to its spatial and dynamic enhancement.

# Dire Straits

Formed 1977—London
The perfect rock band for the "new age era" of rock & roll. The band (really Mark Knopfler) isn't stretching the edges of the envelope, but within the territory they carved out for themselves, they make listenable, relatively sophisticated music.

### Dire Straits

Warner Bros. 3266 (41:28)      **[B]**

From the first note on this recording, it's apparent that Knopfler has assimilated the lessons laid down by the Beatles, Paul Simon, Led Zeppelin, among others—the recording studio is every bit as much a component of a band's sound as its guitars or keyboards. Having come on the scene a few years before digital reproduction became feasible, it appears that Knopfler maintained a keen ear for advances in studio technology. The lush, yet slightly removed, spatial quality of the group's attractive sound is the direct result of these concerns. Musically there is a strong kinship to J.J. Cale's vocal timbre and mannerisms, plus a reliance on his blues-oriented, loping rhythm. Because of Knopfler's limited performance prowess, the elements which lift this recording above the run of the mill are his acknowledged songwriting skills (as illustrated in the album's hit single "Sultans of Swing") and immaculate production values which produce a slightly compressed, but fine sounding CD.

# The Doobie Brothers

Formed 1970—San Jose, California

### Best of The Doobies

Warner Bros. 3112 (45:11)    **[D–]**
To fault their musicianship would be unfair, to fault their product is inevitable; bleached soul/funk sounds geared to meaningless hooks and corporate marketing all presided over by Michael McDonald's adenoidal wail. A prime example of the decline of quality in the seventies version of rock music. The sound is about equal to that of an LP, but who cares?

# The Doors

### Morrison Hotel/Hard Rock Cafe

Elektra EKS 75007-2 (37:27)    **[B]**
The band's apparent concept album that comes close and just doesn't quite make it—the Doors were primarily a singles band. That's not to say this is a failed effort, far from it; outside of their debut recording, it probably maintains the highest level of musicianship from cut to cut of any of the Doors' album releases. As always with this group, Jim Morrison is the center of it all, and as Robert Christgau said: "He's not the genius he makes himself out to be, so maybe his genius is that he doesn't let his pretensions cancel out his talent." The sound is a bit murky, close in quality to that of the LP.

### Alive She Cried

Elektra 9 60269-2 (37:01)    **[C +]**
Released in 1983, the performances that make up this recording took place in '66, '69, and '70. One of the elements that made the Doors so exciting was Morrison's continuing tightrope walk over the abyss of self-parody and wretched excess, particularly in the free-form arena of live performance. On the seven cuts

included on this relatively brief package, he teeters several times, but never hits bottom; or, for that matter, reaches the top. The sound expectedly varies, but a majority of the tracks are excellent: spacious and dynamic, while the others betray their live roots. This CD provides a live look at an important, influential band (though not always a good one), including some of Morrison's brief readings of his strained verse.

### L.A. Woman

Elektra EKS-75011-2 (48:46)    **[B +]**
Blues-based, often tongue-in-cheek, this was the group's last joint effort; prior to its release, Morrison, literate poet and pretender that he was, left for Paris. He never returned, dying of a heart attack there on July 3, 1971, at the age of twenty-seven. About half of this recording works; in part because the band seemed satisfied with simpler approaches and Jim had apparently exhausted his overreaching stage persona, or maybe just his liver. Some cuts continue to hold up, "Love Her Madly," "L.A. Woman," "Hyacinth House," and "Riders in the Storm" among them. Sad to say, the sound is poor—muddy, with some apparent distortion.

# Bob Dylan

### Greatest Hits Volume II

Columbia C2K31120 (78:25—two discs)    **[A]**
Twenty-two examples from an artistic decade marked by Dylan's variety and virtuosity. Five selections were previously unreleased, and the remaining seventeen are all strong statements by the man who did so much to define sixties rock. Simply a first-rate collection. Expectedly, the sound is all over the place, rarely of surpassing quality, and occasionally affected with rough distortion.

### (The Band) Before the Flood

Columbia C2K 37661 (92:40—two discs)    **[A]**
A kick-ass live effort, on which Dylan applied his revisionist approach to his old material, effectively trashing prior meanings and mo-

ments. The Band wails like banshees and Mr. Tambourine Man whips on a new mask for his seventies audience to contemplate. Released in 1974, these recordings were made during the last three performances of his twenty-one city tour with the Band that year (these concerts took place in Los Angeles). Ever since the late sixties, when bootlegs of this musical combination's *Basement Tapes* were widely circulated among aficionados, the opportunity to see these two "naturals" perform together was compelling. Are the revised renditions of his classics successful? Not really, but obviously what matters was his willingness to do it in the first place, and, ultimately, that's what makes this first-rate rock & roll. The interspersed performances of the Band doing their own material are consistent with the whole and burn with raw energy. Given that these are live performance recordings more than a decade old, the sound is surprisingly clear and punchy. There is some compression and some muddiness in the bottom end, but overall, not disappointing.

### Blood on the Tracks

Columbia 33235 (51:55)     **[A + ]**
The snarl was still there, but the shift in Dylan's attitude was marked and perceptible. The spotlight is completely on Dylan here, because the backup musicians added nothing but the briefest sort of filler sound. Dylan filled that spotlight with the best songwriting he'd done in years—honest, poetic, the voice of a survivor hopefully headed for less traumatic times, but carrying the scars and bitterness of savaged love. The music is lilting and haunting, making this Dylan's best release of the decade (acknowledging that the *Basement Tapes* were really sixties material, release date notwithstanding). His singing is stunningly honest which adds dimension to his most mature musings about love lost, both personal and for a time gone by—too quickly. Its folkish sound hearkens back to the sixties; its heart is the perspective it places on times recently past, irrevocably gone. The sound on this disc is wonderful, open, and full. It does have a few moments of overbrightness and slight compression is perceptible, but the vocal detail is greatly enhanced.

### Desire

Columbia CK33893 (56:15)     **[B]**
A return to topicality and a movement away from the more personal stance of *Blood on the Tracks*. While it is a quality work of ambitious scope, it somehow has an unfinished quality about it; probably attributable to the less than polished instrumental "assistance" that lends little of positive value to the proceedings. Still, one of his better offerings of the seventies due to the inclusion of some fine material: "Hurricane," "Isis," and "Sara" being the highlights. The sound is overbright to the point of harshness on some of the vocal and harmonica tracks, a distinct comedown from the high quality of *Blood on the Tracks*.

### Street Legal

CBS CDCBS 86067 (49:56)     **[D–]**
Dylan's released a lot of recordings over a career now spanning more than two decades, and it would be unfair to expect them all to be good—this one's not. The addition of a female chorus detracts rather than adds to the proceedings, and the band plays like their last gig was a Salvation Army affair. The sound is appropriate to the contents: compressed, muddy, distorted, and frequently harsh in the vocals.

### Slow Train Coming

Columbia CK36120 (46:47)     **[C]**
Dylan reborn, what else? This recording, which heralded his conversion to Christianity (he was born a Jew), created a huge stir in the late seventies (its release date was '78, which probably says more about the sterility of the times than the importance of either the event or the music). Actually, of all his many poses, this one seemed most suspect, but buoyed by the Jerry Wexler/Berry Becket production and the fine Muscle Shoals House Band, it had a professional sound to it that had never been heard on Dylan's work before. It was

enough to earn him a Grammy (which he personally accepted) and to lure Jann Wenner out of his lofty publisher's office of *Rolling Stone* to write an extended review which concluded that this was the artist's pinnacle accomplishment. Time has not treated *Slow Train Coming* quite so kindly. The sound is pretty good—clean, detailed, and somewhat open, though it still is noticeably compressed.

# Eagles

Formed 1971—Los Angeles
Slick urbanizers of the L.A. country sound, the Eagles enjoyed great popularity throughout the decade. In retrospect, their sexist lyrics and commercial orientation lacks sustaining substance.

### Desperado

Asylum 5068-2 (36:02)     [C–]
The perfect band for the self-important seventies. On this, their second album, their adopted conceit was the creation of a Western outlaw concept which was designed to provide historical precedent for their sexist rock hero stance. But glossy production and country hooks aside, the general vapidness of the material undermines the myth. The sound on the CD is severely compressed and often muddy.

### Their Greatest Hits

Asylum 105-2 (43:12)     [B]
These ten selections were integral to seventies rock radio. As an indictment of those times, it's nonpareil; yet, it remains slickly seductive. The sound is all over, mostly compressed, occasionally a bit harsh, though often equivalent to the LP version.

### Hotel California

Asylum 103-2 (43:33)     [B +]
The addition of Joe Walsh brought a harder, more rock edge to the band's material which made this their strongest album statement. Gone are the gunslingers of the past; it's tough enough to stay alive on the mean streets of Beverly Hills. In the end, it's a pretty

hard look at the seamier side of success, still packaged for the adoring mass audience, and it works. They may not have been sincere, but they were pros; and Henley and Fry were among the era's more accomplished writers. The sound, while sometimes a bit bright in the vocals, is big, spacious, detailed, and a decided improvement over the LP.

# Earth, Wind and Fire

Formed 1969—Chicago

### That's the Way of the World

Columbia CK33280 (38:39)     [B]
Among the sleekest seventies funksters, Earth, Wind and Fire created some of the most uplifting and joyous pop music of the decade. Glorious arrangements, crescendos of sound anchored by a tight danceable beat, produced truly irresistible musical moments: "That's the Way of the World" and "Shining Star" being the prime examples from this album. The words are empty, but the energy is contagious. The music is a compelling amalgam of jazz, gospel, R&B, and pure pop. The sound is clean, nicely detailed, and punchy, but still compressed.

# Bryan Ferry

b. September 26, 1945—Washington, England
The image may be rock's original lounge lizard, but, in reality, Ferry is one of the most intelligent, entertaining, and serious musicians the form produced in the seventies.

### These Foolish Things

E.G. 823 021-2 (43:58)     [A +]
One of the most fascinating records in the history of contemporary pop music. On it, Ferry re-invents a baker's dozen pop hits ranging from 1936 (the title selection) to a number of sixties goodies: "A Hard Rain's A-Gonna' Fall," "Piece Of My Heart," "It's My Party" (that's right, Leslie Gore's obnoxious 1963 No. 1 hit), "Sympathy for the Devil," "The Tracks of My Tears," and "You Won't See Me." At first contact it may sound like parody,

but it's really a Master's thesis on the last fifty years of American pop music. It's wonderful! The CD's sound is a real enhancement; clear, clean, and well-defined; it occasionally sounds a bit thin, but that's probably more intended than overlooked.

### Another Time Another Place

E.G. 813 654-2 (42:01)    [C−]
The cover shot is a killer. The contents are an extension of the concept behind *These Foolish Things* through another ten wide-ranging pop songs. It starts strong with a version of "The In Crowd" that justifies the cover, but it's pretty much downhill after that: repetitious in both concept and execution. This one didn't earn him his doctorate. The sound varies substantially from cut to cut, but is often harshly bright in the highs and muddy in the lows.

### The Bride Stripped Bare

E.G. 821 127-2 (42:02)    [B]
This is an admixture, four of the ten cuts are Ferry's compositions with the remainder ranging from R&B to traditional Irish music. The material is strong, and Bryan's singing is more honest and emotive than usual, but the production misses more often than it succeeds, which is too bad because this one had the makings of something special. The sound has punch and dynamics that obviously are an improvement over the LP, but equally as obvious, it is still compressed throughout.

# Marianne Faithfull

b. Circa 1947—London

### Broken English

Island 90039-2 (37:44)    [A]
In 1964, Marianne Faithfull attained pop notoriety both for her well-publicized liaisons with members of the Rolling Stones and for "As Tears Go By," a Top Ten British hit that year. After a decade and a half of living in London's

darker, obscure fringes, and away from the music business, she resurfaced with this recording. It is almost the diametric opposite of the stand she assumed in her first performances (sweet innocence)—her voice had become a husky rasp; her message, vitriolic, obscene, and ultimately cynical. Yet, the overall effect is extremely strong in its message and presentation. This is a potent, though not necessarily pleasant, musical statement, featuring a punk attitude, a strong dance beat, and some fine musical and production values. The CD sound is very slightly compressed, but clean and crisp with enough edge to it to nicely accommodate the spirit of the material.

# Roberta Flack

b. February 10, 1939—Asheville, North Carolina

### The Best Of

Atlantic 19317-2 (43:42)    [B + ]
Perhaps because she recorded for Atlantic in the late sixties to early seventies, or because she scored so strongly on her initial outing with "The First Time Ever I Saw Your Face," with resultant influence on the black pop market, the expectations for Flack's career were extremely high. They were never close to realized. Trapped in the rut of her own success/excess, she apparently lacked either the insight or feeling necessary to capitalize on her undeniable talents. Songs included (some duets with Donny Hathaway) are a fair snapshot of a sadly lackluster career, but, the title notwithstanding, omitted are some of her better efforts: "Hey That's No Way to Say Goodbye" and "Reverend Lee" among them. The sound is all over the place, compressed, harshly bright, dynamic, spacious, and frequently subject to audible hiss ("The First Time Ever I Saw Your Face" being almost, if not, ruined by it).

# Fleetwood Mac

Formed originally 1967—England; this incarnation
formed 1974—California

The remnants of a barely surviving sixties
British blues band (Mick Fleetwood and John
McVie) find sunshine and success with the
addition of California's Lindsey Buckingham
and Stevie Nicks who joined the two surviving namesakes along with Christine Perfect
McVie, who had joined the group in 1970.

## Bare Trees

Reprise 2278-2 (37:17)    [B—]

This band has gone through more cycles than
a modern microwave oven. *Bare Trees* comes
from what might loosely be defined as their
middle period (post-Peter Green, pre-Lindsey
Buckingham/Stevie Nicks), when Christine
Perfect McVie's voice and keyboards brought
a more defined pop sensibility to their work.
It is also among the best releases of this
period, highlighted by the enduring "Senti-
mental Lady." The sound is obviously compressed, somewhat murky, and affected by
hiss.

## Fleetwood Mac

Reprise 2281-2 (43:01)    [A + ]

Timing is everything, and this may have been
one of the best timed releases in the history of
popular music—enormously influential, if not
overwhelmingly substantial. John Rockwell,
writing in *Connoisseur Magazine,* called it a
"rock landmark," one of "seven records that
define a musical age." Rockwell's comments
have the ring of truth; particularly, when one
considers how pervasive the Fleetwood Mac
sound was in the FM-oriented mid-seventies.
And this is material of sustaining value—it
exhibits fine writing, singing, and guitar work
as well as one of the best (and most experienced) bass/drum combos in the biz—and
don't let anybody kid you, the flash may be
out front, but the really great rock bands are
built from the bottom up. The sound does
justice to the material—spacious and beautifully detailed in the vocals and strings.

## Rumours

Warner Bros. 03010-2 (39:42)    [B]

*Fleetwood Mac,* released in 1975, was a
huge selling album for its time, over four
million copies (Michael Jackson's eighties
blockbuster *Thriller* sold over forty million
copies, but then there's no accounting for
taste or the power of the tube for that matter). *Rumours,* released in 1977, sold over
two and a half times as many copies as *Fleetwood Mac* and while it may not have been
two and a half times better, it was an
improvement over its predecessor; all the
virtues of which were preserved, but, this
time out, enhanced by more inventive compositions. The sound is what keeps this
recording from achieving a top rating. It provides some enhanced detailing, but is
burdened with hiss and compression. It's
unlikely that the digital transfer was made
from the first generation source tape.

# Aretha Franklin

## Aretha—Live at the Fillmore West

Mobile Fidelity Sound Lab MFCD 820 (48:12)    [B]

Aretha cooks but something's wrong in the
kitchen. In part, it's King Curtis's fine backup
band which never quite seems in sync, and
that's a shame, because her vocals exude
pure, soulful energy. The recording captures
some strong performances: "Dr. Feelgood,"
"Bridge Over Troubled Waters," "Eleanor
Rigby," and a rare recorded duet with Ray
Charles, an extended kickin' version of
"Spirit in the Dark" (which, unfortunately,
never meshes either), but the remainder of
the material is just okay. The CD sound adds
a bit to the punch of the material, but that
sound is marred by hiss, mike hum, occasional dropout, and distortion. It's still the
best way to hear Lady Soul on one of her
better nights; unless, of course, she happens
to be in the neighborhood.

## Amazing Grace

Atlantic 2-906-2 (86:24—two discs)    [A–]

This is not a rock recording. It *is* a recording of a gospel church service featuring the glorious voice and spirit of Lady Soul returning to her home ground, with a little help from Rev. James Cleveland at the piano and conducting the Southern California Community Choir. It's a beautiful musical experience; but her father, Rev. C.L. Franklin, notwithstanding, Aretha was born to be Lady Soul. The sound is noticeably compressed, occasionally a bit edgy, distorted, and muddy, but the CD does add spatial clarity and some detail.

# Art Garfunkel

b. October 13, 1941—New York City

## Breakaway

Columbia CK 33700 (37:06)    [C + ]

Garfunkel's voice is a beautiful instrument; a fact which has caused the singer to become so concerned with his sound that he ignores the meanings contained within the lyrics. Of course, this strips the recording of any real substance. The pure musicality of it is another matter. Featuring Richard Perry's glutinously rich production deployed with about as much tastefulness as one is likely to hear— glistening mid-seventies pop product at its vacuous best. Overall the sound reflects the care employed in Perry's recording—it's beautifully spatial with lovely clarity and only minimal compression. On the negative side, there is occasional hiss audible in the quiet sections and few overbright vocal moments, but these are minor complaints.

# Marvin Gaye

## What's Going On/Let's Get It On

Tamla TCD 08013 TD (67:22)    [A + ]

You gotta buy this one, not only because it contains two of the seventies best soul albums, but also to encourage Motown and inform the rest of the industry that product for value in the disc market will be positively received. The two albums combined here are the highlights in the career of one of the seventies greatest soul singers. *What's Going On*, a singularly influential Motown recording, represents Gaye's autonomous recording ideas, executed with some distance from the hit factory. It went a long way toward making black pop music meaningful to both its black and white audiences (but primarily the former). It helped bring a social consciousness to Motown, although the tenor of the times was also moving that way, and it delivers three great songs, "What's Going On," "Mercy, Mercy Me (The Ecology)," and "Inner City Blues (Make Me Wanna Holler)." In August, 1987, *Rolling Stone* ranked *What's Going On* tenth in its compilation of the "100 Best Albums of the Last 20 Years," saying of it: "Throw in hints of jazz . . . a pronounced gospel feeling, and you have a singular, exquisitely spiritual album." The "feel" of *Let's Get It On*, his next release, and the second album included on this disc, is not that far afield from *What's Going On*, but subjectwise, it's back to business and Gaye's end of the business was sex. This is music for two and whatever else feels good. The sound on both recordings is much brighter, cleaner, and more dynamic than on the LPs. *What's Going On* sounds better, if a bit compressed and occasionally overbright. *Let's Get It On* is generally overbright to the point of occasional edginess, but is more dynamic. Both suffer from too apparent hiss.

### Live at the London Palladium

Tamla TCD 06191 TD (72:25)     [C + ]

This is Motown showbiz captured in concert—long medleys featuring abbreviated glimpses of classic material and a lack of cohesiveness between the singer and the band, both included. But Marvin was communicating that night and the interaction between artist and audience creates genuine excitement every now and again, particularly on "Trouble Man." The sound is boxy and compressed. It's also overbright on some vocals, but never truly harsh. Still an improvement.

# Grateful Dead

Formed 1965—San Francisco

Either you are or you're not—I'm not. So "Dead Heads" be warned; you won't be real pleased with the following reviews, but you may find the comments about the sound quality helpful.

### Workingman's Dead

Warner Bros. 1869-2 (35:55)     [B]

Probably the musical highlight of the band's career—but it won't blind you. Yet, this one comes closest to capturing the ambiance that has made the Grateful Dead more extended family than musical formulators. The sound quality varies from cut to cut, in some cases providing nice open clarity and in others detailing, but compression. Still, overall, a noticeable improvement.

### American Beauty

Warner Bros. 1893-2 (42:28)     [C]

It features a couple of slightly above average compositions (including their trademark "Truckin'") and the ambiance is fairly rustic/hippie. But the ideas are far from original and the "sound" is purveyed far better by other nonlegendary bands. The singing and musicianship remain vaguely communal. The sound is a marked improvement over prior reproductions, providing a clear spacious feel, and some dynamic enhancement—some hiss too.

### From the Mars Hotel

Mobile Fidelity Sound Lab MFCD 830 (37:38)     [C]

The songs are a little better than those on some of the seventies recordings, and the playing is not as viscous as they have frequently exhibited. But it's still the Dead with all their limitations and all their meanings. The sound is like that of a very clean LP, hiss and all.

### Shakedown Street

Arista ARCD 8228 (39:28)     [D]

From about 1970 on, everything the band produced was severely lacking in musical value—they don't sing very well, and while they are competent musicians, that about describes it. The sound is clean, occasionally a little thin, spacious, and well-detailed, but overall, a little bright.

# Al Green

b. March 13, 1946—Forrest City, Arkansas

A great soul singer in an era when the competition was still pretty fierce. Probably underappreciated because he wasn't associated with a "major" label. He recorded for Memphis-based Hi Records where his fine producer, Willie Mitchell, still insisted on using tube amps and twenty-two mikes on the drum kit to get the sound just right.

### Greatest Hits

Motown MCD 0611MD (55:32)     [B + ]

Admittedly, Al worked in a narrow spectrum of material, but with his wondrous, elastic voice, he worked every nook and cranny of it. The fourteen cuts cover all of Green's seventies hits, and while their sonic sameness discourages repetition, they all contain a sinuous sensuality that is compelling and makes them ripe material for certain of life's moments. Willie Mitchell's production precision pays dividends on the CD reproduction—the drums, always a sound marvel on his recordings, have a lifelike presence, and there is an open, smooth quality to the overall sound that is noticeably superior to the LP. Several tracks are marred by hiss, however.

### Call Me/Living For You

Motown MCD 08040MD (73:24)    **[A]**
Another dynamite two-fer from Motown. *Call Me* is easily this fine artist's best release and *Living For You* isn't that far behind. From the original music written by Green's producer, Willie Mitchell, with words penned by Green and arrangements sparked by Al Jackson's tailored drumming, to covers of country classics (à la Ray Charles), Green insinuates himself into a lyric like a serpent, with some truly breathtaking results. This is premier slick seventies soul with some overtly religious overtones that foreshadowed Green's 1977 change from secular to religious material, corresponding with his ordination as a minister. Whatever his guise, the man can sing. The sound on both recordings is fine—clear, defined, and subtly dynamic, all with an easy flowing naturalness that nicely complements the material. There is some slight hiss, but it's negligible.

### Let's Stay Together/I'm Still In Love With You

Motown MCD 08018MD (68:37)    **[A]**
Green's surface vocal sheen can seem like a be-all, end-all because it's so smooth and easy. But, beneath that surface is a man who knows and respects his roots. This is best illustrated by the more emotive vocals and rougher instrumentation reflected on *Let's Stay Together. I'm Still In Love With You* has an overall sound not unlike its companion on this two-fer, only this time, the writing and production failed to quite measure up, though it still has its moments. Soundwise, *Let's Stay Together* generally evidences a detailed, open clarity which is very appealing, but on a few cuts (e.g., "Judy") the sound is compressed, muddy, and noisy. *I'm Still In Love With You* suffers from more hiss (particularly on the otherwise wonderful title selection) and is generally a bit over-bright. Still, the overall sound of the CD is a major improvement over that previously available.

# The Jacksons

Formed 1967—Gary, Indiana

### Michael Jackson and the Jackson Five
### 18 Greatest Hits

Motown MCD06070MD (59:43)    **[B]**
The Jacksons have sold well over 100 million records as a group and Michael, alone, has sold over half that many again. They've done it with well-produced, seamless, eminently forgettable pop music. This disc brings a complete overview of the group's most memorable moments, and while their roots may be funk, the results ain't. The sound quality of the disc is a real plus: clean, spacious, and clear.

# Joe Jackson

b. August 11, 1955—Burton-On-Trent, England
Another intellectual New Waver who brings taste, chops, and respect for popular music to all that he does.

### Look Sharp!

A&M CD-3187 (36:40)    **[B]**
New Wave was punk for the masses and it never really caught on, but Jackson's brand, particularly as exemplified on *Look Sharp!* was about as popular as it got, with "Is She Really Going Out With Him?" included here, being a major hit for him. Joe Jackson is a calculated musician of talent but little exposed soul. Still, this recording is filled with bright, catchy music and is a prime example of the seventies New Wave movement. The sound on the disc is very bright, at times to the point of harshness at volume, and the sound stage is somewhat confined. Other than that, it is clear and clean.

# Rick James
# (James Johnson)
b. February 1, 1952—Buffalo, New York

### Reflections (All The Greatest Hits)
Gordy GCD06095 CD (57:22)    [C]
Producer, writer, and performer, James began
his musical career in Canada fronting the
Mynah Birds which included Neil Young and
Bruce Palmer who both went on to Buffalo
Springfield and beyond. But by the seventies,
Rick was fronting his Stone City Band extoll-
ing the virtues of partying in all respects, and
laying down what he dubbed punk/funk—
really just more slick, techno-black seventies
sounds which did enjoy strong support from
the black audience plus some crossover success. The eleven selections cover most all of
the group's seventies to early eighties successes. The sound varies some from cut to
cut, generally in degree of clarity and
dynamic enhancement, but overall, it's pretty
clean and detailed, if not very spacious.

# Dr. John
# (Malcolm "Mac" Rebennick)
b. 1941—New Orleans

### The Ultimate Dr. John
Warner Special Products 9-27612-2 (54:43)    [A]
A fixture in the fertile New Orleans music
scene from the mid-fifties forward, Dr. John
has written, produced, played, and sung on
countless records for almost thirty years. With
his drawling "N'Orleans" rough, ragged
voiced vocals, respected musicianship, and
voodoo preoccupations, he's an often overlooked musical natural. With production
assistance from the likes of Allan Tussiant,
Jerry Wexler, Tom Dowd, and Harold Battiste;
and musical contributions from Plas Johnson,
the Meters, David Spinoza, and Shirley Good-
man among others, the good Doctor whips up
a spicy brew of New Orleans R&B roots
gumbo. This is year-round Mardi Gras from
the soul of the city where the rhythm never
stops. Sound quality varies from the thin and

slightly harsh to the fat and detailed, but it
remains a marked improvement over vinyl
versions, and the subtleties of the lead vocals
are consistently improved.

# Elton John
# (Reginald Kenneth Dwight)
b. March 25, 1947—Pinner, England
Heralded at the beginning of the decade as
the next wave of the British Rock invasion,
John, while wildly successful, proved to be a
bit of a Trojan Horse spearheading the glitter-
pop ethic takeover of seventies rock. With his
excessively camp stage extravaganzas, gos-
pel-based piano, and Bernie Taupin's sopho-
moric, but sometimes effective lyrics, over his
hook-filled melodies, John scored fifteen Top
Ten hits (five went to No. 1) during the decade
of the seventies.

### Elton John
DJM CD8 (39:31)    [B–]
The first of Elton's 1970 releases (the other
being *Tumbleweed Connection*), it introduced
American audiences to his chunky piano,
enthusiastic vocals, and the juxtaposition of
yearning ballads with all-out production rockers. It was obviously a formula whose time
had come. The musicianship is polished and
tight; the Gus Dudgeon production precise
and complementary, all of which resulted in a
massively appealing pop product. John's
recorded work has always been notable for its
sound quality, and given the vintage of this
material, it doesn't sound that bad on disc.
That doesn't mean that compression and
occasional harshness aren't evident; they are,
but detailing and dynamics are also
improved.

### Tumbleweed Connection
MCA MACD37199 (46:57)    [B]
The songs have more structure and the production, again by Gus Dudgeon, shows a
lighter more varied touch. The fictional Western slant to the lyrics and packaging (not
uncommon to rock at the time, but from Eng-

land with specs?) is not an enhancement. That conceit appeared to have come primarily from lyricist, Bernie Taupin, but Elton was also, obviously, a willing participant. Weak as the early sections of the recording may be, the two bring the proceedings to a strong conclusion. The final two selections, a ballad ("Talking Old Soldiers") and a rocker ("Burn Down the Mission") rank among the duo's best efforts. The sound isn't that clean or dynamically enhanced, and it does suffer from some hiss, but it has nice spatial attributes and greatly enhanced vocal clarity.

### Madman Across the Water
DJN CD5 (45:19)     [C + ]
The opening cut, "Tiny Dancer," for all its lyrical foolishness, is still one of the most compelling cuts John has ever recorded. Unfortunately, it's pretty much downhill from there, although "Levon" isn't that bad. While there still is some evident compression (the recording was released in 1971), the overall sound quality of the disc is impressive.

### Honky Chateau
MCA MCAD 16111 (45:04)      [B + ]
More slickly produced music for the masses, but this time out the whole affair is more crisp and up-tempo; less impeded with obvious filler. In addition, the piano playing and overall tone of the work take on the old English music hall sound (à la *Sgt. Pepper*) and because it's all so obviously showbiz, it works. There is nothing momentous or even very meaningful here—but when some good time, silly pop music will fill the bill, look no further (and it does have the absurdly wonderful "Rocket Man"). The production is impressive in its crisp, spatial definition, but suffers from a slight overbrightness.

### Don't Shoot Me, I'm Only the Piano Player
DJM CD10 (42:54)     [C–]
The songs—"Daniel" and "Crocodile Rock"—are every bit as good as those on *Honky Chateau* as far as the writing goes. The performance, unfortunately, is a different matter. For some reason, on this album,

Elton is just going through the motions (a fact which is highlighted by the clarity the CD imposes on the vocals). Now some would say that is all he ever does, but sometimes he did it with more feeling than others, and this ain't one of those times. The production often sounds forced. The sound is nothing to write home about, its sharp clarity being more than offset by brightness which is often excessive to the point of harshness. They ought to try this one all over again, from scratch. The material deserves it.

### Goodbye Yellow Brick Road
MCA MCAD6894-2 (76:21—two discs)     [A–]
Edited down to one disc, this would easily be John's recorded pinnacle. *Goodbye Yellow Brick Road* somehow managed to blend Taupin's lyrical fantasy and Elton's grandiose musical melanges into something greater than the sum of their parts—the romantic spirit of seventies pop captured in all its excessive, multicolored glory. The title song, the opening instrumental, "Funeral for a Friend," followed by the vocal, "Love Lies Bleeding," and "Candle in the Wind" are the highlights, with the remainder made up of some strong material as well as some pretty forgettable exercises. The sound is a great enhancement over the LP, clear, detailed and dynamic with nice spatial quality, albeit with a slight tendency to overbrightness.

# Rickie Lee Jones
b. November 8, 1954—Chicago

### Rickie Lee Jones
Warner Bros. 3296-2 (42:16)     [A]
One of the seventies' better debut releases, featuring the hit "Chuck E.'s In Love" and including a number of Rickie's quirky, jazz-tinged sagas of losers on the loose: "Easy Money," "Last Chance Texaco," and "Coolsville" among them. It all sounds a bit like John Steinbeck writing for a hip Broadway fifties musical. The arrangements are spare and tasty, focusing on Ms. Jones's throaty, expressive interpretations of her off-

beat but compelling material. The sound has an intensely intimate quality about it, with effective enhancement of the subtle vocal shadings augmented with nice instrumental spacing and clarity. It's not quite as clean as it might be and at times feels a little compressed, while at others a little vocally harsh, but these are minor complaints.

# Janis Joplin

b. January 19, 1943—Port Arthur, Texas
d. October 4, 1970—Hollywood

During the halcyon days of the mid/late sixties in San Francisco, Janis stood as the queen of that area's acknowledged and thriving rock community. A truly talented blues shouter, she came to personify the female rock star of the era, but her life was probably best summed up by her own quote: "On stage I make love to 25,000 people, then go home alone."

### Pearl

Columbia CK 30322 (34:20)　　**[B + ]**
Clearly Janis's best recorded effort after her original Columbia release, *Cheap Thrills*, done with Big Brother and the Holding Company. Sadly, the stature of Joplin's myth is not matched by either the stature or the quantity of her recorded output, so, not even all of this relatively brief outing captures the legend at her best. But on "Me And Bobby McGee," "Mercedes Benz," and "A Woman Left Lonely" she manages to convey the nakedly honest intensity that, at its best, made her work incendiary. Even though the Full Tilt Boogie Band provides first-rate instrumental assistance, too often, the cuts seem either slightly out of sync or overly marred by excessive vocal hystrionics. The sound isn't great, marred by a general muddiness, consistent hiss, and occasional excessively bright upper mid-range.

### Janis Joplin's Greatest Hits

Columbia CK 32168 (41:52)　　**[A]**
It's a good career overview, including both live and studio work with all three of her major backup aggregations, Big Brother and the Holding Company, Kozmic Blues Band, and the Full Tilt Boogie Band, represented. Unfortunately, nothing on record really captured this blues urchin's awesome musical moments. For that you might want to check the Monterey Pop Video to see and hear Janis give one of the most electrifying performances in the recorded history of rock & roll, as witnessed and attested to by Mama Cass Elliot (the rest of the film is prime as well). The disc's sound is, as expected, all over the place; much of it sounding pretty dated. But sonic imperfections duly noted, it is still superior to its vinyl counterparts.

# B.B. King

### The Best Of

MCA MCAD 31040 (40:33)　　**[A–]**
The Blues Boy whose guitar (Lucille) only plays leads, usually searing, soaring ones at that—B.B. King is the standard by which urban blues guitar players have been measured for literally decades. His influence on both the white rock and black blues communities is obvious and extensive. B.B. is also a great blues singer and innovator. This collection of late sixties/early seventies songs, is a fair sampling from a long and prolific career. It includes some fine workouts: "How Blue Can You Get," "The Thrill Is Gone," and "Nobody Loves Me but My Mother," and there are no dogs included (B.B. may never have recorded one). Frankly, his best recordings are the concert releases with *Live at the Regal* leading the list. The sound quality is a bit dynamically enhanced over the LP, but hiss and compression are still evident and the quality does vary substantially from track to track.

# Carole King (Carol Klein)

b. February 9, 1942—Brooklyn, New York

### Tapestry

Ode EK 34946 (44:49)     **[A]**

In the sixties, she was an integral part of the Brill Building's brand of hot pop product, participating in writing over 100 hits, including "Loco-Motion," "Up On The Roof," and "Will You Love Me Tomorrow." In the seventies, she moved into the spotlight with this recording which was on the charts for almost six years, in the process selling over thirteen million copies, making it one of the most commercially successful pop albums ever released. It isn't a fluke. King has written or cowritten these twelve sensitive, yet streetwise, pop vignettes, representative of the best of the form. She sings them straight at you, without artifice or affectation, all backed by simple but very effective instrumental settings. In the seventies, rock branched into a number of subforms and this recording was instrumental in establishing (both artistically and commercially) what has come to be known as the singer/songwriter form of pop rock music. The sound is not real clean, and is marred by insistent hiss, but it's superior to the LP, both in its dynamics and spatial attributes.

# The Kinks

Formed 1962—England

During the halcyon days of the mid-sixties British Invasion, the Beatles and the Stones vied for the championship, with third place a distance back. But the Kinks and the Who stand as the bands most deserving for the bronze. Ray Davies's quirky, absolutely English lyrical perspective, plus performance problems, kept them from achieving major stardom in the United States, but their sophisticated, often cinematic music, has maintained a substantial world following for over two decades.

### Backtrackin Vol. I

Starblend CD Track 1/1 (40:48)     **[F]**

You can't fault the fourteen selections covering this eccentric, creative group's best known singles from the mid-sixties to the early seventies. But you can fault the production—it's godawful. The masters must have been third generation cassettes originally recorded off AM radio. It's a shame; the material merits much better.

### Lola Versus Powerman and the Moneygoround

PRT CDMP8836 (40:17)     **[B–]**

The band's 1970 concept release. The concept involved was the story of a group trying to get a No. 1 hit record. The best thing about the whole affair is the "record" they're promoting: "Lola," one of the decade's best rock songs. The rest of it is OK, but a bit heavy in the tone, both of the singing and the lyrics sung. To appreciate the Kinks, one has to have a certain intimacy with their large body of recorded work. Unfortunately, because the band has not garnered a world of U.S. commercial success, their better early LPs are frequently deleted, and very little of that material has reached CD yet. It's anyone's guess if it ever will. This album is a fair sampling of one facet. The sound is about equivalent to that of a clean LP.

### Come Dancing With the Kinks (The Best of the Kinks 1977-86)

Arista AZCD 8428 (69:51)     **[B–]**

The band's output of the last ten years or so has retained their appealing quirkiness, both musically and lyrically, but their classic work was done in their first decade. This is emphasized by the less than wondrous live versions of earlier classics "Lola" and "You Really Got Me" included here. Ray Davies still tracks the same themes with his unique musical approach, but they fail to resonate any longer, valid though they still may be. The sound is all over the place with newer items having a fine aural sheen ("Don't Forget to Dance" and "Livin on a Thin Line"), but earlier material obviously suffers from analogic shortcomings and muddy digital conversions.

# Gladys Knight and the Pips

### The Best of Gladys Knight and the Pips

Buddah BCD 68001 (67:50)     [C +]

Gladys Knight can sing and when she gets a good song and a solid arrangement, she and the Pips make some sweet seventies' pop/soul sounds ("Midnight Train to Georgia" and "I've Got to Use My Imagination"). Unfortunately, during the seventies Buddah phase of their career, the group consistently settled for production over purpose. However, even in the lesser material, there are times when Knight's warmly sensual voice raises things to a level to be reckoned with. The CD does add a half-dozen "bonus" cuts to this compilation which was originally released on LP. The sound is relatively clean and spacious, but not particularly dynamic or detailed. ("Midnight Train to Georgia" remains one of the great pop/soul songs of the era.)

# Led Zeppelin

### Untitled (IV)

Atlantic 19129-2 (42:40)     [A +]

It all culminates here. Ponderous as it may sometimes be, Led Zep's powerful, mythic thunder is rock & roll (unfortunately, the same can rarely, if ever, be said about their legions of heavy metal successors). This time out they were in full control of their dynamic vision and the end result is an early seventies classic highlighted by "Black Dog," "Rock And Roll," "When the Levee Breaks," and what became the anthem of the decade, "Stairway to Heaven." Of course, Zeppelin's music was about much more than a bombast; it was music of shading and contrast, of instrumental and production precision, all of which are generally well-displayed on the CD. Its dynamics and clarity will make you a believer. It does have slight flaws, some hiss and some vocal compression, particularly on the Joni Mitchell tribute "Goin' to California," but these are ultimately inconsequential.

# John Lennon

b. October 9, 1940—Liverpool, England
d. December 8, 1980—New York City

The rock & roll soul of the Beatles who tried to fulfill that role for all mankind. One of the truly great artists to have expressed his very personal vision through the medium of popular music.

### Shaved Fish

Capitol CDP 7 46642 2 (41:42)     [A–]

A collection of post-Beatles sloganeering—but the message is so important and the artist was so sincere, that it rises to pure rock & roll. While not everything included is of sustaining quality, each cut does evidence the rock production sensitivities of one of the best to ever record within the form. Until they do a digital *Plastic Ono Band*, this will just have to suffice. And it will. The sound varies appreciably from cut to cut, i.e., at times it is a bit bright, at others it's afflicted with hiss and some compression, but, on average the dynamic punch and enhanced clarity make it a clear choice over the LP.

### Live in New York City

Parlaphone CDP 7 461962 (42:20)     [B]

Recorded on August 30, 1972, at a Madison Square Garden benefit concert, but not released until 1986, this is music that's as rough as a cob. As Lennon says between the cuts, "Welcome to the rehearsal." Perhaps it was the vibe that night, perhaps it was just because it was John Lennon in America, New York in 1972; whatever the reason, the performance often rises above its too apparent limitations. The very "live" sound on the disc captures it all, poor musicianship and everything—mike hum and occasional distortion included. But through the entire proceedings shines John's sincere desire to touch all who heard his song. The medium may have been flawed that August night, but the message sounded loud and clear.

# Lynyrd Skynyrd

Formed 1966—Jacksonville, Florida

## One More For the Road

MCA MCAD6897 (71:17)      [B + ]

The height of mid-seventies southern rock, served up live and kickin' by the band that earned its reputation doin' it live on the road. Covered among its twelve strong selections (almost totally drawn from their hot first and second album releases, *Pronounced Leh-Nerd Skin-Nerd* and *Second Helping*) are "Saturday Night Special," "Sweet Home Alabama," "The Needle and the Spoon," and "Free Bird," each an enduring testament to the power of Ronnie Van Zant's writing and performance. This is definitely a live outing, albeit a well-recorded one. The band and the crowd cook—this was stirring southern rock with a gritty edge, but, on record, the studio cuts of these songs remain definitive. The sound is clean, live, obviously lacking in studio sheen and definition, but, nonetheless, a plus.

# Bob Marley

b. April 6, 1945—Rhoden Hall, Jamaica
d. May 11, 1981

Though his musical career began in the early sixties, it was during the seventies that Bob Marley, and with him, reggae, began to permeate the world of popular music. In its native form, it has achieved great popularity, not only in Jamaica (its home ground), but also in England, Europe, South America, and Africa. During this decade, its influence was felt throughout the pop music of the Western world, either through straight cover versions of the material by white stars (e.g., Eric Clapton's rendition of Marley's "I Shot the Sheriff") or more pervasively, through incorporation of its distinctive rhythm/instrumentation into the framework of white/black artists' musical canvases, e.g., Paul Simon, the Clash, the Rolling Stones, and the Police, among many others. Musically, reggae is marked by an inversion of the standard rock instrumental format, i.e., the guitar is used as a rhythmic rather than melodic voice and the bass becomes a melodic as opposed to rhythmic instrument, both playing over a complex/hesitation percussive beat. Lyrically the music combines the concepts and vernacular of the Rastafarian faith as well as the politics of oppressed, deprived minorities, specifically, in cultures still suffering from the financial dislocations of colonialism. Marley, by virtue of his charisma, intensity, and total commitment to both the music and its meanings became the form's one true superstar with a worldwide following. Because of its protest-message lyrics and R&B roots (derived from U.S. records and radio received in Jamaica since the forties), reggae represents a valid permutation of the rock sound and spirit and reflects rock's absorption as a part of the popular culture of the Third World. Marley's death from cancer at age thirty-six was a tragedy perhaps not fully appreciated by the American audience, only a small portion of whom had truly identified with pure expressions of the form.

## Natty Dread

Island 7 90037-2 (38:56)      [B + ]

Recorded after Peter Tosh and Bunny Livingston (nee Wailer) left the group and were replaced with the effective support of the female I-Threes, all of which placed Marley's vocals at center stage illuminating raw passion bubbling over the music's laconic beat. This is one of the first American Marley releases, if not *the* very first to begin to attract more than a hardcore audience; it contains his classic, "No Woman, No Cry." Soundwise, there is obvious compression throughout, but the vocals suffer most; the disc's overall sound is clean and while the rhythm tracks remain a bit murky, they do receive a dynamic lift.

## Rastaman Vibration

Island 7-90033-2 (35:10)      [B]

From political passion to more laid-back social commentary, *Rastaman Vibration* provides a continuation of the smooth groove that Marley and the Wailers had defined and occupied since earlier in the decade. While it lacks a single "classic" track, the recording is of consistent high quality. The sound is obviously compressed with some added detail in the upper mid-range, but it's really not much different from the LP; only a little cleaner.

### Live!

Island 7 90032-2 (40:34)    **[B+]**
Recorded in London in July, 1975, this concert release features seven classic Wailers' songs, some of which go back to the original group that featured Tosh and Livingston. Marley was a hypnotically enthralling performer whose status went beyond the music to that of accepted spokesman for Third World political positions (he was wounded when he became the object of an assassination attempt in Jamaica) and that intensity shows on this release, perhaps better than anywhere else on record. Both the sound (very "live" but muffled, dirty, and severely compressed) and the performance are on the ragged side. However, Marley's intensity more than carries the day, particularly his very moving reading of "No Woman, No Cry."

### Legend (The Best of Bob Marley and the Wailers)

Island 7 90169-2 (50:26)    **[A+]**
The fourteen selections, released originally between 1972 and 1982, provide a fair overview of the career of one of the decade's most influential musical figures. From "Get Up, Stand Up," "Stir It Up," and "I Shot the Sheriff" through the live version of "No Woman, No Cry" to "Buffalo Soldier" and "Jamming," the collection captures the highlights of a man who understood the politics of his music and performed for much more than monetary sustenance. The sound is erratic, exhibiting both the positives and negatives of digital conversion in abundance. However, if you're looking for a one-disc sampler of the work of a reggae artist of first-rank importance, this would be the one.

# Dave Mason
b. May 10, 1947—Worcester, England

### Alone Together

MCA MCAD-31170 (35:06)    **[B–]**
Mason's first solo effort after leaving the legendary Traffic, *Alone Together* is a good, but not great record—too well-crafted, too safe. Nonetheless, his reputation as a composer, guitarist, and singer of the first rank is both merited and in evidence here. In addition, Mason is supported by first-rate musicians who work effectively together. The highlights include: "Only You Know and I Know," "World in Changes," and "Look at You Look at Me." The sound is essentially equivalent to that of the LP.

# Paul McCartney
b. June 18, 1942—Liverpool, England
The son of a twenties jazz band leader, McCartney is a nonpareil writer of polished pop material. While his association with John Lennon in the Beatles provided a musical balance that turned the world of pop music on its ear, on his own (and with his traveling band, Wings), his lack of incisive lyrical intelligence and passionate commitment to more than commercial success has left a residue of eminently listenable, but forgettable material.

### Band on the Run

Parlophone CDP 7 46055-2 (41:13)    **[B]**
Easily, McCartney's most successful and listenable outing, *Band on the Run* was recorded in Nigeria in 1974-75 and reflects both his fine pop sensibility and production acumen (most of the sounds that make up the recording were, in fact, done by McCartney alone in the studio). It does contain some strong seventies pop product: "Band on the Run," "Jet," and "Let Me Roll It" are the highlights. While it goes beyond mere aural wallpaper, it isn't any masterpiece either. The sound, marred by some hiss as well as harshness and distortion, is more open, dynamic and warm than that of the LP.

## Venus and Mars

Columbia CK36801 (43:30)    **[B–]**
Released in 1973, *Venus and Mars* was the follow-up to *Band on the Run* which was basically all McCartney in the studio. With this recording, Wings again became a real rock band, notably through the addition of guitarist Jimmy McCullogh and drummer Joe English. For this outing, the group went to New Orleans and availed themselves of the local musical riches, notably Allen Toussaint. The result is probably the best rock & roll that McCartney has made since departing his original group, particularly in the selections, "Rock Show" and "Listen to What the Man Said." In no small part this is because Paul's songs here also have more spine than most of the post-Beatles saccharin pop with which he has been associated. The sound of the disc generally leaves a bit to be desired—heavy hiss, buried vocals, and occasional distortion are too much in evidence.

# Harold Melvin and the Blue Notes

Formed 1956—Philadelphia
Originally a doowop group, in 1970, Teddy Pendergrass moved from drums to lead vocal and the group signed with Gamble-Huff's Philadelphia International label.

## Collectors Item (All Their Greatest Hits)

Philadelphia International Label CK 34232
(46:51)    **[C +]**
For the four years (1972-76) that Teddy Pendergrass's voice burned through the lovely Melvin vocal arrangements and Gamble and Huffs' overburdened strings, Harold Melvin and the Blue Notes created some of the better disco/soul sounds to be heard. But Harold kept trying to hide Teddy until he finally lost him. While Pendergrass was not featured on every cut on this collection, he is what elevates it above the run-of-the-mill. The man can emote with one of the biggest voices in the biz. The sound is generally clean (there is some very audible hiss in the quiet sections), but clear and dynamic; although some com-

pression also remains evident, it is still a marked improvement over the LP.

# Joni Mitchell (Roberta Joan Anderson)

b. November 7, 1943—Alberta, Canada
One of the most respected, covered, and influential of the singer/songwriters; her intelligently personal lyrical statements and sophisticated folk/jazz voicings have created a readily identifiable, honest body of sustaining work.

## For the Roses

Asylum 5057-2 (40:36)    **[A–]**
Often complex, introverted, and confessional, this is arty (as opposed to emotional) folk music for moderns. Joni's work exhibits a certain pristine, strongly feminine quality. On *For the Roses,* her vocals are set amidst beautifully conceived, almost classical instrumental accompaniments. This is music which, for the most part, demands more attention than what usually is marketed under the "pop" label. It is also music that rewards the attentive listener. The sound, while sometimes disclosing slight hiss, is, overall, clear and the disc accords the acoustic instruments full and detailed clarity with Joni's unique voice preserved with all its idiosyncrasies.

## Court and Spark

Asylum 1001-2 (37:00)    **[A +]**
Because of the more melodic nature of the material and its less intricate lyrical convolutions, this is the highlight of Joni's major musical career. It is also as fine an example of the singer/songwriter genre as you will ever hear. Fortunately, the sound of the CD is clean, clear, and warm; of the same consistent high level as the rest of the package, making this a "must" disc.

## Miles of Aisles

Asylum 202-2 (74:07)    **[B–]**
The eighteen selections, providing almost an hour and a quarter of early seventies concert

performances, cover Joni's most popular material: "You Turn Me On I'm a Radio," "Big Yellow Taxi," "Woodstock," "Blue," "Circle Game," "Real Good for Free," and "Both Sides Now" among them. Also included are lesser known, but high-quality compositions such as, "Cold Blue Steel and Sweet Fire," "The Last Time I Saw Richard," and the fascinating "Jericho." Her performance supported by Tom Scott's jazz-oriented L.A. Express and by her own solo accompaniment on piano, guitar, or dulcimer has a very "live" feel in its straightforward unpretentiousness. The sound is definitely concert quality, not bad, but very compressed; somewhat noisy and occasionally strident. The CD sound emphasizes both the strengths and the weaknesses, and there is a fair share of both here.

# The Modern Lovers

Formed 1972—Boston
Hans Christian Andersen discovers the Velvet Underground. Leader Jonathan Richman is an unselfconscious, natural contrarian who has joyously preserved the wondrous eye of a child for us all to see through. This is fragile rock & roll. Jonathan Richman loves Jonathan Richman and through his music, he communicates that love on a truly universal level that transcends explanation. Warning: This may be an acquired taste.

### The Beserkley Years (The Best of Jonathan Richman and the Modern Lovers)

Rhino RNC 75889 (59:45)     [A +]
This collection covers multiple versions of the Modern Lovers. The first incarnation (which included Jerry Harrison, later of Talking Heads, and Dave Robinson, later of the Cars) featured the production of John Cale (the original Velvet Underground cellist) resulting in the classics: "Roadrunner" and "Pablo Picasso" (included), as well as first-rate live and studio takes of material performed by Jonathan with subsequent versions of the band. The sound had to be tough to work with. Some cuts were literally recorded in a bathroom (Richman liked the echo), and

Harrison has stated that the original band's recording philosophy was that "anything that was worked over lost its energy." Rhino's usual first-rate production efforts result in a detailed, spacious, nicely dynamic sound that is seriously marred with hiss and a generally noisy background.

# Van Morrison

### Moondance

Warner Bros. 3103-2 (39:17)     [A +]
Robert Christgau said it best: "Morrison's soul, like that of the black music he loves, is mortal and immortal simultaneously; this is a man who gets stoned on a drink of water and urges us to turn up our radios all the way into . . . the mystic." This is as good as it ever gets. The CD suffers from consistent hiss and a slight tendency to overbrightness in Van's vocals, but, on the positive side, it's detailed and dynamic with a warm, spacious sound.

### His Band and the Street Choir

Warner Bros. 1884-2 (42:22)     [A–]
The mystical Irish minstrel of rock & roll mixes some contemporary soul with some Crescent City rhythms as a follow-up to his formidable *Moondance*. It's a comedown; it almost had to be, but, it's still a damn fine outing. The tone is less visionary and more soul party, which yields some rousing up-tempo numbers, notably the hits, "Domino" and "Blue Money." Sound quality varies (actually it's easy to distinguish between the various recording sessions); most cuts are compressed with little, if any, enhancement over the LP, whereas others are marred by very audible hiss and edgy overbright sound, but exhibit more dynamics and detail.

### Into the Music

Mercury 800 057-2 (49:50)     [A +]
After 1972's *St. Dominic's Preview,* Morrison released four albums (one of which, *It's Too Late to Stop Now,* was a live double-record set) over the next six years which declined in both content and popular acceptance. The

1979 release *Into the Music* celebrated a
resurgence of the creative powers which he
had exhibited at the end of the prior decade.
On this recording, he sounds more in com-
mand of his prodigious talents than, perhaps,
anywhere else on record. His singing is a
testament to the expressive powers of the
human voice and the instrumental combination of strings (Toni Marcus on violin, etc.)
and R&B horns (beautifully arranged by Pee
Wee Ellis and Mark Isham) has proved to be a
resonant background for Van's religious and
fleshly visions since the time of this release.
The whole thing is great, but the last four
selections, concluding with the almost eleven
minute "It's All in the Game/You Know What
They're Writing About" may be his recorded
tour de force. The sound is clean and nicely
detailed, though the "stage" is not overly spacious and there is an overall tendency toward
too much brightness, particularly on the
up-tempo numbers, but these aren't major
complaints.

## New Riders of the Purple Sage

Formed 1969—Marin County, California
The country offshoot of the Grateful Dead.

### The Best Of

Columbia CK34367 (30:50)      [D–]
Second-rate country by ersatz second-rate
country players. Suffice it to say, their timing
was about the only thing right about this
group. The sound varies, from roughly LP
equivalence to some cuts with slight detail
and dynamic enhancement.

## Graham Parker

b. 1950—London
The largely undiscovered major talent to
arise out of the later seventies British musical
renaissance.

### Squeezing Out Sparks

Arista ARCD 8075 (34:59)      [A + ]
This is hard-assed, hard-edged, hard-workin'
rock & roll in the fullest classic, yet current,

sense. The Rumour, one of the era's best pub-
rock bands, drives with near manic intensity
while Parker spews out his truthful, honest
anger above it all. R&B-based, rock-rooted,
these are the outpourings of a man who be-
lieves in the power of rock & roll with all the
fervor he possesses. Sheer excitement
enhanced by bright, hard, crisp dynamic
sound. There wasn't a lot of great rock & roll
made in the latter half of rock's transitional
decade, but this was some of it, and it's tough
stuff.

## Gram Parsons (Cecil Connor)

b. November 5, 1946—Winter Haven, Florida (raised
   Georgia)
d. September 19, 1973—Joshua Tree National Monu-
   ment, California
The son of country singer/songwriter Coon
Dog Connor, Parsons came by his roots legit-
imately. During his sadly brief career, he
proved to be one of the least recognized but
most influential figures of the late sixties and
early seventies musical scene. Parsons's brief
association with the Byrds resulted in 1968's
*Sweetheart of the Rodeo,* the seminal country
rock album that gave rise to an L.A.-based
genre that became a dominant strain in early
seventies rock music.

### Gram Parsons and the Fallen Angels Featuring Emmylou Harris Live 1973

Magnum CD5D 003 (47:23)      [A + ]
Parsons's heartfelt, haunting music is a true
expression of an American cultural heritage
which he made compatible to the rock era.
These sounds have bound people and re-
gions together for generations and Parsons,
Harris, and crew perform them with a commitment and respect that establishes both
their history and immediacy. This live album
contains many of his and other writers' contemporary country classics, and with the
exception of his wondrous "Hickory Wind," is
essentially comprehensive. The sound is
obviously from live performances, but it's

open, clear, and generally first-rate. One listen to this fine recording should explain Dave Marsh's observation that, "Parsons's influence is wide, deep, and likely to last."

# The Pentangle
Formed 1967—England

### Basket of Light
Transatlantic TRACD 205 (41:04)     **[B–]**
This band attempted to preserve the English folk music tradition and instrumentation by enhancing it with modern recording technology tinged with some jazz overtones and rhythms. The result is apparently souless, beautiful music that sounds like fine crystal. The disc does nothing to diminish the extraordinary sound quality that made the LP an audiophile favorite for years. It's clean, amazingly detailed, and spacious, with marginal hiss.

# Tom Petty (and the Heartbreakers)
b. 1952—Gainesville, Florida
  Formed 1975—Los Angeles
One of the forms of rock to take shape in the seventies has been dubbed "arena rock"— potent, anthemic statements delivered with sufficient impact and sonic drive to be heard in the huge venues to which the rock promoters moved the audience during the decade. Petty, along with Springsteen and Seger, represented the best examples of the genre.

### Damn the Torpedos
MCA MCAD5105 (36:54)     **[B + ]**
Classic late seventies American rock & roll— bright, tight, forceful, well-written and produced music, played by a first-rate group of musicians whose joy comes through. Quality rock anthems for the assembled masses. The sound is clean, punchy, and well-defined,

with a slightly edgy overall brightness that sometimes teeters on the edge of discomfort.

# Pink Floyd

### Dark Side of the Moon
Harvest CDP746001-2 (42:58)     **[A + ]**

### Dark Side of the Moon
Capitol CDP746001-2 (42:54)     **[A–]**
Released in 1973, this album was still on the *Billboard* pop charts in 1986 after selling more than ten million copies in the United States alone. The original, and obviously most enduring, of the seventies English concept art rock albums. The eclectic techno sound was very much attributable to the contribution of Alan Parsons, the project's Abbey Road engineer, the saxophone of Dick Parry, and Clare Torry's expressive, wordless vocals. *Dark Side of the Moon* has become, perhaps, the essential icon of seventies rock. The sound quality depends on which of the two versions (Capitol or Harvest) is heard. The import Harvest release is now almost impossible to find (unless one is willing to pay a hefty price), but it affords much the superior sound—fuller, more rounded with significantly reduced tape hiss. The Capitol version is still a spatial and dynamic enhancement over the LP, but suffers from some muddiness and much more annoying hiss than the Harvest recording which, interestingly enough, runs four seconds longer.

### The Wall
Columbia C2K36183 (81:23—two discs)     **[B]**
It's overlong, and won't bear close scrutiny, either musically or (especially) lyrically, but it is listenable. *The Wall* is the pinnacle of English art rock at the end of the decade; it bears testament to an obscure and/or minimal concept. Yet, this is a band that understands the art of the recording studio with more acumen than most; thus, if only on

a sonic level, it succeeds. The CD adds marvelous dynamics, clarity of detail, and stage/depth to all the ingenious sound effects.

# Lou Reed

b. March 2, 1943—Brooklyn, New York
Reed, principle writer and lead singer of the massively influential Velvet Underground, is that rare animal possessed of a rock & roll heart and a poetic mind. Not everything he had done since leaving the Underground in 1972 has worked; in fact, most hasn't.

### Transformer

RCA PCD14807 (37:03)      [C–]
While the Summer of Love and Me Decades passed merrily by, Lou Reed continued to sing about the seamier side of things. In the case of *Transformer,* the premise is "affected trendiness." Aided and abetted by David Bowie and Mick Ronson, this results in some engaging moments, "Walk on the Wild Side" being the obvious one. The rest of the recording delivers more of the same, but it's not nearly as well realized. The sound varies, with some muddiness and compression evident, but a number of the cuts, (notably "Walk on the Wild Side") are beautifully rendered on disc; clear, detailed, and open.

# The Rolling Stones

### Get Yer Ya-Yas Out!

abco 852 (47:54)      [B + ]
It was Madison Square Garden. The playlist is perfect. They were the greatest rock & roll band in the world. They were playing hot and nasty—scurrilous, biting, blues-based rock & roll. Yet somehow the recording never really ignites; there's not a definitive Stones version of any of this material. That said, it's still easily the best concert recording made by a great rock band. One of the reasons that *Get Yer Ya-Yas Out!* never fully realized its obvious potential was its sound quality, which was poor on record and isn't much improved on disc. Jagger's vocals are almost lost in the

mix and the guitar sound is dirty, while the bottom succumbs to murkiness. There's also some dropout and distortion.

### Hot Rocks (1964-1971)

abco 2CD606/7 (86:42—two discs)      [B + ]
If you're looking for a sampler, here it is; a little bit of everything. But work of the magnitude done by the Stones during the period covered by this compilation has too much richness and complexity to be properly served in a listener's digest rendering. The sound varies, but is generally several cuts above the LP version.

### Sticky Fingers

Rolling Stones Records CK40488 (46:26)      [A]
This is unrepentant, unregenerate, arrogant Stones' style rock & roll at its best (well, maybe not "Wild Horses"). From "Brown Sugar" to "Moonlight Mile" with eight soulful, nasty numbers in between, this is the music that made them the kings (or at least the Dark Princes) of early seventies rock & roll. With this release, the Stones changed labels to Columbia for scandalous sums of money and their own label. This is mentioned because the digital conversions of this label's material are generally not of the audio quality of the previously reviewed London (abco) earlier releases. The sound on *Sticky Fingers* is reed thin and overbright. But it provides more clarity and detail than are available on the LP.

### Exile on Main Street

Rolling Stone Records CGK40489 (66:35)      [A + ]
Rock verité—basement rock & roll, call it what you will—it is the scuzziest, dirtiest, most chaotic album release of a great rock band at the height of its powers, driving home ironically detached cynicism with undiminishing arrogance. It is one of the ten greatest rock records of all time (*Rolling Stone* ranked it third in its August 27, 1987, critics' survey of the best recorded releases of 1967-87). Literally recorded in a basement with a mobile unit, it may have been another calculated statement, but like most of the Stones' messages at the time, this one rang

true on many levels. *Exile on Main Street* is tough, dense music which pertains to its times and to the continuing spirit of rock & roll. The CD improves the clarity of the sound (which some may find equivalent to the color-izing of a black-and-white movie), but the murky power persists, pulsing with its carnal rhythms. All that, and it's got "Tumbling Dice," too.

**Some Girls**

Rolling Stones Records CK40449 (40:46)   **[B]**
Probably the last gasp of a once great band. They were playing tighter than ever, particu-larly Watts (drums) and Wyman (bass), but with this band that's not necessarily a virtue. This is stripped-down, straight-ahead Stones' rock & roll, and it still resonates with the echoes of their former dark grandeur (it was the group's best-ever selling album), but the intensity has been replaced with something more commercially akin to the disco sen-sibility of the time. The sound is punchy, crisp, and terribly overbright.

# Linda Ronstadt

b. July 15, 1946—Tucson, Arizona

**Heart Like a Wheel**

Capitol CDP7 46073-2 (31:45)   **[D]**
Her strength is her achingly pure, perfect pitched voice which is truly a remarkable instrument. Her devastating weakness is an inability to convey, or worse, comprehend the meaning of the lyrics she performs. *Heart Like a Wheel*, which was the initial move away from the more country sounds of her prior records, is probably her strongest recorded outing—good song selection, excel-lent musicianship, and more vitality in her lyrical interpretations than she's displayed before or since. Sadly, this one shining re-corded moment has been butchered in its conversion to disc; the mix is muddy, thick, distorted, and generally inexcusable.

# Santana

Formed 1967—San Francisco

**Caravanserai**

Columbia CK31610 (51:23)   **[C–]**
What had begun in the late sixties as an improvisational Latin rock band, became, with this release, a Latin jazz/rock fusion experiment. *Caravanserai* has its moments, but it's mostly ambling, formless, and lacking in central theme or meaning. The recording is plagued with hiss and, overall, has roughly the same sound characteristics as its LP predecessor.

# Boz Scaggs
# (William Royce Scaggs)

b. June 8, 1944—Ohio
Boz got his start as the singer in the Steve Miller Band and ultimately migrated with Mil-ler from Texas to San Francisco in 1967. Over the next decade or so, Skaggs developed into one of the smoothest, white soul singers around. In recent years, he has quit recording and now owns the Blue Light Cafe in the City by the Bay.

**Slow Dancer**

Columbia CK32760 (36:38)   **[B–]**
Working with former Motown producer, Johnny Bristol, Scaggs lends his smooth voic-ings to ten soul selections, largely written by the artist and Bristol. This is slick, listenable, ballad-to-medium tempo white soul music performed by one of the better practitioners of the form. The sound is generally very good; nice separation among the instruments and slightly enhanced dynamics with some compression and occasional distortion on a few vocals.

**Silk Degrees**

CBS CK33920 (41:33)   **[A–]**
In addition to being one of the more polished, white soul/rock vocalists of the seventies, Boz has a knack for writing strong, hook-filled material. On *Silk Degrees*, he had a

hand in eight of the ten selections which include his one major hit, "Low Down," as well as "Georgia" and "Lido Shuffle." It all adds up to a fine recording of mostly up-tempo, R&B-based rock & roll, that is easily Scaggs's best album effort (although "Loan Me a Dime" from 1971's *Boz Scaggs* is the single high point of his recordings, but it's not currently available on disc). The guy is slick, but he's also good. The sound, while a bit compressed, is clean and nicely detailed.

# Bob Seger

b. May 6, 1945—Ann Arbor, Michigan

It's almost un-American not to like Bob Seger. The blue-collar, truckin', hard-rockin', hard-workin' rock & roller who just kept bringing it to the people; working the toughest gig in the biz—the road—more days than not, year in and year out. He ain't what he used to be, but, then, who is?

### (And the Silver Bullet Band) Night Moves

Capitol CDP7 46075 2 (36:59)      [A + ]

There's nothing new here; just the best of the fifties and sixties rock & roll and soul music restated with honest currency and sung by one of rock's best voices. The years of dues behind *Night Moves* cling to it like grime on flesh. Dave Marsh described it best: "That wonderful chronicle of moments when age becomes irrelevant and innocence gains experience." There really isn't a bad cut on the album. The sound is a joy, not perfect, but a joy—bright, full, detailed, clean, and very dynamic (it does have some compression and occasional distortion in the vocals).

# The Sex Pistols

Formed 1975—London

The epitome of Britain's 1960's rock bands, the Beatles and the Stones, have both been identified with a Svengali who guided them to greatness. As Brian Epstein packaged the Beatles and Andrew Loog Oldham the Stones, Malcolm McLaren provided that service and much more to the Sex Pistols. The

idea was simple enough. Create a band that would be the turd in the palace of smug success-smothered music that was then impersonating rock & roll. McLaren's genius was in finding the right turd.

### Never Mind the Bollocks Here's the Sex Pistols

Virgin CDV 2086 (38:54)      [A + ]

It's an assault. A remembrance of things past and of a spirit almost lost. You feel the Sex Pistols. The hearing is almost irrelevant. This is dissolute, daring music that isn't easy in any way, but it is one of those rare recordings that somehow affects the way everything after it is heard. *Never Mind the Bollocks* was the one unchallenged rock & roll album of the seventies. Nihilistic, nasty, neurotic, and pnuematic, it was/is the spirit incarnate. The sound is tight, driving, and abrasive, just as was intended.

# Simon & Garfunkel

### Bridge Over Troubled Water

Columbia CK9914 (37:29)      [B + ]

Well-crafted as they are, the lyrics haven't worn all that well; perhaps because of overexposure due to the tremendous popularity the album initially enjoyed in 1970 and its continued playability. What sustains are the lush melodies, superbly produced. Overall, the CD's sound revitalizes this old chestnut providing a precise, yet warm, dynamic rendering of the craftsmanship displayed by the duo and their wonderful producer/engineer, Roy Halee, in the recording studio. The sound is sadly afflicted with consistently audible hiss and some distortion and/or muddiness in its loudest passages. Yet, on balance, the digital conversion is a substantial improvement; in fact, it offers several truly stunning moments.

### Greatest Hits

Columbia CK31350 (44:32)      [D−]

You certainly can't fault the song selection on this first-rate compilation. But on most cuts the sound is incredibly poor, thin and shrill with some distortion thrown in for good measure. This is one disc where the record wins hands down.

# Paul Simon
b. October 13, 1942—Newark, New Jersey
While his body of work is impressive for both its innate quality and its popular acceptance, his ultimate legacy may be as a bridge between the indigenous music of the world's divergent cultures.

### Greatest Hits, Etc.
Columbia CK35032 (51:53)      [A + ]
Just as Garfunkel's musical career plummeted following the duo's breakup, Simon's sharply ascended. As his eclectic craftsmanship became more pronounced, his musical product became more diverse, but always professionally and precisely presented. Simon has managed to extend the Brill Building pop ethic into a valid contemporary popular idiom. Faulting this collection has to be simply a matter of personal idiosyncrasy: "Slip Slidin' Away," "Still Crazy After All These Years," "An American Tune," "Mother And Child Renunion," "Take Me to the Mardi Gras," plus eight other wonderful pop songs. At his best ("An American Tune"), Paul Simon is one of the finest writers of popular music the form has known. If all that weren't enough, the CD is pure sonic joy. This is the best of the seventies pop products through the best of the eighties sound technology.

# Sly and the Family Stone

### Greatest Hits
Epic EK30325 (40:04)      [A + ]
This recording coalesces the upbeat sounds and sentiments of the Woodstock era through the exuberant, innovative, creative genius of Sly and his "family" that was a real embodiment of the ideals of which they sang. Because Stone had a tendency to try to do it all in each song, too often his reach exceeded his grasp; and, because his mood and music

change radically with his next release (*There's A Riot Goin' On*), this recording, which literally includes every Sly single that successfully achieved his vision, is one of the best compilation rock/pop/funk recordings ever issued. It will make you dance and smile and maybe remind you of what it might have been. It's chock-full of brilliant, influential, and, too often, overlooked pop greatness. The sound, while varying a little, is bright, crisp, clean, clear, detailed, and dynamic—you can't ask for much more.

# The Spinners
Formed 1957—Detroit

### The Best Of
Motown MCD09008MD (30:03)      [C–]
This collection, originally released in 1973, covers this fine singing group's early seventies Motown material and does not include any of the smooth soul hits produced by Thom Bell after the group moved to Atlantic (e.g., "One of a Kind [Love Affair]" or "Mighty Love"). While their appealing vocal skills are evident on some of these brief selections, the whole affair is just too much Motown production-line pop allowing little of the Spinners' unique appeal to shine through. The CD's sound is bright, clean, and dynamic with some harshness in the upper mid-range vocal tracks.

# Bruce Springsteen
b. September 23, 1949—Freehold, New Jersey
In the early seventies, the word leaked out that Columbia Record's late famed talent scout, John Hammond (who had been responsible for bringing Billie Holliday, Count Basie, Pete Seeger, Aretha Franklin, the Four Tops, and Bob Dylan to that label's roster), had made another major discovery, Bruce Springsteen. His first release, *Greetings from Asbury Park, N.J.*, came out in '73 and his greatest, *Born to Run,* was released in 1975 which resulted in Bruce making the covers of both *Time* and *Newsweek,* still a unique

event in rock's brief history. Springsteen represents the reincarnation of rock & roll's basic tenets: escapism and rebellion as product for mass consumption. These attributes, combined with his highly acclaimed personal values which, in many instances, amounted to an endorsement of America's traditional values, as well as a deep concern about this nation's loss thereof, make up the elements out of which he has carved incredible stardom. Devoid of rock-star trappings, Bruce was the blue-collar rock & roller working concerts that generally started on schedule and often ran for more than five breathtaking hours' duration, leaving his audiences sated with the power of the music to redeem the moment and to create a truly meaningful experience. To see "The Boss" in a small venue was as close as most fans ever got to the true power of the music, and it was an unforgettable experience, made palpable by Springsteen's repeatedly proven desire to reach each and every soul who came to hear. The payoff, in a literal sense, didn't come until the 1980s when Bruce reached true super stardom, inevitably sacrificing some of his intimacy, but preserving the best of it all through sheer will, awesome energy, and a genuine, caring talent.

### Greetings from Asbury Park, N.J.

Columbia CK31903 (37:14)      **[B]**
His original '72 release which is divided between acoustic cuts focusing on his then-wordy (Dylanesque) lyrics, and the R&B-inflected power rock upon which his Jersey reputation had been built. While the record never received the acceptance suggested by the hype, it does contain some classic cuts, "Blinded by the Light," "Growin' Up," "Spirit in the Night," and "It's Hard to Be a Saint in the City," which bespoke the teen vision of the times with an intimacy and immediacy that parallels that attained by the first rock & rollers twenty years prior. The recording somehow lacked continuity and suffered from generally crude production values which ultimately undermined the poignancy

of the message. On CD, the vocals become more intimate and the instrumental separation is enhanced, but there is also audible hiss, thin, somewhat compressed sound and a frequent edginess to the stronger vocals.

### The Wild, the Innocent, and the E Street Shuffle

Columbia CK324232 (46:56)      **[A–]**
A clear transition from the individually focused *Greetings from Asbury Park, N.J.,* to the ensemble power of *Born to Run,* this fascinating recording shows the artist groping toward the potent, ultimately romantic sounds which would come to epitomize rock & roll for many young Americans. It is here, also, that his narrative lyrics, studded with quick, canny, compelling characters supported by truly adventurous song structures is first exposed; all to celebrate the glories and the grotesqueries of youth. Included are some transcendant moments: "4th Of July, Asbury Park (Sandy)" and "Rosalita (Come Out Tonight)" being the obvious highlights. While the sound stage is a bit constricted and the vocal tracks more mixed into the instrumentals, the sound is very good, devoid of hiss; dynamic and nicely defined.

### Born to Run

Columbia CK33795 (39:38)      **[A + ]**
It all comes together here—the E Street Band, the drama, the romance, the grandiose vision for the common fan. This is a concept recording which owes a strong production nod to Phil Spector, that distills down to some of the best rock songs of the decade (the title cut, "Thunder Road," "Jungleland," "Backstreets," and "Tenth Ave. Freezeout," among them). It all amounts to a territorial imperative by a man whose vision encompasses all things American. Both the CD and LP suffer from very noticeable compression and some muddiness, but the CD is a bit brighter, with slightly enhanced detail. Considering what has been done with much older, and assumedly more primitive master material (e.g., almost anything Bill Inglott has reworked at Rhino), it is a crime that something sonically

better couldn't have been done with the first CD release of this true seventies classic recording; the heroic nature of which would nicely mesh with more heroic sound. Columbia remastered the digital conversion in late 1987, so more current copies of the CD sound appreciably better than the first disc releases. This was a very difficult, daring recorded statement which Springsteen has called "the most intense experience I ever had."

### Darkness on the Edge of Town
Columbia CK35318 (43:02)     **[A]**
From the cover photos to the contents, it's clear that this is the statement of a changed man; the boyish beliefs have been supplanted by hard-won knowledge of the "real" world. (Obviously, a reflection of two years of court battles with his first opportunistic manager which kept him out of the recording studio where he might have capitalized on the resounding acclamation accorded to *Born to Run.) Darkness on the Edge of Town* echoes with the honed-down grittiness of material that reflects more the reality than the romance of his beloved road. Highlighted by Bruce's painfully potent vocal outpourings and his slashing guitar, it includes some of his strongest material, "Promised Land," "Badlands," "Adam Raised a Cain" and the title cut. The CD sound is uneven, admittedly dynamic and crisp, most of the time, it is impaired by occasional harshness and audible hiss on the quieter sections. Overall, the sound is an improvement over the LP, but would be substantially better if there were clearer separations among the various voicings.

# Squeeze
Formed 1974—London

### Singles—45's & Under
A&M CD-4922 (43:44)     **[B + ]**
The principal writer/composers behind Squeeze (Chris Difford and Glenn Tilbrook) were often critically anointed as the punk Lennon/McCartney of British seventies new wave rock & roll. While their well-crafted hook-filled pop vignettes certainly adhere to many of the tenets established by their illustrious sixties English pop predecessors, the Squeeze's songs certainly remain a far cry from the Beatles in either originality or execution. That said, the band remains one of the most elegantly crafted proponents of the post-punk power-pop sound of the era. Their work is sharp, lustrous, and instantly appealing. This relatively brief compilation, which focuses primarily on their seventies successes, but includes early eighties material as well, works both as an overview of a fine pop band and an introduction to the eighties pop slickness that was to become a principal element of the once vital English music scene. The sound, of course, improves with the advancing date of recording, but overall, while it is more dynamic and spacious than the LP, it is afflicted with noticeable compression and hiss.

# The Staple Singers
Formed 1953—Chicago
A true family group who produced first-rate gospel sounds in the mid-fifties and early sixties. Founded upon Roebuck "Pop" Staple's simple, effective guitar lines and the expressive, unique lead vocals of daughter, Mavis. In the early 1970s, the Staples succeeded in grafting secular "message" lyrics to their infectious poppish gospel sound with appreciable commercial success. (Mavis's voice may be an acquired taste, but once acquired, it's addictive [although her crossover pure-pop efforts in recent years have lacked major acceptance]).

### Be Attitude: Respect Yourself

Mobil Fidelity Sound Lab MFCD832 (41:49)     **[B]**
The two highlights, "I'll Take You There" and
"Respect Yourself" are prime examples of this
seventies pop/gospel sound. The remaining
eight selections all sound great, but they all
sound too much alike and suffer from less
than average lyrics. Spare, minimalistic production sensibility underscores the rhythmic
foundation and the vocal interplay that are
the strengths of the Staple sound. The sound
of this disc is impressive, dynamic, propulsive, with beautiful spacing and clarity.
The mix is a bit strange in that the vocals are
often behind the instruments and there is a
suggestion of vocal harshness at volume, but
these are minor criticisms.

### The Best of the Staple Singers

Stax FCD60-007 (61:14)     **[A–]**
A reasonable argument can be made for gospel as the principle ingredient of that heady
mix: rock & roll. What the Staples provide in
addition to Pop's purefyin' guitar and vocals,
is a lightly bleached gospel sound built on
honest roots and Mavis Staples's wondrous
voice. What they also provide is a truly joyous
listening experience for everyone. This sixteen song compilation, originally released in
1975, includes: "Heavy Makes You Happy,"
"Respect Yourself," "I'll Take You There," "If
You're Ready," and "City in the Sky." The
sound is generally impressive: crisp, detailed,
and dynamic with excellent separation. It
does evidence some hiss and a tendency to
excessive brightness at volume.

# Steely Dan

Formed 1972—Los Angeles

### A Decade of Steely Dan (The Best Of)

MCA MCAD5570 (68:11)     **[D–]**
Muzak for the pseudo-set. I'll bet Horace Sil-
ver's still pissed, not to mention the Bird.
Pompous, pilfered pap. The sound isn't bad,
but noticeably compressed and occasionally
muddy. (This may be the most aptly named
band in rock.)

# Cat Stevens (Steven Georgiou)

b. July 21, 1947—London

### Greatest Hits

A&M CD4519 (39:21)     **[C + ]**
The material sounds dated, but the sound
quality remains impressive. Singer, songwriter, seventies success, Stevens left the
business disillusioned (after a half-dozen gold
albums). The melodies and production are
both first rate, the lyrics tend to be either silly
or a downer, with far too much of the latter.
The CD sounds great.

# Rod Stewart

### Gasoline Alley

Mercury 824 881-2 M-1 (41:57)     **[B + ]**
From compositions by Dylan, to Elton John/
Bernie Taupin and Bobby Womack (plus his
own fine additions), Stewart mixes folk and
pure rock & roll for a heady blend that very
much follows the formula of his critically
acclaimed first release. This time around, the
highlights aren't as bright, but for overall
quality, it is an excellent package. Also, like
the first release, the sound is obviously compressed, but generally clear.

### Every Picture Tells a Story

Mercury 822 385-2 M-1 (40:43)     **[A + ]**
One of the truly great rock & roll albums; in
part, because here is where it all came
together for Stewart, and, in part, because of
Mickey Waller's stupendous drumming. This
is the essence of what once made Rod Stewart
great. His compositions (the title cut, "Maggie
May" and "Mandolin Wind") are the highlights; his singing is sublime, and his
production, utilizing both pedal steel and
mandolin to augment a basic rock & roll
lineup, created an English country rock classic that easily withstands the test of time. It
never was this good again for Rod, but then
there are very, very few who achieve a creative pinnacle equal to *Every Picture Tells a*

*Story.* (But, oh, how the mighty have fallen.) Thankfully, the sound on CD maintains the same high standards as the material: clean, crisp, dynamic with decent separation, it does exhibit some compression (particularly on the drums) but it isn't that bad, and where there is distortion, it is minimal. This one is a must.

### Never a Dull Moment

Mercury 826 263-2 (33:11)     **[B + ]**
The package comes pretty close to *Every Picture Tells a Story,* minus the mandolin, and it results in fine listening, but its predecessor was so damn great! Still, "You Wear It Well" and his cover of Sam Cooke's "Twistin the Night Away" would hold up anywhere. This, to date, sadly also represents his last real quality recorded effort. The sound has an overall muffled, dirty quality to it, that still reflects greater dynamic enhancement than the LP, but it's not much improvement over the vinyl.

# Donna Summer (Donna Gaines)

b. December 31, 1948—Boston
The crowned queen of disco, who survived to build a successful seventies pop career.

### The Summer Collection (Greatest Hits)

Mercury 826 144-2 M-1 (40:23)     **[C + ]**
Bright, brash, and brassy—Summer brought an appropriately cool persona and hot voice to the disco demimonde that signaled the nadir of seventies pop music. Obviously, it wasn't Donna's fault; she was, and is, just a fine pop singer looking for an audience. There's not much here in the way of soul or intent, it's just glossy pop product designed to accompany the Me Decade's dance to artificial decadence. Formula material worked by talented professionals who end up with sleekly packaged instant fun—for somebody somewhere? The CD's sound is reflective of the overall production sensibility; bright, punchy, and spacious.

# Talking Heads

Formed 1975—New York City
Dance music for the mind. Or, as England's *Record Mirror* said of this extraordinarily influential American punk/new wave quartet: "After all these years, someone can still take the five basic components of rock—a singer, a song, a guitar, bass, and drums—and come up with something totally fresh."

### Talking Heads: 77

Sire 6036-2 (39:02)     **[A]**
One of the most original debut albums of the decade, if not in the history of rock & roll. Providing civilized techno-tension that is palpably real, the Heads firmly affix themselves to the classic traditions of the form while giving it a contemporary vernacular. Truly the music of its times. On *Talking Heads: 77,* David Byrne utilizes his performance and conceptual genius to create simple melodic underpinnings that reverberate with the tension of his petrified, edgy vocals. The sound is bright, crisp, dynamic, and clear; nicely enhancing Byrne's quavering vocal inflections.

### More Songs About Buildings and Food

Sire 6058-2 (41:48)     **[A]**
The experimentation begins. Brian Eno becomes the fifth Head, at least for a while. The textures and tonalities of the band's sound expand, but the stance (modernism, minimalism) and central musical element (the tension between Byrne's vocals and the music) remain a constant. *More Songs About Buildings and Food* also introduced an R&B aspect to the Heads' sound that would endure. The album produced their first hit, a cover version of Al Green's "Take Me to the River." The CD's sound is, again, an enhancement: beautifully spaced and defined with a slight tendency to some overbrightness.

### Fear of Music

Sire 6076-2 (40:43)     **[B]**
As the musical values move forward and became more edgy and rhythmically propulsive, the tension between the music and

Byrne's uniquely fascinating vocals has diminished. There are moments when everything coalesces ("Life During Wartime") and rises to the level of the band's best, and that's a fairly potent level. While this is still a fascinating and effective musical statement by one of the few original groups creating in the late seventies, too much of the material doesn't quite measure up and too much of the production is intrusive. The sound is first-rate, with great separation and clarity.

# James Taylor

b. March 12, 1948—Boston

Taylor has proved to be one of the most talented, genuine (though troubled), and sustaining members of the early seventies singer/songwriter movement.

### Sweet Baby James

Warner Bros. 1843-2 (31:54)      **[B]**

Taylor's second album release, this is the recording that garnered his first real commercial success, based principally on the popularity of the confessional "Fire and Rain." Also included on this enduring release are the fine title cut and "Steamroller." Taylor expresses some intense emotions here, but always with the surface control that, at its best, heightens the impact of his harrowing messages but, too often, drains meaning from the lyrics. The recording remains a seminal example of the male singer/songwriter school. Sadly, the sound is consistently accompanied by some of the most audible hiss available on disc. On the positive side, the CD provides amazing vocal intimacy (with a slight tendency to overbrightness) as well as good dynamics, openness, and precision of detail.

### JT

CBS CK34811 (38:01)      **[A + ]**

The culmination of Taylor's recorded output, featuring fine compositions and restrained but expressive vocal readings. His folk/jazz/R&B-derived pop productions perfectly showcase the direct appeal and strength of the

material and are beautifully rendered. While every cut offers quality, the highlights include the hit, "Handy Man," as well as "Another Grey Morning," "Bartender's Blues," "Traffic Jam," "Terra Nova," and the simple but inordinately valid "Secret of Life." The sound of it all is little short of revelatory: remarkably clean, spacious, warm, intimate, and detailed. This is one of the best sounding pop discs available.

# Richard Thompson

b. March 3, 1949—London

# Linda Thompson (Linda Peters)

Born out of the traditional English folk roots of Fairport Convention and shaped by their Sufi beliefs, Richard and Linda Thompson's modal folk rock may well be the single greatest undiscovered joy of seventies pop music. There are many who believe Richard is the finest living electric guitarist. He writes some of the most intelligent, compelling (and frequently witty) music around. Linda, who has now divorced him and attempted a currently aborted solo career (although it did yield one wonderful, but largely ignored album, *One Clear Moment,* Warner Bros. 25164-1, LP only), has a haunting, full, expressive voice that perfectly complements Richard's lyrics and musical textures.

### First Light

Chrysalis CCD1177 (43:22)      **[C + ]**

All the elements that made the Thompsons one of the decade's most compelling, but least acknowledged performers, are included here but, in what appears to be a rare nod to commercial appeal, the background musicians and instrumentals are more American than English. The end result is a substantial diminution in the potency of the product. It's not a bad collection, and it does have some fine moments—"Restless Highway," "Layla," and the haunting "Strange Affair"—but, somehow, their unique magic is never really expressed; probably, in no small part, because Richard's amazing guitar work is submerged in weaker ensemble playing. The sound on the CD is clean and clear, but noticeably compressed, resulting in sound analagous to that of a slightly enhanced, good quality LP.

# The Velvet Underground

### Loaded

Warner Special Products 9-27613-2 (39:20)    [A]
Easily the band's most accessible and "musical" record; it, of course, wasn't released until after Lou Reed, the center of it all, had abandoned the group. This is not the abrasive, seamy sound with which the band first lashed its miniscule but devoted audience; hell, this is almost gentle, yet made special by Reed's lyrical character studies of some fascinating fictional creations. Perhaps if *Loaded* had been the Velvet's first, instead of final release, their audience would have achieved its deserved dimension, but by the time this album hit the racks (with the band itself in final disarray), the abrasive power and sonic experimentation of their earlier work had pretty much alienated most of their not too numerous original following. That's a shame. As it is, *Loaded* has become an enduring final testament to the work of one of the most influential and important bands in the history of rock & roll. The CD sound, while not revelatory, is both a dynamic and spatial improvement over the LP, but is afflicted with occasional distortion and frequently heavy hiss.

# Muddy Waters (McKinley Morganfield)

b. April 4, 1915—Rolling Fork, Mississippi
d. April 30, 1983—Chicago
One of the first, and probably the best, of the fifties Chicago electric urban blues purveyors whose influence on rock & roll (particularly the members of the original British Invasion) is incalculable.

### Hard Again

Blue Sky ZK34449 (45:40)    [A]
Produced by Texas albino blues guitar great Johnny Winter, this is the blues: urban and hard. Waters's singing is majestically powerful, painful, and expressive, and Winter's guitar burns while James Cotton's harp defines the sound. One listen and it's easy to understand what made the Rolling Stones do what they did. The CD adds punch, clarity, and some separation to the sound which is also a bit compressed with a tendency to muddiness in the band's sound. There's also an occasional harsh edge on some of Waters's definitive vocals.

# The Who

### Who's Next

MCA MCAD 37217 (43:15)    [A+]
*Tommy* was the Who album that garnered all the hype (rock opera!) and became a motion picture but, *Who's Next* is their classic—the recording by which this powerful band will be measured and remembered. This effort represents the best that each member had to offer, but in the end, it is Daltry's triumph. His vocals soar over and slice through the dense driven sound of a first-rate rock band at the peak of its power, ultimately capturing the pure animal ecstasy at the heart of great rock & roll. "Baba O'Riley," "Bargain," "My Wife," "Goin' Mobile," "Behind Blue Eyes," and one of rock's all-time great anthems "Won't Get Fooled Again" are the highlights, but there's not a selection on the album which isn't first-rate. The sound is as close to a perfect fit to the material as is likely to be captured—powerfully dynamic, with wonderful separation and openness as well as precise individual detailing. Yes, there is occasional audible hiss, but let's not be nitpicking in the face of great rock & roll.

### Meaty Beaty Big and Bouncy

MCA MCAD37001 (42:18)    [A–]
The Who were the garage rock singles band of the British Invasion, making this compilation of those singles almost an essential rock album. "I

Can't Explain," "Pictures of Lilly," "My Generation," "Pinball Wizard," "Magic Bus," "I Can See for Miles," "Substitute," and "Anyway, Anyhow, Anywhere" rank with the best releases of their era. Townshend has called it "the greatest of Who albums" noting that "it reminds . . . [the band] . . . who we really are." Sadly, the sound is inconsistent, but is generally very compressed, often abrasive and distorted, muddy, and afflicted with constant, noticeable hiss. It's still wonderful.

# Stevie Wonder (Steveland Judkins or Morris)

b. May 13, 1950—Saginaw, Michigan
A true musical genius whose career began as a Motown child star, but whose real influence dates to his mature work done in the early seventies when he made the synthesizer and the studio his personal instruments. Wonder created a funk-based pop sound that enjoyed strong popular acceptance, widespread critical acclaim, and immense influence on the pop product that followed. His strength is in the sound and structure of his music; his lyrics often tending to veer off into some personal, flaky neverland.

### Talking Book

Tamla TCD06151TD (43:30)     [A–]
With this release, Wonder not only forever established his independence from Motown's traditional hit-making formula, he also entered the first rank of popular recording artists on the strength of its two major hits, "You Are the Sunshine of My Life" and "Superstition." Unfortunately, a part of the legacy he created was an excessive reliance on synthesizers in pop/rock music (thereafter generally used by those who lacked either Wonder's genius or vision with expectedly dire results). The sound on this disc is pretty clean, somewhat dynamically enhanced, but lacking spatial benefits, because overall compression keeps it from escaping the bounds of LP sound.

### Innervisions

Tamla MCD09052MD (44:12)     [A + ]
This recording represents the pinnacle of a very important artist's career and of his physically blind but nonetheless extraordinarily humane vision. For all intents and purposes, and for all of its richness and variety of texture, it is essentially *all* Stevie Wonder. He personally created and arranged every sound heard. His canvas stretches from the tough realities of ghetto streets to the transcendent joy of spiritual acceptance, each rendered in an original, musical palette. The feel is a little more jazz than funk, the result is simply glorious pop music—uplifting in sound and message. The CD sound is a marked improvement over the LP, with greater clarity, definition, and dynamics; although hiss remains fairly evident throughout.

# Neil Young

### After the Goldrush

Reprise 2283-2 (35:15)     [A–]
The eccentric rock & roller in the guise of singer/songwriter. This is a recording which was intended as the soundtrack to a movie that was never made, which, in retrospect, somehow seems totally appropriate. It is at once dense and simple, prophetic and mundane. What really matters is that after more than a decade and a half, it retains a uniqueness of vision and sound that still holds interest. It is also the record which, probably more than any other, established Young's star status. The disc has dynamics and clarity which are markedly superior to the LP, but it is afflicted with excessive and pervasive hiss.

### Tonight's the Night

Reprise 2221-2 (45:01)     [A + ]
Young is an acquired taste, primarily because of the nasal whine which he uses for a voice; also because of his propensity to employ distortion as an element of his sound tapestry. His vision and wide-roving intensity, however, cannot be doubted. Written in part as a

response to the drug-related deaths of two members of his musical touring aggregation, *Tonight's the Night* is a dark, rough, less than pleasant experience which Young's record company held for two years before offering it to the market. With this release, Young may have been motivated by very personal losses, but the end result is a conceptual elegy to the youth and dreams that buoyed the great sixties myths. This isn't easy music either to hear or to listen to, but it is redemptive—it is pure rock & roll, in the fullest sense. Or, as Young himself has said of it, "I probably *feel* this more than anything else I've ever done." The sound, which features continuous, obvious hiss, is a bit more dynamic and defined than the LP, but the digital conversion is murky, dirty and distorted which may, in this case, represent perfect reproduction.

### Harvest

Reprise 2277-2 (37:38)    **[D + ]**
This difficult artist's most popular album, probably alienated the listening/buying public from the rock record reviewers more than any other major release. The former loved it, the latter were cool to, or disdainful of, it ("puerile, precious, and self-indulgent, not to mention musically insipid," John Mendelsohn said). The critics may have overstated the negative, but they were on the right track. The CD sound adds nothing to that of the LP; very compressed, dirty, and lacking in articulation.

# Warren Zevon

b. January 24, 1947—Chicago
The enfant terrible of the seventies LA music scene, whose lyrical occupations run from British werewolves to headless mercenaries; while his music is based upon the rock format, often inflected with symphonic colorations. A prodigious talent whose promise has never been fully realized.

### The Best Of Warren Zevon—A Quiet Normal Life

Asylum 9 60503-2 (47:34)    **[A]**
Zevon's personal vision reveals a style more akin to pulp detective fiction than pop lyrics, redeemed by a bizarre, literate sense of humor. Additionally, he has captured the sun/smog-drenched seamy decadence of lotus land more effectively than any other LA habitué. This fourteen-song collection, which opens with his one quasi-hit, "Werewolves of London," is an excellent overview of a promising, flawed career that has produced more than a few brilliant and beautiful moments ("Desperados Under the Eaves" and "Accidently Like a Martyr"). The compilation also includes the original version of Zevon's composition, "Poor, Poor, Pitiful Me" which, in itself, should be enough to keep Linda Ronstadt in Gilbert & Sullivan for the rest of her natural life. The sound varies, but overall, is somewhat compressed, roughly equivalent to that of a dynamic LP.

# SEVENTIES COLLECTIONS

"I have no use for bodyguards, but I have a very specific use for two highly trained certified public accountants."

—Elvis Presley

### Heartbeat Reggae

Ryko RCD219 (64:14)  **[B + ]**

A first-rate compilation of seventies and eighties reggae and dub material from a variety of reputable practitioners of Jamaica's principal cultural export to the modern "third" world. Among the artists included: Big Youth, Black Uhuru, Burning Spear, Gregory Isaacs, the Mighty Diamonds, Mutabaruka, and Lee "Scratch" Perry, all rendered in Ryko's generally first-quality digital sound.

### Out of the Blue

Ryko RCD20003 (62:19)  **[A–]**

A little Zydeco, a lot of blues and R&B; it all boils down to over an hour of good times/bad times Saturday night roadhouse music in first-quality digital sound. The seventeen selections include works by Buckwheat Zydeco, the Night Hawks, Roomfull of Blues, George Thorogood, John Hammond, Duke Robillard & the Pleasure Kings, Clarence Gatemouth Brown, Johnny Copeland, and Solomon Burke.

### More Reggae Music

Sound REG CD5 (59:30)  **[C + ]**

Aptly titled, this sixteen-song set includes efforts by Bob Marley and the Wailers, UB40, Jimmy Cliff, Desmond Dekker, Peter Tosh, and Yellowman. Both the sound and musical quality varies substantially. Of the included classics, Dekker's "Israelites" and "You Can Get It If You Really Want It" both suffer from excessive hiss and bad distortion as does Cliff's "Many Rivers to Cross;" the sound quality of the remainder is pretty good given some compression and fairly frequent hiss.

### Rhythm Come Forward

Columbia CK39472 (39:40)  **[C + ]**

The nine reggae selections include work from Bob Marley and Peter Tosh to Aswad and Jimmy Cliff, although none of them are the best material from these artists. The Marley cuts are marred by overly bright sound, and the rest of it varies from LP quality to fairly impressive sound (if not content). A decent, but far from outstanding, collection.

## Stax Greatest Hits

Special Import (Fantasy) JCD-702-1110 (65:20)　　[B]
In the late sixties and the early seventies—
slightly pre-disco times—black popular music
began to soften as the raw power of the earlier
R&B influence gave way to a sleeker more
urban pop sound that mirrored changes in
the black listening audience. Stax led the
move with the sounds captured here—the
Dramatics, Isaac Hayes, and Johnny Taylor
epitomized the Stax product. Today, its primary relevance is historical, but it still provides pleasant listening. Included on this
compilation are some cuts which retain the
drive of prior mainstream black music—
the Staple Singers' "Respect Yourself,"
Rufus Thomas's wonderful "Do the Funky
Chicken," and Little Milton's "That's What
Love Will Make You Do." It should be noted
that the disc reviewed is a Japanese import
and the sound it provides is first-rate—clean,
crisp, and dynamic.

## Storytellers: Singers & Songwriters

Warner Special Products 9-27615-2 (69:28)　　[B]
Despite the corny title, this is a pretty tolera-
ble collection; eighteen songs by the likes of
Joni Mitchell, James Taylor, Arlo Guthrie, Tom
Waits, John Prine, Randy Newman, Judy Col-
lins, John Sebastian, Tom Rush, Steve Good-
man, Tom Paxton, Jerry Jeff Walker, Phil
Ochs, and various and sundry others. In most
cases, the song performed by each is familiar
and representative. As was inevitable, the
sound quality is erratic; the nadir being the
hiss afflicting Prine's "Sandstone," and (sadly)
Newman's "I Think It's Going to Rain Today,"
while Tom Rush's "Circle Game" is a sonic
wonder. The rest of the cuts sound OK; not
great, not awful, more like lightly compressed, relatively clean LPs. A fair sampler
of contemporary folkish sounds.

# THE
# EIGHTIES

"In the eighties rock & roll went to work
for corporations and got up at 6 A.M.
to go jogging."

—Bono

If the seventies marked the beginning of the decline in pop/rock music, then the eighties certainly have produced little to reverse that direction; the dominant themes of the decade being marketing and technology.

However, all is not without hope. The same artists who have come to realize the power of their communicative abilities (through their obvious commercial rewards), have, in some cases, chosen to exercise those awesome powers to advance humane causes and needs. It should never be forgotten that this most often vilified form of popular culture has not only been at the forefront, but has also been the most potent, of all the arts in the advancement of the human condition. Whether it be the starving millions in famine-plagued Africa or a heroic few men and women deprived of basic human rights, rock & roll performers have taken up the gauntlet while others in the arts have too often merely chosen to observe.

Apart from that more elevated preoccupation, on an "artistic" level, technology has dominated the rock music industry in the eighties. The synthesizer, which literally put almost all known, as well as some previously unknown, sounds at the fingertips of a keyboard player, along with the ability to modulate or modify those sounds at whim, replaced the electric guitar as the principle instrumental voice of much of the decade's pop product.

Added to this is the now almost ubiquitous drum machine: the computerized metronome that guarantees perfect *time*; hell, it guarantees the best recorded licks of the great drummers of rock's past. Yes, at the time of this writing, the latest technological "tool" in the arsenal of the recording industry is the Digitizer. This electronic "wonder" allows those hidden souls in the techno end to "borrow" a sound, a phrase, or any other recorded effect from anyone, anywhere, and add it to the sound of today's hit record.

It may be entertainment; it sure ain't rock & roll. It's more like a game of Pavlovian chess played among the hidden stars of the eighties' mostly mediocre record (CD) business, i.e., the producers and engineers ably assisted by the radio programmers, demographers, and marketing experts who all account to the finance department of their respective conglomerates.

Probably, the ultimate perversion of it all is reflected in the merger of audio/video technology manifest in MTV: the bastard merger of video technology and the popular recording arts. The latest techno development on the immediate horizon being the CD-V, a modification of the digital disc which will provide (with the addition of a new piece of hardware) a disc that plays a music video plus several selections of pure digital sound in the newest marketing package.

MTV, which has promoted mostly recycled, synthesized Motown in video perfect packages, also resulted in the elevation of eighties "stars" who were more notable for their physical attractiveness than their musical abilities. As usually is the price of the decade's more dazzling, diverting entertainments, the loss has been in the capacity of imagination, perhaps humanity's most precious part.

In an age when the anti-heroes of yesterday's pop culture (or at least their contemporary successors) have embraced marketing/commercialization to a shocking degree with various and sundry commercial tie-ins between bands and products becoming the unfortunate norm, the music, itself, has not been particularly notable. The decade has seen the rise of Michael Jackson whose *Thriller* is the runaway bestseller of all time, proof that Jackson represents the perfect eighties synthesis rock star—his appeal being as much visual as aural.

The era's other major superstar, and, like Jackson, a man whose musical beginnings precede the current decade, Bruce

Springsteen established the canonization of blue-collar American rock. Springsteen, who first achieved fame in 1975-76, has managed to attain almost heroic stature in the Reagan resurrected eighties reenactment of the Eisenhower fifties with his monster mega-seller, *Born in the U.S.A.*

Prince has probably provided the most innovative and creative music of the decade, although his skin color and performance affectations and attitudes have prevented him from attaining truly mass commercial acceptance. (They have not, however, prevented nearly everyone else in the industry from mining his creative genius.) And his motion picture debut, *Purple Rain,* may well be the definitive rock movie.

Perhaps another seventies group, Talking Heads, may represent the ultimate current incarnation of the rock group that best personifies the spirit and nature of its moment.

Don't assume that the glorious river of sound begun in Memphis over thirty years ago has run aground. There is still good music, rock & roll music, being made today. There's just less of it, making it harder to find. But what does come through loud and clear is the fact that it has now been over two decades since anyone added anything major to the mix.

The music, obviously has, and will, continue to change. Yet, the spirit that sparked it in the first place is a recognizable constant in the best of it all; whether made in Memphis in '55 or Minneapolis in '85.

In the end, it's probably wise to remember that real understanding and evaluation can only come from the perspective of time passed, even for a medium whose principal currency is currency.

# THE
# EIGHTIES
## on Compact Disc

"If you want something for nothing,
go jerk off."

—Bob Weir

## King Sunny Ade and His African Beats

### JuJu Music

Mango CCD9712 (43:07)    **[A]**

JuJu is the name given to the "popular" music of Nigeria which is based upon Yoruba tribal roots. Ade, or Chairman King Sunny Ade as he is locally known, builds his intricate sounds upon the classic call and response approach (in this case between singers and African talking drums) employing modern sounds and technology (electric guitars, synthesizers, and even Hawaiian slack string guitars) to achieve what he accurately calls "a very rich music." Sinuous, elegant, and compellingly rhythmic, it's not difficult to understand how the King and his large band could have made over forty albums (with average sales of a couple hundred thousand per release). The CD's sound is wonderful, precise, spacious, instrumentally defined, clean, warm, and all supported by dynamic percussion.

## The Alarm

### Declaration

IRS CD70608 (46:14)    **[C–]**

Empty sloganeering by another of the new guitar-driven eighties rock revolutionaries. Anthems devoid of meaning other than as an opportunistic location to hang the hooks. The sound is relatively clean and dynamic, but with a marked tendency to shrill overbrightness.

## Laurie Anderson

b. 1947—Chicago

Conceptual musician/artist who has succeeded in effectively merging contemporary music and theater for a broader than normal audience for this genre.

### Home of the Brave

Warner Bros. 9 25400-2 (34:53)    **[B + ]**

It may not be rock & roll music, but in a way, Laurie's work is defined by a rock & roll sensibility. This is the soundtrack to her concert film and is a trip into techno-, electro-, voice-modulated eighties multimedia expression.

Ideally suited to the digital medium, this all-digital recording is nothing less than a pure sonic delight. Experimental, yes, but witty and ultimately compelling listening.

# Anita Baker

**Rapture**
Elektra 9 60444-2 (37:35)     [C +]
A major '86 soul/jazz/pop hit from an artist with one of the loveliest, most supple, and expressive voices currently around. The weakness in the song selection and sameness of the slick, lush production, ultimately drain the life from a fine vocal effort. The sound is eighties clean, albeit with a slight tendency toward edgy brightness.

# Bangles

**Different Light**
Columbia CK40039 (38:48)     [C +]
In an earlier part of the decade, the Go-Gos achieved brief stardom, the first all-woman rock band to do so. The Bangles, who have followed the same path, achieved justifiable success in the mid-1980s through bright vocal harmonies, strong song selection, and an energetic guitar-based sound. It's not memorable, but it's sure listenable, light rock/pop. Clear with excellent separation, the sound mix tends toward the bright, thin side.

# Blondie
Formed 1975—New York City

**The Best of Blondie**
Chrysalis VK41337 (44:12)     [B]
Bleached, bouncy, ultimately insulated American New Wave by a late seventies/early eighties band that managed to ride that New Wave to a pop crest with "Heart of Glass" in the spring of 1979. Drawing on a broad pastiche of sixties and seventies strains and supported by Clem Burk's power drumming, the group achieved more recognition than

most of the bands who attempted to bring the "new sound of the seventies" to the charts. This album presents a fair overview of their slick, but not sustaining product (note that the mixes have been changed in some of the hits included here). The sound is clean, generally well-defined, and punchy, but it suffers from some hiss and that brittle, overbright radio mix.

# The Blue Nile

**A Walk Across Rooftops**
Linn Records LKHCD1 (38:11)     [A–]
Minimalist, techno-rock from a band notable for its intelligence and restraint. As *Melody Maker* accurately said of *A Walk Across Rooftops,* "nostalgia, romance, elation, and reflection are woven into the fabric with gossamer delicacy." Music for contemplation, it is recorded with beautiful spaciousness, precision, and clarity resulting in a premier example of CD sound.

# The BoDeans

**Love & Hope & Sex & Dreams**
Slash/Warner Bros 9 25103 2 (41:54)     [B]
The '86 debut by a Wisconsin-based retro-rock band whose music echoes with the classic strains of Dylan and the Band. Heightened by T-Bone Burnett's simple, clean production values, the BoDeans don't break new ground, but amply illustrate a proficiency to make known elements insinuatingly memorable. The CD sounds very clean, defined, and dynamic.

**Outside Looking In**
Reprise/Slash 25629-2 (48:56)     [C–]
A lot has changed for this promising young group from Waukesha, Wisconsin, between their 1986 debut release and this, their second recording. The original quartet is now a trio (albeit one abetted by a number of guest artists on this release) and production has moved from T-Bone Burnett to Jerry Har-

rison, Talking Heads' keyboard player. The result is another slice of eighties heartland retro-rock, although this time around, the sound is a bit more atmospheric and dense. Highly listenable, but lacking in any real outstanding specific selections and somewhat weak lyrically. The all-digital sound is excellent.

# James Brown

### Gravity

Scotti Bros. ZK40380 (39:44)    **[B]**
Producer (and soul singer) Dan Hartman brings Mr. Dynamite's sound into the eighties, which means that the funk is programmed as well as played, with mixed results. It did produce Brown's first major hit of the decade, "Living in America," which featured Stevie Ray Vaughn on lead guitar; while it's great to hear James's driving sounds in a current context, the whole enterprise has a bit of the feel of current convenience packaging. Yet, Soul Brother No. 1 still has his moments, a quarter of a century after the original fact. While the mix has a slightly overbright edge to it, it also leaps off the disc with dynamic intensity.

# Buckwheat Zydeco

### On A Night Like This

Island 7 90622-2 (35:16)    **[B]**
Best described by David Browne in *Rolling Stone* as "the dance hall music of French-speaking Louisiana blacks," Zydeco is designed for one thing—a good time, party-down from the City that earns its keep, keepin' on. The central elements to the Zydeco sound are the accordion (played here by Stanley "Buckwheat" Dural, the acknowledged successor to the contemporary master, Clifton Chenier), rub boards (breastplates ribbed like metal washboards and played with finger thimbles), and absolutely contagious dance rhythms. Dural seasons his musical mix with electric guitars, synthesizers, and

horns. It's a good time in French and English (strong covers of the Blasters' "Marie" and Dylan's "On a Night Like This"). The sound is clean, clear, and dynamic, but retains some compression and tape hiss.

# Solomon Burke

b. 1936—Philadelphia
Preacher and soul music pioneer, purveyor of "rock & roll soul music," his first R&B hits date back to the early sixties.

### A Change Is Gonna Come

Rounder CD2053 (42:41)    **[B + ]**
At the half-century mark, Burke can still preach a lyric with heartfelt fervor and one big voice. This set of smooth soulful sounds was recorded in New Orleans in 1984 and it doesn't disappoint. Highlighted by Paul Kelly's "Love Buys Love" and Sam Cooke's "A Change Is Gonna Come" (a definitive contemporary version), the sound is spacious, clean, well-defined, and only slightly occasionally compressed. The surface may be smooth, but the roots are still there.

# T-Bone Burnett (J. Henry)

b. St. Louis; raised in Texas
This lanky, laconic reborn classic/country rocker first achieved notice as a part of Dylan's Rolling Thunder Review and then as a part of the short-lived Alpha Band. In the eighties he has enjoyed limited success with a few recordings of his well-written contemporary parables, but his star has ascended in recent years as a sought-after record producer.

### Truth Decay

Takoma TAKCD7080 (43:08)    **[C + ]**
Straight-ahead rock propels T-Bone's twelve compositions notable for his pithy, yet trenchant, vocal observations and the monotonal voice in which he delivers them. The initial release of one of the brighter minor luminaries to arrive on the American music scene in the last half of the seventies, this recording

of what Dave Marsh labeled, "mythic Christian blues" is loose, but somehow tired. The sound is OK, occasionally overbright and occasionally subject to hiss; however, it is more dynamic and defined than on the LP.

## T-Bone Burnett

MCA MCAD5809 (44:33)    **[A]**
Over four days in the early summer of 1986, Burnett gathered a half-dozen "country" oriented musicians (including David Hidalgo, Byron Berline, and Billy Swan) in a digitally equipped studio where they laid down these thirteen tracks on this "live" studio recording with obvious feeling and affection. This is a contemporary country sound that lies close to its roots and the artists' hearts with a resultant timeless sound. A gentle but deeply moving effort that feels almost like eavesdropping on the private ruminations of people playing for the love of a music that is integral to their being. The all-digital sound is a revelation: quiet and clean with beautifully defined shadings.

# Alex Chilton

b. December 28, 1950—Memphis
Both a founder and the lead voice of the legendary Box Tops, Chilton has scuffled in and out of the music scene since that band's demise in 1970 and the subsequent creation and demise of his follow-up group, Big Star.

## Stuff

New Rose Rose 68 CD (57:58)    **[D+]**
This compilation is made up of nine cuts recorded in 1986 in New Orleans and seven others recorded in the late sixties through the mid-seventies, most of which were written by Chilton. It's generally clean, straight-ahead rock (with the newer work reflecting a certain punk sensibility), but is more of minor historic interest than current musical validity. The sound on the more recent recordings is clean and dynamic, but with a marked tendency to overbrightness. The older selections are sonically pretty weak, muddy, and compressed.

# The Clash

## Sandinista!

Epic EZK37037 (144:33—two discs)    **[A−]**
Sprawling, formless, excessive and frequently bursting with greatness ("The Magnificent Seven," "Charlie Don't Surf," "Junko Partner," "Hitsville U.K.," "Ivan Meets G.I. Joe," "Something About England," "Washington Bullets," and "Police on My Back"), *Sandinista!* is another (in this case punk) example of a great single album buried in the wretched excess of multiple sides. It's still memorable, but simply too diluted. The sound is clean enough, but subject to obvious compression.

## Combat Rock

Epic EK37689 (46:05)    **[A]**
The last (and most commercially successful) gasp of this mid-seventies British punk aggregation whose popular success doomed their aesthetic principles. This is punk polished with Glyn John's fine production hand and also with a bow to the New York rap scene. An arty and explosive mixture of their reggae, funk-based rock, *Combat Rock* produced the band's ultimate audience acceptance as evidenced by several genuine hits, "Rock the Casbah" and "Should I Stay or Should I Go?" In retrospect, this is probably a perfect eulogy for one of the most vital exponents of the English seventies punk explosion. The sound is clean and spatially well-defined, although it occasionally tends to overbrightness, but never excessively.

# Class of '55 (Carl Perkins, Jerry Lee Lewis, Roy Orbison, Johnny Cash)

## Memphis Rock & Roll Home Coming

Polygram 830 002-2 M-1 (37:12)    **[B]**
Legendary is the operative word for this Chips Moman-inspired recorded gathering, thirty years after the fact, of four of the original Sun artists that helped begin it all in the first place. They all take a turn (singly and

together) at some new compositions and some classics (Jerry Lee Lewis's rendition of "Sixteen Candles" being the most successful) all with a deep bow to the King departed, and often with obvious feeling. The spark has not gone out, but the fire has been banked now for a few years. All in all, *Class Of '55* does offer more than just nostalgia, and it was obviously a meaningful moment for all involved (and that included John Fogerty and Dave Edmunds). The sound is clear and clean, though lacking somewhat in separation and evidencing some minimal compression.

# Elvis Costello and the Attractions

### Taking Liberties

Columbia CK36839 (51:37)    **[A–]**

A bit of a hodgepodge, twenty tracks culled from the B-sides of singles and songs included on English but not American versions of earlier album releases. Sprinkled with marvelous moments ("Girls Talk," "Radio Sweetheart," "Stranger in the Dark," "My Funny Valentine," [yes, *that* "My Funny Valentine"], "I Don't Want to Go to Chelsea," "Night Rally," and "Getting Mighty Crowded"); the recording is ultimately chaotic, but exhilarating. The sound varies, but is roughly equivalent to LP quality.

### Trust

Columbia CK37051 (41:45)    **[B–]**

The complexities of modern romance shrouded in the tense mysteries of sex remain Costello's principal lyrical preoccupation, but this time around, they failed to produce any specifically memorable songs, though the quality of the material is pretty high. Somehow, one gets the feeling that at this point in his career, Costello, while still bitingly energetic, was somewhat stuck. The CD's sound is much punchier and better defined than on his prior

disc releases, but it still suffers from compression and overbrightness.

### Almost Blue

Imp Records Imp Fiend CD33 (32:34)    **[C–]**

Punk goes to Memphis for twelve country classics produced under the aegis of impresario Billy Sherrill, and the general critical consensus is that Elvis and the boys should have stayed on the other side of the pond. The pathos too often sounds like bathos, although "Good Year for the Roses" works like a charm. The sound is clean, well separated, but clearly compressed.

### Imperial Bedroom

Columbia CK38157 (51:04)    **[A + ]**

The band plays better than ever before, and Geoff Emerick's deeply layered production has received frequent critical kudos, often invoking favorable comparisons to *Sgt. Pepper.* Costello's songs here move away from his often abrasive punk stance to pure Tin Pan Alley, making this perhaps his most listenable album. However, his lyrical preoccupations, paranoia and guilt, tend to lend an overall insularity to it all that retains the integrity of Costello's original stance. The sound is great: clean, defined, dynamic, and appreciably more open than on the LP.

### The Best of Elvis Costello and the Attractions

Columbia CK40101 (64:25)    **[A]**

The CD version adds three bonus tracks ("The Angels [Want to Wear My Red Shoes]," "Man Out of Time," and "A Good Year for the Roses") to the sixteen originals included on the LP version of this fairly representative collection of the work of this most prolific of punk's pioneers. An effort has been made to clean up the mixes on the tracks included and the result is a uniformity of sound usually not heard from such divergent sources. Overall, it's dynamic and fine, with some expected compression and a tendency to edgy brightness. As single disc collections go, this one is a winner, particularly considering the vast body of work from which it was drawn.

## Punch the Clock

Columbia CK38897 (45:34)    **[A]**
For this guy, the word "prolific" is an understatement. The pop propensities evidenced on *Imperial Bedroom* continued unabated here. This time around, certain big band colorations and punctuation have been effectively added. Highlights include "Every Day I Write the Book," "Shipbuilding," "Pills and Soap," and "The World and His Wife." Surface and sound notwithstanding, Costello's acerbic, painful lyrical preoccupations remain at center stage. The sound, while not quite as remarkably transparent as that on *Imperial Bedroom,* is still a substantial improvement over the LP, adding a punch to the proceedings which are otherwise clean and fairly well defined.

## The Costello Show (Featuring Elvis Costello)
## King of America

Columbia CK40173 (57:59)    **[A–]**
This time around, Elvis trots out a new/old (short-lived) persona, i.e., Declan McManus, but the music is clearly of a piece with that which preceded it. T-Bone Burnett's clean, open production highlights Costello's voice and the underlying material. On this outing, Elvis (oops, sorry, Declan) employs backup musicians who are principally drawn from the cream of contemporary American studio veterans (Jim Keltner, Mitchell Froom, James Burton, Ray Brown, and Earl Palmer among them) rather than the Attractions, a few of whom join on a couple of the selections. All said, it's a somewhat ambiguous effort which certainly has its moments, but one that doesn't rank with the best of Costello's work. (It probably sounded better initially than it really was because of the paucity of the competition at the time of its release.) The sound displays slight hiss and compression but retains the punchy definition that is the earmark of a good digital recording.

## Blood & Chocolate

Columbia CK40518 (47:49)    **[A]**
Back with the Attractions (and his "old" name), Elvis is as biting as ever. Dense, murky, and driving, this release hearkens back to the harrowing days of yore when Costello rode punk's screeching mayhem to personal stardom. Complex and ultimately aching music from a man whose misery is apparently constant, but whose talent is overwhelming ("I Want You"). The sound is clean, but its stage is a bit compressed.

# The Robert Cray Band

## Bad Influence

Hightone HCD 8001 (42:46)    **[A–]**
Almost singlehandedly, Robert Cray has spearheaded a late eighties American blues resurgence. His work is dependant upon a smooth singing style and terse, but effective, guitar work, frequently employed in the service of his eighties-style sensitive, somewhat self-effacing, blues originals. Competent, quality work, the best selections are "Phone Booth," "So Many Women, So Little Time," and "Share What You've Got and Keep What You Need." This may well be Cray's finest outing. The sound is afflicted with some slight hiss and compression, but it is detailed with nice separation.

## False Accusations

Hightone HCD 8005 (38:13)    **[B]**
More modern, melodic upbeat blues material that is very much of a piece with its predecessor, providing clean playing and songs reflecting the moods of the modern world. The material is not quite as strong as that on *Bad Influence,* but the sound is cleaner and more dynamic; in other words, excellent.

## Strong Persuader

Polygram 830 568-2 M-1 (39:26)    **[A]**
Riding the strength of a major label and resultant hit single, "Smoking Gun," this 1986 release brought Cray's economical, current sounds to the American mass audience. The record showcases all of his substantial strengths and features a more assured, emotive singing style with some fuller R&B-sounding strains overlaid on the basic blues

foundations. Again, the principal strength may be the material which features consistently excellent writing. Bright and appealing, the CD's sound is extremely dynamic, intimate, and well-separated; although, it exhibits a slight tendency to shrillness in its highs.

# Marshall Crenshaw

### Maryjean & Nine Others
Warner Bros. 9 25583-2 (42:22)    [D]
Promise, promise—all we get is promise. The sound is muddy too.

# David & David

### Boomtown
A&M cd5134 (41:04)    [A]
From L.A. (where else?)—modern fables of sterile times in a world where reality is often consumed with escape from the real thing. Melodically compelling, lyrically intelligent, and supported by sympathetic, effective production values, this is about as appealing as the personal apocalypse is ever going to sound. While some have said that the vocal approach of the two Davids resembles that of Hall and Oates, in fact, the material is much more strongly reminiscent of that produced by the Squeeze. The sound is open, precisely detailed and dynamic; perhaps a bit bright, really only marred by pervasive hiss.

# Dire Straits

### Making Movies
Warner Bros. 3480-2 (37:41)    [B−]
Blues-based, guitar-centered pop sounds from Mark Knopfler, a man who has found his vein and mines it effectively. Knopfler's strengths are his compositional abilities and understanding of effective use of the modern recording studio. The former are best illustrated on "Tunnel of Love" and "Romeo and Juliette" (two of his better all-time songs), and

the latter is evident throughout the recording. The CD's sound, while afflicted with some hiss, is beautifully open and dynamic with each voicing firmly centered in its own specific location.

### Love Over Gold
Warner Bros. 9 23728-2 (41:24)    [B−]
More easy listening; romantic, elegantly produced sounds from Knopfler and his ever-changing band of backup players. This time out, there are only five selections, so each contains more space for instrumental meanderings. The sound effects are lovely; the substance is questionable. As always their attention to detail in the recording studio pays off with a fine-sounding product, consistently among the best in the current pop scene.

### Brothers in Arms
Warner Bros. 25264-2 (55:12)    [B]
The accurately aimed, but ultimately blunted, barb at MTV, "Money for Nothing" was the single that brought such great success for what is really a rather mediocre album. Knopfler does have the knack for writing engaging melodies and strong narrative lyrics, and he also has the ability to create a spacious, newish-wave, soft-rock sound which has found a receptive audience. If the music is less than first-rate, the sound quality is another matter. This all-digital disc is simply one of the best-sounding pop CDs around.

# Bob Dylan

### Real Live
Columbia CK3944 (52:21)    [D−]
There's obviously some talent at work here, but it's pretty well hidden. It too often sounds more like a hootenanny than a rock concert. Dylan's recorded live efforts have rarely been successful, and this is no exception. The disc sound is simply terrible—constant hiss, murky, muffled vocals, heavy compression, and a band that sounds like it didn't make it to the stage from the bus. There may have

been some quality moments on this tour, but you won't hear them here.

### Empire Burlesque

Columbia CK40110 (46:56)     [C–]
The born-again phase had passed, but the female backup singers hadn't. Neither the material nor the performance provide much of sustaining value. It's not that it's that bad, it really isn't; it's just that it's Bob Dylan, and, right or wrong, the measure of quality is pretty high. The sound, while slightly compressed, is pretty dynamic and clean; it's also subject to fairly continuous hiss.

### Infidels

Columbia CK38819 (46:15)     [B–]
Dylan's only all-digital recording, *Infidels* sounds great, particularly in the subtleties of the vocals, but the material is a different matter. This is gospel/pop/rock with a little politics thrown in for old time sake. The motivation behind it feels more like a desire to continue a career than a need to express much of deep conviction. *Melody Maker* was singularly unimpressed calling it "as stimulating as an evening in a laundromat," but who knows what kind of laundromats they frequent. Because of its pop sensibility, fine production values, and polished musicianship, *Infidels* is appealing albeit watered-down Dylan, with a couple of stronger inclusions: "Sweetheart Like You" and "Don't Fall Apart on Me Tonight."

### Knocked Out Loaded

Columbia CK40439 (35:34)     [B–]
The mix came out of a dance club and the song selection is weird; much of it recorded with an echo-chamber effect around the lead vocals which, with the female and children's choirs, gives many cuts an ordained quality. Forget the first five selections; the interest lies in the final three, each written by Dylan with a different cowriter. "Brownsville Girl," on which actor/playwright Sam Shepard is the collaborator, is an eleven-minute surreal cinematic montage that manages to somehow reflect a resonant American strain. Tom Petty

provides that function on "Got My Mind Made Up," an honest-to-God rocker on which Dylan sings with some real intensity. Finally, the fascinating collaboration with mainstream popster Carol Bayer Sager, "Under Your Spell," has the feel of pure pop product (with a slight gospel tinge), but in some subtle lyrical manner sustains the nervy quality that was the key to Dylan's classic work. The sound is punchy and dynamic, with nice instrumental separations, a strange vocal mix, and a lightly noisy background.

# Steve Earle

### Guitar Town

MCA MCAD-5713 (34:33)     [A]
The seventies and early eighties brought commercialization to Nashville with the same vengeance that it attacked the rock community. The result was string-drenched music that was incredibly vapid, even measured by the usual soap opera norms. The last half of the decade has brought the inevitable backlash—the return to scrawny, leather-lean, honest-to-God, roots country sound. The kind of music to drive your truck to (*big* truck). Earle is at the forefront of this hard-edged, hard-voiced resurrection. Earthy, well-honed lyrics two-steppin' across a lonesome twang—that's Steve Earle, and he's damn good. This is country music for a changed country—it sounds familiar, but it sounds fresh as well. The CD provides clean, crisp, well-defined, and nicely spaced sound qualities.

### Steve Earle and the Dukes Exit 0

MCA MCAD5998 (38:42)     [A]
This one proves that *Guitar Town* weren't no fluke. The band plays simple, tight, kick-ass, pedal steel country music while Earle brings a hard-edged drawl to his acutely observed, well-wrought lyrics that define a part of the contemporary American scene as well as any being written today. The sound is excellent, exhibiting all the positives of digital reproduction.

# Joe Ely

b. 1947—Amarillo, Texas

The varied textures of the cultures which coexist in the Lone Star State have bred a kind of regional music rich in its sources, e.g., Tex-Mex, Western Swing, rockabilly, and honky tonk among them. The music that Ely plays reflects all those influences with some R&B and rock & roll thrown in for good measure. He received his widest exposure when he opened for the Clash, both in England and the United States, on their 1980 tour.

### Lord of the Highway

Hightone Records HCD8008 (44:05)    **[B]**

This isn't Ely's best recording, but it is the only one currently available on disc. *Lord of the Highway* is a fair introduction to a fine artist about whom *Melody Maker* said, "He has everything going for him except success." While the band touches upon the dark swamp power at the soul of rock & roll, Ely's vocal restraint keeps it all just this side of the edge. Still, there are some good moments, "Me and Billy the Kid" and "My Baby Thinks She's French," among them. The sound is first-rate: warm, open, and detailed with excellent separation.

# The English Beat

Formed 1978—Birmingham, England

A band of young and old, black and white, English and Jamaican players who rose out of the English late-seventies ska revival with a danceable beat, a proclivity for Motown covers, and a punk/political stance.

### What is Beat?

IRS CD70040 (46:09)    **[B + ]**

A compilation of some excellent late seventies/early eighties English ska-based pop music. A danceable, insistent beat propels bright melodies and lyrics that manifest the appropriate amount of political awareness. The Beat was one of the original, and most enduring, of the brief-lived two-tone movement that arose, in part, from England's substantial Jamaican population and the punk awareness of a socially stratified society. Good stuff. The sound varies with its divergent sources; overall, it's fairly clean, lightly dynamic, but primarily reflective of its mostly analog ancestry, hiss and all.

# Brian Eno
# (Brian Peter George St. John de Baptiste de la Salle Eno)

b. May 15, 1948—Woodbridge, England

### Thursday Afternoon

EG EGCD64 (60:58)    **[B]**

Eno has employed his tape loops and other studio wizardry to create this composition specifically written for the uninterrupted one hour-plus playing time of the CD. Similar to his other "ambient" compositions; what at times feels like formless pleasantries of electro sound, does exhibit a subtle, almost organic pattern as melodic repetitions ebb and flow through these contemplative forms. The sound is all you can ask for from disc reproduction, even with its analog sources.

# Eurythmics

### Revenge

RCA PCD1-5847 (44:10)    **[D]**

More synthesized, programmed pop pap by a group whose appearance remains more interesting that its sounds. (Hooray for MTV!) England's *New Musical Express* said it all: ". . . the triumph of the mediocre art thief over the sources that arouse his envy more than they inspire him." Nonetheless, Dave Stewart's production is as predictably polished as ever, and Annie Lennox does her usual effective vocal job, but the material is far from exceptional, resulting in another bright, quickly forgettable pastiche. The CD sounds crisp, clean, and dynamic, although it's a bit overbright in the highs.

# The Everly Brothers

### (Highlights) The Reunion Concert

Mercury 824 476-2 (68:36)     **[A]**

After growing up and performing together for over thirty years (their singing careers having begun when they were children), on July 14, 1973, in Hollywood, Phil literally smashed his guitar on stage in mid-show and walked out on what had been one of the most successful and enduring partnerships in rock music's history. On September 23, 1983, in London, Dan and Phil Everly reunited on stage for the first time. This recording commemorates that occasion. As pure rock history, the event has sufficient stature to stand on its own, but, gloriously, it proved to be much more. The Everly's sound was undiminished; if anything, there was an added richness to their soaring harmonies, which may, in part, be the result of the digital sound used for this recording. Whatever the reasons, *The Reunion Concert* is a pure nostalgic delight. Given the fact that this was a live event, the sound is a blowaway. Clean, crisp, defined, and detailed, it's hard to fault. Sure the drums and bass are mixed too far forward and Don's guitar sound tends to overbrightness, but that's nitpicking. Two notes: (1) five songs included on the double LP album are deleted from the disc, leaving twenty; and (2) the accompanying liner text is very informative.

### The Everly Brothers (EB/84)

Mercury 822 431-2 (33:22)     **[B]**

Not really a debut recording, but it is the Everlys' first studio release after a ten-year hiatus. It clearly establishes that the quality of their uniquely beautiful, influential harmonies remains undiminished. In addition to three fine new Don Everly compositions, the album, produced by Dave Edmunds, includes first-rate material from Paul McCartney ("On the Wings of a Nightingale"), Jeff Lynne ("The Story of Me"), and Bob Dylan ("Lay, Lady, Lay"). It also strongly reaffirms the duo's Kentucky country roots. Unfortunately, the weakest aspect of this fine album is the CD sound, which while far from awful, isn't any addition to the proceedings. It suffers from a bad mix which overly emphasizes the bass/drum sound and too often drowns the vocals in the instrumentals (primarily on the up-tempo numbers) while displaying some muddiness as well as an overall overbright sound.

### Born Yesterday

Mercury 826 142-2 (45:03)     **[B+]**

Another Dave Edmunds's production, this 1985 release is studded with some beautiful country-tinged, current pop material impressively performed. Don Everly's title song again demonstrates his excellent composing abilities, but is, unfortunately, his only song included in this set. In addition to a soaring reading of the Sutherland Brothers, "Arms of Mary" (which sounds like it was written for the Brothers), they also cover Mark Knopfler's lovely "Why Worry" and Dylan's "Abandoned Love." But the real highlight is the bonus CD-only cut, the full-out Everly ballad magic applied to Sam Cooke's "You Send Me"—it does. The sound is a bit of a mixed bag. The ballad material is generally warm, nicely spacious and detailed, but the up-tempo numbers suffer from muddy mixes and too obvious compression.

# Donald Fagen

b. ca 1950—Passaic, New Jersey

### The Nightfly

Warner Bros. 23696-2 (38:56)     **[D−]**

More pallid jazz rock sounds from half of Steely Dan (the other being Walter Becker). England's *Melody Maker* summed it up, "Musically, lyrically, spiritually, and concept-wise, this album's a bummer." On the other hand, the CD sound is first-rate.

# Marianne Faithfull

### Strange Weather

Island 7 90613-2 (38:15)    [A–]

A haunting excursion to the pre-World War II sounds of Marlene Dietrich—it conjures up a chanteuse, seamed-hose and high heeled, amid a smoky blue melancholy. Three of the cuts date back more than half a century ("Penthouse Serenade [When We're Alone]," 1932; "Yesterdays," 1933; and "Boulevard of Broken Dreams," 1934); while the remainder include compositions by Tom Waits, Bob Dylan, Leadbelly, and Doc Pomus. The high (low) light has to be Marianne's rerecording of her 1964 ingenue hit, "As Tears Go By;" if you don't think that the times have changed, one listen to this late eighties reading will forever dispel that idea. The beautiful Stones' play-mate of twenty years ago has grown into a tough, experienced woman, now possessed of a deep burnished voice, which she employs to effectively explore memories, times past, and the general despair of life's and love's losers. Impressive, but not for sunny morn-ings or springtime afternoons. The sound is pretty decent, but is plagued with hiss as well as occasional muddiness.

# Bryan Ferry

### Bryan Ferry/Roxy Music Street Life (20 Greatest Hits)

Polystar/EG 829 362-2 (74:04)    [A–]

Perhaps Roxy Music's greatest virtue has been its accuracy as a mirror of its moment—unfor-tunately, the image reflected is not always appealing, but, what the hell, that's life. At least life the way England's foremost seven-ties art rock band perceived it. What Bryan Ferry and Brian Eno created in the mid-to-late seventies was some of the sleekest, most fascinating music of a fairly arid artistic period. Dave Marsh called their recording *Siren*, "A touchstone album of seventies art rock." Robert Christgau, on the other hand, observed of their debut release, *Roxy Music*, "This celebrates the kind of artifice that could come to seem as unhealthy as the sheen on a piece of rotten meat." (He liked the album.) This compilation covers both Ferry's and Roxy's recordings from the seventies through the early eighties, twenty selections all told. For the most part, the Ferry cuts are repre-sentative of his better solo work, but the seventies Roxy Music material, while good, omits some classics, e.g., "Serenade" and "The Thrill of It All," while leaning too heav-ily upon eighties material produced by the surviving three original members (Ferry, Phil Manzanera, and Andy Mackay). This most recent material has brought the band its greatest acceptance in both England and the U.S., but, while eminently listenable, it is romantic rock which lacks the inventiveness and stance that made earlier versions of this group so influential. The sound varies mark-edly, as must be expected; the eighties cuts, while exhibiting some compression, are still bright, dynamic, and clear with precise spa-tial separations. The early Roxy Music in-clusions tend to be bright to the point of harshness.

### Boys & Girls

Warner Bros./EG25082-2 (38:24)    [A]

Atmospheric, arty, and appealing, Ferry's very successful 1985 outing (which includes his hit, "Slave to Love") is an aural montage. His principle themes of self-involved melan-choly and romance are expressed through multiple layers of synthesizers and multi-tracked vocals all in the service of mood rather than of message; and they work to per-fection—ambient sounds for *distingué* lovers. The sound quality is almost perfect, marred only by occasional hiss in some of the quieter sections; otherwise, it qualifies as one of the better sounding pop discs around.

# Fine Young Cannibals

## Fine Young Cannibals

London 828004-2 (34:37)     **[F]**

Following the breakup of the English Beat, two of its original members (Andy Cox and David Steele) advertised for a vocalist and came up with a real winner in Roland Gift. Thus, Fine Young Cannibals and this, their 1985 debut, which is first-rate pop product that effectively displays Gift's prodigious singing style. The highlights are the tough "Johnny Come Home" and a rave-up version of the King's "Suspicious Minds." Sadly, the sound on this CD is awful: thin and distorted, with Gift's voice sounding like a trebly rasp. Stick with the LP.

# John Fogerty

b. May 28, 1945—Berkeley, California         .

The essence of Creedence Clearwater Revival which was America's greatest rock singles band.

## Centerfield

Warner Bros. 25203-2 (35:37)     **[A–]**

In 1985, thirteen years after Creedence disbanded and ten years after Fogerty released his last solo recording, John came back with *Centerfield*, which proved to be a breath of fresh air amid the formula pop of the mid-eighties. This album is a one-man studio effort—Fogerty wrote, sang, and played it all, which proved to be a somewhat insular *tour de force*. Highlights are the title (which baseball should adopt as its anthem), "The Old Man Down the Road," "Rock & Roll Girls," and his paean to the King, "Big Train From Memphis." Perhaps there's too much bitterness between the lyrical lines, but the sound is pure car radio rock & roll. The CD is very good (particularly considering the overdubs that must have been required), but reflects a certain compressed sound stage.

## Eye of the Zombie

Warner Bros. 25449-2 (43:56)     **[A]**

From cover to contents, this is a scarifying statement. *Eye of the Zombie* is the second

eighties release for Fogerty who had returned to the world of pop music with full energy. This time out, he mastered the idiosyncrasies of the modern recording studio and its stepchild, the synthesizer. In addition, instead of doing it all himself, he enlisted the aid of other musicians, primarily on bass, drums, and backup vocals. The whole outing has a more open, current flavor than *Centerfield*, and reflects a certain, almost Old Testament vengeance in its seething overview of a technological world frighteningly preoccupied with violence and nihilism. It didn't enjoy the popular success of *Centerfield*, but may well prove more enduring. The sound is great: precise, detailed, and dynamic with wonderful openness and instrumental separation.

# Frankie Goes to Hollywood

Formed 1984—England

## Welcome to the Pleasure Dome

Island 7 90232-2 (70:11)     **[B]**

Frankie say: Trevor C. Horn (producer). Of course, it's all hype. But Horn is nothing short of a production genius; a man who really knows his way around a recording studio. Thus, hype or not, the sound is spectacular. Substance, forget it; this is disposable product for disposable times. If you're looking for a demo disc to show off the wonders of its sound, this all-digital recording would be a prime candidate: clean, tight, open, crystal-clear, and occasionally, sonically dazzling.

# Peter Gabriel

b. May 13, 1950—England

## So

Geffen 9 24088-2 (46:24)     **[A–]**

Eighties power pop by one of its most intelligent, creative, and sincere practitioners. Obviously, the best thing to come out of Genesis, Gabriel is a man of great musical and production sophistication who employs his architecturally structured sounds to exorcise personal demons. While there is an antiseptic, somewhat overworked coolness about it all, this is one of those rare recordings that has garnered both critical and popular acceptance. (The latter probably arising out of Gabriel's wondrous video dexterity as well as his musical creativity.) The sound is open, dynamic, detailed, clean, and well-separated, about all one could ask from a CD.

# Art Garfunkel

### Scissors Cut

CBS/Sony 38 DP22 (31:46)    **[D]**
Lush early eighties pop/ballads which attempted to substitute production sheen for personal soul resulting in aural cotton candy. The musicianship and studio perfectionism (thanks to Roy Halee) are evident throughout, but neither the singer nor the songs justify the effort on Garfunkel's fifth solo release since the break-up of Simon and Garfunkel. The sound, given its analog origins, is very good: open and clean. However, some background noise is occasionally evident and the sound stage lacks depth and appropriate spaciousness.

### The Art Garfunkel Album

CBS CDCBC 10046 (50:06)    **[C–]**
If Garfunkel's post-Simon brand of pop pastry is your dish, this fourteen-selection compilation includes most of his better known material, e.g., "Breakaway," "A Heart in New York," "Wonderful World," "I Only Have Eyes for You," and "I Believe (When I Fall in Love It Will Be Forever)". As is always the case with Garfunkel, the sound production values are first-rate resulting in a quality-sounding CD, which does reflect the limitations of its analog origins.

# Marvin Gaye

### Midnight Love

Columbia CK38197 (39:40)    **[A]**
Like most pop stars (black, white, male, and female), sex appeal and love songs were Gaye's stock and trade, but Marvin got more explicit about it than most. This, the last release before Gaye's tragic death, marked a resurgence in a career that had been in disarray for a period of almost ten years, and brought Gaye back to the forefront with its smash hit, "Sexual Healing." While not the equal of his classic *What's Going On, Midnight Love* has to rank with his best recorded work and that automatically places it with the best soul releases of the era. The apparently contradictory themes of sexual and spiritual redemption are the cornerstones of this work and the artist blends them with seemless compatibility. It may not be a totally fitting epitaph, but it comes damn close. The sound is crisp, clean, detailed, and clear with a slight tendency to excess brightness in the highs.

# Georgia Satellites

### Georgia Satellites

Elektra 60496-2 (38:53)    **[C + ]**
Throwback southern rock & roll by a scruffy band from a state that has become a major source of eighties musical talent. The Satellites sound a bit like the London rock scene in the sixties, before psychedelia came along. They don't break any new ground, but there's always a place for good ol' Saturday night kick-ass rock & roll. These guys know that and deliver ten strong doses on this, their debut release, including the hit, "Keep Your Hands to Yourself." The sound is just OK, pretty muddy in the mix and very compressed, given its current vintage.

# Grateful Dead

### In the Dark

Arista ARCD8452 (40:52)    [C + ]

For twenty-two years, these aging hippies
from the Haight have nurtured an extended
family which now has achieved mythical stature. More icons than musicians, the Dead
and their enduring audience represent an
almost perfect commercial/ideological sym-
biosis. *In the Dark* is their first studio effort in
years, and while they still can't sing or play
that well, it just doesn't matter anymore; hell,
it never did (Kharma is Kharma). This *is* their
best recorded outing in years and "Black
Muddy Water" is a good song. The sound is
first-rate: dynamic, open, tight, clean, and
clear.

# John Hiatt

b. 1952—Indianapolis

### Bring the Family

A&M CD5158 (45:33)    [A + ]

Hiatt is one of the undiscovered gems of the
current rock world. He writes some of the
very best lyrics you're likely to hear ("Besides
the buttons on our shirts, girl—what else did
we leave undone?"). And if the buying public
has missed that fact, and, to date, they have,
his fellow musicians haven't. Hiatt songs
have been covered by a number of current
recording artists. In addition to his compositional skills, he is a first-rate interpreter, with
an elastic voice and an honest way with a
lyric. Principally known for his work with Ry
Cooder's touring band, he has now released
eight albums, generally to critical acclaim
and little else. On *Bring the Family,* his 1987
release, he is joined by Ry Cooder on guitar,
Nick Lowe on bass, and Jim Keltner on drums
for what is clearly his strongest album statement, and it's an absolute killer. From the
clever lyrics and good time upbeat sound of
"Memphis in the Meantime" to the aching
beauty of "Lipstick Sunset," the ten selections
reflect the scope of an artist whose concerns
and musical abilities encompass a large spectrum of what is rock & roll music. To top it all
off, the fine musicianship displayed here is
beautifully showcased in some of the best CD
sound you are likely to hear.

# The Honeydrippers

### The Honeydrippers Vol. 1

Esperanza 7 90220-2 (18:20)    [C–]

A negligible but nice idea that was probably
more fun for the participants than for their
audience, although, "Young Boy Blues" has a
certain perverse appeal. The sound is clean
and pretty open, but clearly reflects its analog
roots.

# Chris Isaak

### Chris Isaak

Warner Bros. 25536-2 (36:19)    [A + ]

Swamp rock from Stockton, California. Isaak
is one of the few genuinely exciting artists to
emerge in the mostly arid eighties. He's a
throwback to the sound and image that
arose out of Memphis over thirty years ago.
His voice is strongly reminiscent of Roy
Orbison, his band is tight and true, and his
songs echo with the history of the best of
rock & roll. Buy this disc and maybe Warner
Bros. will release his debut recording, *Sliver-
tone* (Warner Bros. 25156-1) on CD—it's
every bit as good, if not better, than this, and
that's saying a lot. The sound is first-rate:
warm, open, detailed, and dynamic, with
heavy, though intended, echo.

# Joe Jackson

### Joe Jackson's Jumpin' Jive

A&M CD3271 (42:17)    [C + ]

If not in musical form, in spirit, the jitter-bug-
ging era that was the forties bears a certain
kinship to rock & roll. Certainly Louis Jordan
has been referenced by a few rock critics as a
prehistoric progenitor of what has come to be
known as rock & roll. On *Jumpin' Jive*, Joe
Jackson has gathered together a big band that
accurately mirrors the sound of the great
swing bands of that bygone era. In the process, they cover several of Louis Jordan's
classics. Like most of Jackson's work, *Jumpin'
Jive* is a technical *tour de force*, the only missing ingredient is that spark that gave rise to
the adage "it don't mean a thing if it ain't got
that swing." The sound is clean and nicely
separated, but it's thin and obviously compressed, resulting in a small stage—music
confined by the speakers.

# Ladysmith Black Mambaza

### Shaka Zulu

Warner Bros. 9 25582-2 (36:48)    [A]

This ten-voice, male, church choir under the
leadership of Joseph Shabalala has had
import recordings available in the United
States for a number of years. But it wasn't
until 1986 when they joined Paul Simon on
his classic *Graceland* that their wondrous
vocal prowess received anything like mass
exposure. This 1987 release was produced by
Simon and engineered by the extraordinary
Roy Halee with results that are among the
best pure vocal music on record. Eight of the
ten songs are sung in English (the other two
in their native Zulu), but Black Mambaza's
voice is universal—music from the heart to
the heart that celebrates life as majestically as
you are ever likely to hear. An amazing
record by an amazing group. The sound is
perfect—crystal-clear and as open as the spirit
of the music.

# Cyndi Lauper

### She's So Unusual

Portrait/CBS RK38930 (38:37)    [A]

It may have sold as much on visual image as
musical content, but those who bought the
package got a bonus—Cyndi Lauper is a natural; one of the most engaging pop talents to
emerge in the eighties. *She's So Unusual* is a
class debut release—good songs (some written by Lauper, with inclusions from Prince
and Jules Shear among others), great singing,
and bright supportive production. "Time
After Time" is among the best ballads to come
out in the decade; "She Bop" and "Girls Just
Want to Have Fun" brought feminist values
(both personal and social) to a teen audience
in positively compelling form—a delight that
sustains. The sound is dynamic and fairly
clean, but a bit overbright and somewhat
compressed, very analagous to the sound of a
good quality LP.

### True Colors

Portrait/CBS RK40313 (38:08)    [A]

Cyndi's second, released in 1986, reaffirms
her status as one of the major female pop
talents of the decade. She sings her heart out,
whether it be a ballad or up-tempo number,
and she communicates both her unique personality and emotions through every lyric.
Ably assisted by such diverse talents as the
Bangles, Adrian Believ, Nile Rodgers, Billy
Joel, Aimee Mann, and Pee Wee Herman,
Lauper has produced an album that covers a
wide range of pop territory, and all of it well.
The centerpiece is her cover of Marvin Gaye's
"What's Going On" segueing into the New
Orleans classic, "Iko Iko," which is inspired
in both concept and execution. The sound is
a revelation: spacious, clean, open, and
dynamic with precise separation. The vocal
mix is set back a bit, but Cyndi's penetrating
voice still gets through.

# Lone Justice

## Lone Justice

Geffen 24060-2 (36:09)    **[B–]**

This pop countryish album is principally notable for one thing: Maria McKee, who happens to be one of the hottest female voices to hit rock in recent memory. She's not a bad writer either, having had a hand in the writing of half of the disc's ten selections, the most notable being "After the Flood." This is the recording that produced the driving hit, "Ways to Be Wicked" written by Tom Petty and Benmont Tench, the Heartbreakers' talented keyboard player who contributed substantially to these proceedings. The sound has its moments, but generally is analagous to that of a clean LP.

# Los Lobos

### How Will the Wolf Survive?

Slash/Warner Bros. 9 25177-2 (33:29)    **[A]**

This is pretty impressive stuff. Its roots are real, and so are the dues it took to get this L.A.-based Chicano band acceptance within the mostly white mainstream of pop success. From straight ahead Saturday night rockers through traditional Mexican folk material, to contemporary compositions that express the valid and growing point of view of one of America's largest minorities (and one that has not as yet made that much impact on its adopted culture), Los Lobos brings absolutely first-rate musicianship, real sensitivity, and obviously heartfelt meaning to whatever they perform. They are one of the most valid of the decade's new rock bands, and the title selection on this collection is their greatest recorded work yet. The sound quality reflects excellent instrumental separation, T-Bone Burnett's straightforward, clean production values, relatively clean sound, and some evidence of analog compression.

### By the Light of the Moon

Slash/Warner Bros. 9 25523-2 (40:37)    **[A–]**

The worthy follow-up by David Hidalgo, Cesar Rosas, and company suffers from dichotomy of intent, i.e., it's partially made up of Rosas's energetic rock numbers and partially of Hidalgo's lyrical expressions of the difficult aspects of life for many Spanish-speaking immigrants in America in the 1980s. But these concerns are every American's because the problems addressed involve universal disillusionment, heightened by proximity to the world's most affluent culture ("The Hardest Time"). That aside, on a track-by-track basis, each selection reflects this fine band's strengths which are considerable. It is arguable that the future hope for real creativity in rock (and maybe for the nation) may depend upon the continued diversity of a society that draws fresh inspiration and attitudes from a multiplicity of cultures—Los Lobos certainly supports that premise. There is a realness to their music which transcends language or cultural boundaries and assures it continuing currency. There is no single cut on *By the Light of the Moon* to rival "Will the Wolf Survive?" but the overall quality of the release is almost the equal of its fine predecessor. Again, T-Bone Burnett's direct, open production pays dividends in the sound, which is clear and separate, and this recording reflects dynamics and openness that are markedly superior to that of their first full album release.

# Los Lobos, Bo Diddley, Howard Huntsberry, Brian Setzer, and Marshall Crenshaw

### La Bamba—Original Soundtrack

Slash/Warner Bros. 25605 2 (31:26)    **[A + ]**

Almost thirty years ago, Ritchie Valens came out of the large Los Angeles Mexican-American community to achieve national celebrity at the age of seventeen in the second wave of fifties rock & roll. "La Bamba," "Come On, Let's Go," and "Donna" rocketed him to fame—a small plane, Buddy Holly—the Big Bopper—and a snowy night in Iowa established his epitaph: "The day the music died." The year 1987 brought the movie version of this tragically brief story with Los Lobos paying musical homage to an acknowledged inspiration with intensity and integrity. While the eight cuts performed by Los Lobos are the core of the recording, the remainder isn't filler by any means. Bo Diddley's "Who Do You Love" by itself is almost worth the price of admission; and the Crenshaw, Setzer, and Huntsberry covers, particularly the latter doing Jackie Wilson's "Lonely Teardrops," maintain the excellent musical standards established by Los Lobos. The sound on this all-digital disc is a major plus: clean, dynamic, and spacious.

## Nick Lowe

b. March 25, 1949—England
He got his start in Brinsley Schwarz, the seventies British pub-rock band whose alumni have proved extremely influential in the rejuvenation of the seventies and eighties English pop scene. He has also been a mainstay (on bass) of Rockpile, as well as handling production chores for both Elvis Costello and Graham Parker.

### 16 All-Time Lowes

Demon Fiend CD20 (47:43)    **[B]**
This compilation provides a fair overview of the witty, facile pop playfulness of one of the most ubiquitous members of the late seventies and eighties English music scene. His talent is undeniable, but his stance is sometimes questionable. It would have been nice to have "Rollers Show" among the disc's included selections, but otherwise it does cover most of his highlights; including the hit, "Cruel to Be Kind" and the bizarrely funny, "Marie Provost." The sound varies, but is, overall, equivalent to that of a clean LP, hiss and all.

## The Lucy Show

### Mania

Bigtime 6012-2-B (39:52)    **[B–]**
The Lucy Show sounds a bit like REM on speed, but it's a good sound from a tight, energetic band working the punk New Wave side of the eighties American musical street. The twelve brief selections reflect a promising young band on the verge of establishing an individual identity—here's hoping they make it. The sound is clean, but compressed, rarely escaping the speakers. It is also afflicted with constant, if not overwhelming, hiss.

## John Martyn

b. 1948—Glasgow, Scotland

### Piece by Piece

Island 7 90507-2 (58:44)    **[B + ]**
Martyn weaves highly individualistic tapestries of sound, which include folk, jazz, blues, and light rock elements. There is a kinship between these sounds and the haunting works of Nick Drake. Since the late sixties, this individualistic artist has created a series of atmospheric recordings reflecting diverse influences, but resolving them in cohesive, appealing works which have enjoyed critical accolades and created a cult following. But they still remain outside of the ever-changing mainstream. While marred with continuous hiss, the CD's sound is very open, clean, and dynamic; a notable enhancement.

## John Cougar Mellencamp

b. October 7, 1951—Seymour, Indiana
Originally, little more than another Midwestern Bruce clone. By the mid-eighties, he had turned his composing skills to his Midwestern, small-town roots becoming a part of what has recently been dubbed "Heartland Rock."

## Scarecrow

Mercury 824 865-2 M-1 (41:10)    **[B + ]**

*Scarecrow* is music concerned with the economic hard times and loss of traditional rural values that has affected much of America's midsection. The subject matter is valid, obviously heartfelt from Mellencamp's perspective (he still resides in his home state), and is presented on this, his critical breakthrough album, with power and precision. Musically, this artist doesn't break any new ground (Springsteen's powerful, romantic rock echoes from every note), but he writes some decent lyrics and his spirit appears to be more consistent with what was behind it all in the first place. The title cut is the best item on the record, and it's a winner. The sound is dynamic, crisp, and relatively open, with an unfortunate tendency toward overbrightness.

### The Lonesome Jubilee

Polygram 832 465-2 Q-1 (39:47)    **[A]**

If rock & roll is any kind of political harbinger, then this fine recording may presage a populist revival to be reckoned with in November of 1988. With *Scarecrow*, John Mellencamp turned his lyrical focus to the life and concerns of America's rural heartland. Since the artist's feelings seem heartfelt, this redirection has increased the stature of his work significantly. Yet, populist ideals are only one facet of this complex effort. Mellencamp is dealing here with questions pertaining to the essence of the life experience itself, its joys, despairs, and ultimate inevitability. This context is presented within simple, yet sophisticated, musical settings that employ a number of classic American folk instruments, e.g., Dobro, accordion, and violin in addition to the standard rock band lineup, all of which connect the songs and themes to their somewhat obvious, but nonetheless enduring antecedents. Don Gehman's production has an energetic immediacy which the excellent digital sound fully communicates.

# Joni Mitchell

## Dog Eat Dog

Geffen 9 24074-2 (43:34)    **[A]**

A dense, multilayered, complex, and ultimately very satisfying recording. This is the seventies singer/songwriter embracing the synthesized techno-rock of the eighties, which she employs with great dexterity and assuredness. Her lyrical preoccupations have moved from the self-confessional to the political. The melodies here aren't exactly hummable, but her vision is acute and her presentation ultimately sophisticated. The sound of the disc cuts the LP all to hell—its dynamic, precise openness adds an entire additional dimension, allowing the CD listener to hear the material the way it was intended.

# Van Morrison

## Inarticulate Speech of the Heart

Mercury 811 140-2 (47:01)    **[A]**

Van as ecstatic Irish spiritual visionary. *Inarticulate Speech of the Heart* is a beautifully conceived and executed homage to the "auld sod." Notable for its orchestral textures (a number of the cuts are instrumentals), it has a conceptual completeness which is rare in pop music. Van's return to his ancestral homeland seems to have had a salutory effect on both the man and his music. Thus, while the mood is often almost elegaic, and there is not a cut on the album that even approximates a "rocker," *Inarticulate Speech of the Heart* proves to be an uplifting, even joyous listening experience with the highlights being "River of Time," the instrumental "Celtic Swing," "The Street Only Knew Your Name," and "Cry for Home." The CD's sound is open, expansive, clear, and defined—it completes an almost perfect recorded presentation.

### A Sense of Wonder

Mercury 822 896-2 (43:39)    **[B + ]**

Morrison's most specific, spiritually directed recording. The sounds of a sensitive, caring man dealing with the cosmic wonders of pure spirituality. As such, it is generally about as far from rock & roll as anything this fascinating artist has recorded. The usual diversity of influences (blues, rock, jazz, and traditional) is clearly reflected here, and Van is singing at the height of his powers, which is about as good as it gets. The sound is a revelation: open, spacious, defined, warm, and clean.

### Live at the Opera House Belfast
Mercury 818 336-2 (52:05)     [A–]
Morrison's discomfort in live performance is legendary. This is only the second release of concert material in a recording career that spans more than twenty years (the first being *It's Too Late to Stop Now*). With the exception of the briefest instrumental reference to "Into the Mystic" in the intro, the eleven selections are drawn from Van's post-1978 recordings. While nothing included is an enhancement over the studio originals, it is a polished, well-received performance on which Morrison sounds confident, if not exactly comfortable. The CD sound is excellent for a live recorded effort, with clear separation, impressive dynamics, and a tendency to overbrightness in the vocals and brass.

### No Guru, No Method, No Teacher
Mercury 830 077-2 (51:14)     [A + ]
Rich instrumental textures, some great songs ("Got to Go Back," "A Town Called Paradise," and the best upbeat song he has done in years, "Ivory Tower"), plus some of the most impressive singing of anyone in pop music, make this Morrison's strongest album in years. His influence within the world of pop music has been incredibly direct and broad, but it is only a hardcore cult within the mass market that appreciates and supports this man who is a treasure in our contemporary musical culture. The sound is crystal-clear, defined, open, and warm.

### Poetic Champions Compose
Polygram 832 585-2 (48:13)     [A]
Stilted title notwithstanding, this is one of Morrison's most lyrical outings—more song cycle than collection of disparate elements.

*Poetic Champions Compose* opens ("Spanish Steps") and closes ("Allow Me") with lovely instrumentals featuring Van's alto saxophone and is intersected by a third ("Celtic Excavation"). While there are no individual selections that stand out (with a possible exception of his evocative reading of the traditional "Motherless Child"), it is precisely the flowing continuity of the work that ultimately provides its special appeal. The instrumentation employed is very consistent with all of this artist's post-eighties recordings, featuring both strings and horns to create almost orchestral textures. Morrison's singing is direct and natural. All of this adds up to lovely music for a Sunday morning or an autumn evening. The sound is well-defined, smooth, and generally clean. The only real criticism is a certain lack of spaciousness which an all-digital recording might well have added.

# The Neville Brothers
Formed 1977—New Orleans
As much a part of the Crescent City's R&B scene as the gumbo or crawfish pies for which this most fertile of American musical cities is justifiably famous.

### Fiyo on the Bayou
Demon Fiend CD65 (35:44)     [A–]
Dave Marsh said it as well as it could be said: " . . . as fine a set of New Orleans rhythm and blues workouts as anyone's put together in the past decade." The CD sound is clean and generally clear, but reflects some slight muddiness in the mix and an overall compressed LP-like quality.

# The Nylons
Formed 1979—Toronto, Canada
An a cappella quartet whose repertoire runs from doowop to gospel and pop.

### One Size Fits All
Open Air OD0301 (30:24)     [C + ]
Slick, proficient, eminently listenable vocal music by four guys who are at least keeping

the idea (if not the spirit) of the fifties great street corner harmonies alive and well. The standouts on this, their debut release, are "Silhouettes" and "Bop! Til You Drop." The sound is simply faultless—this is a demonstration-quality disc.

### Seamless

Open Air OD-0304 (33:48)     **[B–]**
Aptly titled, although soulless is equally applicable. They sing four-voiced harmony with dynamic precision, but there is little beneath the shimmering surface. *Seamless* is their best recorded effort as a result of the superior song selections. "The Lion Sleeps Tonight" ("Wimoweh") even garnered commercial airplay, no mean feat for an almost a cappella group. Again, the sound quality is extraordinary.

### Happy Together

Open Air OD 0306 (33:51)     **[C–]**
At least they didn't call this one *Support*. More of the same, with a few more sound effects added to the mix. The title cut is as good as anything they've recorded, the rest of it is more shiny surface without sustaining substance; pop music for the new-age, no-soul crowd. If it's possible, the sound is even better (more definition) than on their two earlier disc releases.

## The Persuasions

Formed 1962—Brooklyn, New York
The only known surviving U.S. sixties doowop group, the Persuasions (with help from Frank Zappa, who gave them their first recorded exposure) have maintained a career doing pure a cappella music for more than a quarter of a century.

### No Frills

Rounder 3083 (35:52)     **[B + ]**
This 1986 release isn't the equal of the 1977 classic, *Chirpin,* but it provides the CD buyer a historic footnote—the unaccompanied street corner (so-called "doowop") harmonies that fueled much of the fifties nascent rock

sounds. Built on one of the most resonant bass voices you'll ever hear (Jimmy Hayes), their repertoire runs from gospel, to pop and doowop (all of which are fairly represented here). The pure expressive joy of the human voice raised in song is their stock-in-trade. The sound is clean, but it exhibits the limitations of its analog roots in its compression and somewhat closed space. If you want to know what real doowop is all about, this is as good as you'll find on disc.

## Tom Petty and the Heartbreakers

### Hard Promises

MCA MCAD37239 (40:09)     **[A]**
This is top-quality American mainstream rock & roll performed with a hard edge and honest intent. Perhaps not the equal of *Damn the Torpedos* (its immediate predecessor), but it's close enough. Highlighted by "The Waiting," "The Insider," "King's Road," and "A Thing About You," this recording, along with *Damn the Torpedos,* constitutes the best work by one of the most powerful late seventies/early eighties rock bands working. Jimmy Iovine's deft production captures every nuance. *Hard Promises* on disc reveals a clean open sound, precise separation, and sparkling dynamics that bring new life to a fine outing by a first-rate band working at the top of its not inconsiderable powers.

## Pink Floyd

### The Final Cut

CBS CK38243 (43:28)     **[C–]**
Subtitled "A Requiem for the Post War Dream" this is Roger Waters's musical eulogy to his father. It is also Waters's last effort with Pink Floyd. *The Final Cut* is a somber, heavy record with a few memorable moments, but overall, it sinks under Waters's gloomy, vaguely cosmic visions. The sound is clean and open, but its compression impedes the

dynamics upon which much of its production punch is predicated.

### A Momentary Lapse of Reason

Columbia CK40599 (51:16)     [C + ]

The rock album as an aural movie. This is Pink Floyd devoid of Roger Waters, which means that it is principally a David Gilmour recording. Once again, it isn't *Dark Side of the Moon,* although it's an obvious descendant of that landmark recording. Sonically, this is an extraordinary outing. Recorded digitally (except for the bass and drums which were done on analog), the sound is the best part of it all. (It should be noted that there is a slight tendency to occasional overbrightness even on this all-digital effort.) The lyrics have all the stilted banality we have come to expect from England's pioneer art rockers, and its musical attributes are, for the most part, clearly secondary to the sonic effects upon which this band has built its not inconsiderable reputation.

# The Pogues

### Rum, Sodomy and the Lash

Stiff 2223270 1 (43:07)     [A]

Traditional Irish folk music dragged screaming through the punk dump. If *Rum, Sodomy and the Lash* proves anything, it is that the spirit of rock & roll lives in many guises. By infusing the old songs with that irreverent spirit, those songs regain the currency that gave them original meaning. Lead singer Shane MacGowan is the living incarnation of the Irish hooligan as the devil incarnate; and, he sings just like you hope he will. The Pogues are six Irish lads and one woman, Cait O'Riordan, who is Elvis Costello's wife. Produced by Costello, this sometimes crass album is infused with his sense of edgy anger, but what lingers is the passion and the caring. Also what lingers is one of the strongest anti-war songs ever recorded, "And the Band Played Waltzing Matilda." The sound is clean, clear, and "live."

# The Pointer Sisters

Formed Oakland, California

### Breakout

RCA PCD1-4705A (43:45)     **[D]**

Packaged pop for a packaged age. Mostly studio technique and production in which the three female voices are one more element. Slick and senseless. The CD sound is extremely overbright, subject to hiss, distortion, and compression in both dynamics and space.

# The Police

Formed 1977—England

### Synchronicity

A&M CD-3735 (44:30)     **[D]**

Pseudo-music by intellectual and emotional poseurs who enjoyed a brief vogue, but have thankfully managed to cash in their numerous chips and go their separate ways. (That said, "Every Breath You Take" is a stunning pop song.) The sound is an almost state of the art analog to digital conversion with barely noticeable compression.

# The Pretenders

Formed 1978—London, England

### The Pretenders

Sire 6083-2 (47:15)     **[A + ]**

Chrissie Hynde, whose vocals, rhythm guitar, and songwriting define the Pretenders, is one of the most honestly real artists to come along in the last decade. She makes rock & roll; no apologies, no regrets. This debut recording is stunning in its power, intimacy, directness, and variety. There's not a weak cut, but the standouts, "Precious," "Stop Your Sobbing," and "Brass in Pocket" were the reason this release established the Pretenders as one of the most successful of the New Wave bands to come out of England in the late seventies. Hynde is a major contributor and this is a major work. The sound is pretty much the equivalent to that of the LP.

## Get Close

Sire 25488-2 (45:22)    **[A]**

Working with three premier producers, Jimmy Iovine, Bob Clearmountain, and Steve Lillywhite, and a variety of musicians, including the only other surviving member of the original group, Martin Chambers, on drums, on one number, Chrissie Hynde has again fashioned a first-rate release. All the attributes which the original band exhibited six years previously remain, albeit softened with a more pop-oriented sensibility. Yet, there is no sense of compromise—Chrissie's too blunt and basic for artifice; that's why she consistently makes great rock & roll. This time around, the sound, too, is great—clean, defined, open, and dynamic.

# Prince
# (Prince Rogers Nelson)

b. June 7, 1960—Minneapolis

The brief history of rock music has included a handful of black artists (Ray Charles, James Brown, Sly Stone, and Stevie Wonder) who, while enjoying various degrees of crossover recognition have, in fact, had immense impact on the form of all the pop music that came after them. Prince clearly is the latest to enter this august group. The son of musical parents, he signed with Warner Bros. at age eighteen, releasing his first one-man album (he plays all the keyboards, guitars, and other instruments as well as multi-tracking his vocals) the same year. Before he was twenty-one, he had been credited with creating the widely influential "Minneapolis Sound" with his inventive pop/funk/rock blend.

### Dirty Mind

Warner Bros. 3478-2 (30:18)    **[A +]**

Talk about truth in labeling, this one lays it right out up-front and then delivers. Prince's amorous preoccupations, ranging from oral sex to incest, make up the lyrical subject matter here. Make no mistake, he doesn't pull any punches. This recording had been called "positively filthy" even before the PMRC had

been heard from. However, by flouting his explicit lyrics over a synth-based, propulsively insinuating pop/funk sound, with hooks aplenty and a danceable beat, the Minnesota *wunderkid* established his own very influential niche in the eighties pop market ("When You Were Mine" from this release was covered by a number of other artists, and over the ensuing years, he's given songs to numerous artists in both the pop and funk markets). Subject matter aside, these are simply some of the freshest, brightest, most engaging sounds to have entered the pop mainstream in years. The CD sound is clean and clear, but also reflects some compression in both dynamics and audio stage size.

### 1999

Warner Bros. 23720-2 (62:19)    **[A +]**

If there was any question about Prince's musical stature and true genius, it was this recording which resolved the matter in his favor, once and for all. Masterfully building upon funk, soul, disco, rock, and pop sounds and influences, Prince has constructed an album of refreshing dance music, that manages to sound totally fresh and is consistently inventive. "Little Red Corvette" and "1999" are the popular highlights. But his unstoppable groove runs through the ten irresistible selections (one less than the original double LP collection, "D.M.S.R." having been omitted by Prince to get the double LP package on a single CD), resulting in a landmark eighties effort. The sound is more open and dynamic on CD, but is impaired by continuous hiss and background noise, overbrightness, and noticeable weakness in the drum sounds.

### Prince and the Revolution Purple Rain

Warner Bros. 9 25110-2 (43:55)    **[A +]**

In 1984, his purple majesty brought out the soundtrack to what may well be the definitive rock movie, and delivered one of the best pop records of the year. A major aspect of this highly visible genius's music is his ability to create songs which sound totally new, yet manage to be accepted and retained on first hearing. This is well illustrated here with

"When Doves Cry." As usual, Prince's music runs the gamut among multiple, currently popular forms (soul, funk, psychedelia, etc.) and he handles each with freshness and individuality. The addition of the Revolution on this disc, while mostly functioning as a backdrop for the master's performance, does open up the feel and texture of the sound. It is here, also, that Prince demonstrates his guitar prowess, which alone would grant him major status in the current music scene. The CD sound is clear, open, dynamic, and well-separated, but does have a tendency toward excessive brightness and retains some noticeable hiss.

**Prince and the Revolution Parade**
Warner Bros. 25395-2 (41:0)    [A + ]
The follow-up soundtrack to the follow-up film ("Under the Cherry Moon"), the soundtrack fares much better than its celluloid counterpart, but that's not saying much because the movie was a bona fide bomb. Actually, it's a shame the movie came out, because the record, standing alone, clearly does. The music on *Parade* reflects an even broader musical palette than Prince had demonstrated on prior recordings, with an overall somewhat sweeter sound. Upon its release, it met with mixed critical and public response, but after the passage of about a year, it seems clear that this represents another massively creative musical step for a young man who continues to dazzle with his unceasing inventive freshness. True, one of the cuts is so tied to the film that it doesn't really work on the recording ("Sometimes It Snows in April"), but the rest stand up in any context, particularly "Girls & Boys," "Kiss," and "Anotherloverholenyohead." The sound is an unreserved success—open, crystal-clear, and beautifully spaced and defined.

**Sign O the Times**
Paisley Park/Warner Bros. 25577-2 (80:03— two discs)    [A]
The prolific one returns this time with a double-disc outing that once again explores the multiple sounds and nuances of current (rap) and past (funk, soul, you name it) popular music. This time around, it's mostly Prince working solo (but who can tell?), although some additional musicians do make an occasional appearance. It's simply another brilliant *tour de force,* although, in all honesty, it would probably have been the ultimate pop statement that the critics have been awaiting from him if it had been edited into a single disc recording. As it is, it's a little bit of a lot of things with some dross, but more than its share of brilliant gems. The sound is first-rate—clean, very open, crisply dynamic, and nicely detailed.

# Lou Reed

**New Sensations**
RCA PCD1-4998 (43:02)    [A−]
Reed has adopted a lot of personas in the recording career that he fashioned for himself since departing the Velvet Underground in the early 1970s. This, the eighties model, may well be the most accessible yet. It's true that the brutally edgy guitar sound is buried in the mix, along with female backup singers; and the lyrical preoccupations are now concerned more with the elements of middle-class pleasures than underclass horrors, but there is still some bite left. His eye for lyrical detail may also be a little diminished, but he's far from blind. Yeah, it could be a bit nastier and angrier, but everybody grows up sometime, for better or for worse. The sound isn't bad, except for too noticeable, too frequent hiss.

# R.E.M.
Formed 1982-83—Athens, Georgia
Clearly, one of the most influential and important of America's new eighties rock bands. Their sound is built upon the chiming guitars pioneered by the Byrds almost two decades before, but R.E.M.'s sensibility clearly looks forward.

## Murmer

IRS CD70014 (44:09)    **[A–]**

The band's first recording was an EP (now included as a part of their 1987 compilation release, *Dead Letter Office*, IRS CD70054), but this is the album that began the accolades that have helped this band rise above cult status in the latter half of the eighties. Their sound has a timeless, atmospheric quality about it that defies literal explanation, but it is nonetheless palpably real. While they work in a rather narrow spectrum, and Michael Sipe's ambivalent, hidden vocals lend little "explanation" to it all, there is, at the core of it, a coiled energy that ultimately proves irresistible. The sound on this disc is equivalent to LP quality, compressed with constant hiss.

## Reckoning

IRS CD70044 (38:13)    **[A + ]**

More of the same muffled intensity and atmospheric energy. This time around, the individual tracks have a more defined separateness which ultimately sustains greater interest. The album produced the "hit" "(Don't Go Back to) Rockville" which is excellent, but so are the rest of the selections. R.E.M. has taken some of the best of the music's glorious past and made it current in a manner that preserves, yet validly updates, its antecedents. The sound is an improvement over *Murmer* in terms of both clarity and dynamics, but it still suffers from some compression and hiss.

## Fables of the Reconstruction

IRS IRSD-5592 (39:46)    **[B + ]**

With this release, there is a subtle change in the subtle music—it remains enigmatic as ever, but *Fables of the Reconstruction* is, if anything, more dense and obtuse than its less than transparent predecessors. The sound is roughly equivalent to that on *Reckoning,* but the content isn't as good.

## Life's Rich Pageant

IRS IRSD5783 (38:33)    **[B + ]**

A brighter, more dynamic version of the band. A bid for more commercial acceptance? Perhaps one can till the same narrow field only so many times. This time, there's more variety in the rhythms and instrumental textures, not to mention almost clarity in the lyrics. The sound is appreciably cleaner and more dynamic than on their earlier recordings, as well as brighter and more defined.

## Dead Letter Office

IRS CD70054 (63:51)    **[B + ]**

A compilation of outtakes and "B" sides that includes several of their Velvet Underground covers which are the highlights, along with the inclusion of their outstanding debut EP, *Chronic Town.* You have to respect any group that will hang this much personal laundry on one line. Obviously the sound is all over the place, some distortion, some muddiness, and lots of hiss.

## Document

IRS IRSD-42059 (39:51)    **[A + ]**

This amazingly prolific band has previously maintained a murky, dense chameleon-like persona which made them many things for many fans. *Document,* while a studio effort, is really their first recording that communicates their live energetic intensity—it's also the first that clearly communicates the words. Both elements prove to be a plus, resulting in their strongest release since *Reckoning,* and, perhaps, their best ever. Described by David Fricke, writing in *Rolling Stone,* as "A clench-fist manifesto of rebel bravado," *Document* is a searingly haunting experience that conjures up rock's classic moments, but ultimately echoes nothing but itself, again and again. The CD's sound is perfectly mated to the material: clearer than ever before, yet still possessed of felt, but unheard, energies.

# The Replacements

### The Replacements

Sire 9 25330-2 (37:06)     [B + ]
Bright, brash, highly energetic pop product from one of the many exciting young groups to come out of Minneapolis in the eighties. Punk though they may be, you can't take them too seriously, since they don't allow themselves that treacherous luxury. This is good time music that works. The sound is very bright.

# The Rolling Stones

### Emotional Rescue

Rolling Stones Records/CBS CK40500 (41:18)     [D]
A little look backward, a little grungy, a little going through the motions. Yet, when you've got a contract, you've got to deliver, but does this really count? Eminently forgettable, if not forgiveable. The sound is a bit brighter than the LP, otherwise it's a toss-up.

### Tattoo You

Rolling Stones Records/CBS CK40502 (43:00)     [B–]
This may prove to be ultimately the last viable gasp by a once nonpareil rock band. The fans loved it anyway; it's probably the all-time best-selling Stones' release (topping *Some Girls*). It's not a bad Stones album by their standards of the last fifteen years, but who can forget what once was? Clearly, its one truly outstanding moment is "Waiting for a Friend," both because of its mature lyrical stance and, especially, because of Sonny Rollins's sax solos. While it evidences some compression and hiss, the disc does have a cutting dynamic edge to its open sound, which is an enhancement.

### Dirty Work

Rolling Stones Records/CBS CK40250 (40:05)     [C]
This 1986 release is primarily a Keith Richards/Ron Wood guitar record, but the real punch comes from the Wyman/Watts bass/drum that just seems to improve with age.

Clearly, the emphasis here is more on the instrumental than vocal attributes of the band. Measured by the stature this once great group had attained, *Dirty Work* is an obvious disappointment (eighties pop in the guise of rock & roll). Measured by the standards of its current competition, it just ain't that bad. Besides, it might be the final chapter (but don't bet on it). The sound is open, driving, and clean, with a slight edge to the upper mid-range.

# Roxy Music

### Avalon

Polydor/EG800 032-2 (37:25)     [C + ]
The spark and intensity that made Roxy Music the great British seventies art rock band had passed. In its place appeared a sleek, sophisticated sound that, while utterably listenable (preferably as background music), offered little in the way of substance or meaningful intent. It is a lovely sound, precisely produced and packaged. The CD provides an excellent complement to the sound of the music—very open, relatively clean and nicely defined with excellent separation.

# Boz Scaggs

### Hits!

Columbia CK36841 (43:13)     [B + ]
First-rate compilation of some of the smoothest white soul music to come along in the seventies. Scaggs is both a fine, easy vocalist and an excellent soul/pop writer, both of which are amply illustrated on this ten-selection package which includes "Lowdown," "You Make It So Hard (to Say No)," "Lido Shuffle," and "Dinah Flo." Given the differences in the age and source of the included recordings, the sound is a model of consistency and it's smooth, detailed, open, and well-defined with excellent separation.

# Paul Simon

### One Trick Pony

Warner Bros. 3472-2 (38:18)     **[B–]**
The soundtrack to the movie of the same
name that Simon wrote and in which he
starred. This isn't vintage Simon by any
stretch of the imagination, but he's too fine a
craftsman for it to be without merit; however,
most of the material is fairly forgettable. "Late
in the Evening" became a bit of a hit in 1980,
but the highlight is "Ace in the Hole," one of
the best songs ever written by one of America's best contemporary song writers. The
sound is generally impressive: dynamic, very
open, and detailed, but it does have a less
than clear background, and occasional distortion. However, in this case, these are minor
complaints.

### Hearts and Bones

Warner Bros. 9 23942-2 (40:45)     **[A–]**
Simon's 1983 release, which was probably the
least commercially successful recording of his
long career. This was the case even though
it contains all the elements common to his
well-received work: fine songs sensitively performed set against the best pop production
values. The obvious answer is that it lacked
the hit song necessary to make the album a
success. Yet, there are some great songs
included here: the autobiographical title cut
that chronicles his marriage to and divorce
from Carrie Fisher, as well as the more obvious potential hit, "The Late, Great Johnny
Ace." Perhaps it's all just too grown-up for pop
success; *Hearts and Bones* again demonstrates pop craftsmanship of the highest order
as well as ingenious lyrics sung with genuine
feeling. As is usually the case with Simon's
work, the sound quality is a major addition to
the proceedings and so it is with this CD.

### Graceland

Warner Bros. 9 25447-2 (43:10)     **[A + ]**
Throughout his lengthy career, Simon has
been an eclectic craftsman. Prior to this
release, his pop music has incorporated
sounds from South America and Jamaica as
well as American blues and gospel material.
In late 1985 and early 1986, Paul Simon dis-
covered the current popular music of South
Africa and it inspired this truly wondrous
recording. Working with a number of native
musicians whose roots-oriented material represents the best of South Africa's current pop
sounds, Simon has grafted his fine melodic
sense to the extraordinary harmonies and
complex rhythms which represent the source
material for much of American popular
music. Perhaps because of its political
aspects, *Graceland* represents a rock & roll
album in the truest sense. Beyond these political considerations, musically it is perhaps
the finest pop album to be released in the
decade of the eighties. Consistent with its
moving, meaningful, and melodic contents,
the sound quality of the compact disc is
excellent.

# Simple Minds

### Once Upon a Time

A&M CD5092 (40:17)     **[B]**
A big eighties anthemic rock sound, musically
originally derived from Roxy Music's fine seventies work, but which has now reached a
point where the message is almost lost in the
grandeur of the sonics. *Once Upon a Time*
remains a prime example of eighties arena
rock with substance in addition to waves of
pounding sound. Jim Kerr is a passionate performer with the ability to communicate his
obviously sincere humanistic messages. The
sound quality on this disc is excellent:
extremely dynamic, vastly open, and also
providing excellent clarity and detail.

# Simply Red

### Picture Book

Elektra 9 60452-2 (44:30)     **[C–]**
*New Musical Express* summed this one up,
". . . soul-by-the-numbers is as cliché-ridden
as the ugliest offspring of gothic interbreed-
ing." The sound, however, is first-rate.

# The Sir Douglas Quintet

### "Live"

Takoma TAKCD7095 (41:14)    **[B + ]**

Doug Sahm is another of the many Texas musicians who moved to California in the early 1960s. His music reflects his "roots," incorporating country, Tex-Mex, jazz, blues, and Western Swing into a unique "rock" sound that was notable for the introduction of the vox (farfisa) organ sound which Augie Meyer brought to the original Sir Douglas group. The result was a distinctive sound that propelled the band to its two most memorable hits, "Mendocino" and "She's About a Mover" (both included here). This '86 release captures the band doing ten selections recorded "live" in Austin and Los Angeles. Something of the grungy sixties charm may be missing, but Doug's got a great rock voice and there is an honesty of intent about it that remains compelling. Given the source locales, the sound is pretty impressive; a bit compressed and subject to constant hiss, but otherwise, it's clear and dynamic with a nice open spacious feel.

### The Collection

Castle CCSCD 133 (55:26)    **[A–]**

Texas has been a major contributor to the rock movement almost from its inception (Buddy Holly was born in Lubbock on September 7, 1938). In large part, this arises because that state's music is, in many ways, a microcosm of rock itself, i.e., the ultimate amalgamation of all forms of pop music. From Tex-Mex through Western Swing to rockabilly, Doug Sahm and his trusty sidekick, Augie Meyer (on the farfisa organ) make music that incorporates all these elements into what is great roadhouse Saturday night listening. Yet, this is no homage to the past; the Quintet's music, made primarily in the late sixties to early seventies, was very much of its time and held its own at a time when the overall quality of rock music was substantially higher than it has ever been since. This is loose (sloppy?) good-time sound enhanced

by a heritage and committed performance. The seventeen selections cover essentially all of the group's vintage efforts. The sound is dynamic and fairly open, but suffers from some heavy hiss and compression from time to time.

# Bruce Springsteen

### The River

Columbia CK36854 (83:50—two discs)    **[A + ]**

This sprawling summation of his seventies work finally brought Springsteen the mass audience he had deservedly been seeking for almost a decade with the hit single, "Hungry Heart." While a majority of the cuts are up-tempo rockers of the first order, included in the twenty selections on this release are a number of Springsteen's personal, moving ballad statements. *The River* is filled with great rock & roll: "The Ties That Bind," "Cadillac Ranch," "You Can Look (But You Better Not Touch)," "I'm A Rocker," and "Ramrod," as well as an excellent sampling of his meaningful narrative ballads: "Independence Day," "The River," "Fade Away," "The Price You Pay," and "Wreck on the Highway." All in all, *The River* is a world unto itself, a world of intense feeling and driving rock & roll. The sound is an improvement over the LP, particularly in the detail afforded Springsteen's vocals; however, at volume the overall brightness tends to harshness which impairs the clarity otherwise found on the discs.

### Nebraska

CBS CK38358 (40:26)    **[A + ]**

In 1982, Bruce Springsteen released this, his most unique and perhaps, ultimately, his most enduring recording. Actually, the release is made up of the demo tapes that Springsteen had done on his four-track home machine utilizing only his acoustic guitar, harmonica, and voice to capture the desolation and despair that he perceived at the heart of America's heartland. This is a portrait of the underside of the American Dream presented in a stark, highly personal style. There are a number of true classics among the ten included cuts, "Atlantic City" (which garnered some airplay), "Highway Patrolman," and "Nebraska" among others. The sound of the CD is defined by the sound of the source material, which means that if you are looking for sonic perfection, this is one to pass by. It's constantly filled with the tape hiss arising out of overdubs, and is fuzzy and murky much of the time. Yet, somehow, the sound seems totally appropriate for the content, making this disc an excellent addition to the 1980s library of American rock & roll.

### Born in the U.S.A.

CBS CK38653 (46:58)    [A + ]
This is the one that did it. *Born in the U.S.A.* is the classic rock & roll album that elevated Springsteen above the rest of the musical crowd to the status of living legend. Energetic, mature, and featuring the E Street Band playing tighter than ever, it is an album composed of consistently outstanding compositions. The title, "My Home Town," "No Surrender," "Glory Days," and "Dancin' in the Dark" (its first major hit) are illustrative of the overall quality to be found here. The sound quality is excellent, particularly in the detailed rendering of the vocals, and impressive separation. However, there is a bit of upper mid-range edge to it, as well as occasional muddiness in the instrumentation, notably the drum track.

### Bruce Springsteen and the E Street Band Live/1975-85

CBS 40558 (216:16—three discs)    [A + ]
From the outset of his historic career, Springsteen's been first and foremost a live performer. To understand this artist's truly awesome power, one just has to experience him live, to feel the energy, to know that it is his honest desire to make every member of every audience feel that they have known the very best that he and the E Street Band have to deliver. Thus, over his lengthening career, his ever-growing audience has craved a live recording in the hopes of catching those magic concert moments once again. Bootleg

copies of various concerts and live radio broadcasts have surreptitiously circulated since the mid-seventies. Finally, in 1986, Bruce set out to remedy this situation with the ultimate concert recording. This compilation is the equivalent of a real Springsteen concert because the total playing time runs over three and a half hours and covers forty selections, a few that are offered here for the first time on record. Musically, the package is uneven. Too many of his older classics are included as they were presented post-1985. This may be a concession to the availability of better recordings in later years, but often results in less than impassioned performances. That said, the set does contain some magnificently inspired moments such as the 1975 ballad rendition of "Thunder Road," several songs from *Nebraska* performed with the band for the first time on record, as well as some smashing rock & roll ("Cadillac Ranch") and the closer, a cover version of Tom Waits's "Jersey Girl." The real greatness of Bruce Springsteen is his strong sense of personal honesty and commitment behind a very humanistic concern. These attributes come through, in part, on this live release but, unfortunately, the principal thing that echoes through the music is a sense of "event" rather than the substance of the its message. Given the fact that these are live recordings, the overall quality of the CD sound will simply blow you away. It is almost as if one were sitting with the band given the degree of detail and the intimacy afforded by this release.

### Tunnel of Love

Columbia CK40999 (46:27)    [A + ]
There had been much speculation about how Springsteen would follow up *Born in the U.S.A.*, the album that led to his deification. There had been concern expressed about how his mega-stardom would impact on the man and his work. The answer lies in *Tunnel of Love*, in which Springsteen turns to his greatest resource, his honest artlessness, now deepened with understanding and acceptance born out of survival. Somewhat akin to

*Nebraska* in its intimacy, though very different in stance and coloration, *Tunnel of Love* is a subtle triumph in the face of incredible odds—a testament to the traits and talents that have placed Springsteen in the unique company where the only standards are self-defined. *Tunnel of Love* is ultimately about survival on all levels, and Springsteen provides both truth and poetry, augmented by spare but effective instrumentation to help us along the way. Various members of the E Street Band add effective, but relatively minimal, tints to Springsteen's songs and stories—Max Weinberg, Bruce's longtime drummer, appears on almost all the cuts, again demonstrating his ultimate tastefulness. The all-digital sound is beautifully natural, open, and clear—essentially flawless.

# Squeeze

### Eastside Story
A&M CD3253 (48:39)     **[A]**
Once again, Dave Marsh summed it up best, this '81 release " . . . is a near perfect pop-rock album of pithy vignettes that fuse Beatlesesque lyricism with New Wave wit." The sound, while slightly compressed, is spatially open, crisp, dynamic, and well-defined.

# Talking Heads

### Remain in Light
Sire 6095-2 (40:10)     **[A–]**
New Wave meets African polyrhythms and performance techniques. In a sense, *Remain in Light* is a single continuum of song, a fact which the complete playability of the CD enhances. A fascinating recording, which reflects the conceptual genius of the band as well as its impressive musicality. Its rhythmic appeal is totally seductive, and the recognizable, fragmented phrases which make up the floating lyrics, create a strange reality. The sound isn't wonderful, far too much hiss and obvious compression.

### Speaking in Tongues
Sire 9 23883-2 (41:16)     **[A+]**
The Heads' most fully realized album. It retains the potent, rhythmic underpinnings that had been the essence of *Remain in Light* and overlays them with the best set of songs the band performed. Melodically pop-oriented with more narrative congruity to the lyrics, this is a more accessible release than its predecessors. A great album of eighties New Wave techno-pop music. The sound quality of the CD is almost flawless.

### Stop Making Sense
Sire 25186-2 (46:33)     **[A+]**
The soundtrack to what is probably the best rock concert film ever made. The academic background of all the band members was in the visual and architectural arts; thus, the concert setting with its audio/visual aspects seems to bring out their best. In addition, by this time, 1984, Byrne had grown comfortable with his uncomfortable performance persona, and his vocal confidence and weird expressiveness are a highlight of one the best live albums released. The nine selections cut across the entirety of the band's recorded history, making this an excellent career overview as well as providing new insights into the older material. The sound is extraordinary with excellent imaging.

### Little Creatures
Sire 25305 (38:46)     **[A+]**
Swell pop fantasy; the ultimate eighties jukebox sound. Consistently inventive, hook-filled, and melodic, the Heads again display a stylistic dexterity rare in the history of rock & roll. The sound (all digital) is as good as it gets.

### True Stories
Sire 25512-2 (46:35)     **[A–]**
The soundtrack to Byrne's bizarre motion picture. Musically, it marks a return to the less pop-oriented, more frenetic New Wave sounds upon which their original work was based. This band seems incapable of making boring music; and while *True Stories* may not

represent the change or growth that has been reflected on each of their previous releases, it still rewards repeated listening. The sound, while not quite as impressive as *Little Creatures,* is still almost flawless.

# 10,000 Maniacs

### In My Tribe

Elektra 9 60738-2 (46:58)     **[B]**
This release represents the coming of age of an excellent pop/folk/rock eighties band and particularly its lyricist and lead singer, Natalie Merchant, who is one of the most fascinating female leads to come along in recent years, although she really needs to be seen to be fully appreciated. This is very listenable, intelligently accessible modern pop music which promises an interesting future. Credit should be given to Peter Asher for his immaculately direct production which brings the band clearly into focus and is also reflected in nearly flawless all-digital sound.

# Richard Thompson and Linda Thompson

### Shoot out the Lights

Hannibal HNCD 1303 (40:55)     **[A +]**
Simply the great undiscovered, rock masterpiece. Music of power the equal of anything recorded in the last fifteen years or so. Linda's vocals are majestically beautiful, Richard's guitar uniquely eloquent. At its best, it has moments of terrifyingly magical potentcy ("The Wall of Death" and "Shoot Out the Lights"), as well as transcendental beauty ("Just the Motion"). Conceived and recorded during the final death throes of their marriage, the music vibrates with incredible tension and energy. The sound is excellent. While slight hiss and minor compression are occasionally evident, the clarity and spatial definition are a perfect enhancement. (As an

added plus, the CD contains a track not included on the LP, "Living in Luxury," which isn't bad, but isn't necessary either.)

# Richard Thompson

### Across a Crowded Room

Polydor 825 421-2 (41:49)     **[A]**
In 1982, Richard and Linda Thompson released *Shoot Out the Lights,* one of the most powerful recordings in rock history. Part of its potency arose out of the final tensions of the destruction of their marital relationship. *Across a Crowded Room* is Richard's first recording following their divorce. Thompson is one of the largely undiscovered giants of the current rock scene, and, perhaps, the best guitarist working, a fact which this release doesn't belie. But it must be remembered that much of this album concerns itself with the pain of separation ("Ghosts in the Wind") and the bitterness, too ("When the Spell Is Broken" and "She Twists the Knife Again"). It also includes some strong, driven rock & roll ("Fire in the Engine Room"). *Across a Crowded Room* is not necessarily an easy or pleasant listening experience, but it is a potent one. The sound, while a shade thin, is clear, open, defined, and extraordinarily precise.

### Hand of Kindness

Hannibal HNCD1313 (41:23)     **[A +]**
From the rocking opening chords of "Tear Stained Letter" (a great rock number by any standards) to the polka-driven craziness of "Two Left Feet" that closes *Hand of Kindness,* Thompson delivers music of power, integrity, and majestic intensity. "How I Wanted To" may be one of the most intimately searing laments on record. Throughout it all, Thompson's incredible, modal guitar playing and John Kirkpatrick's buoyant accordion, keynote music of variety, texture, and tension. The sound is warm, clean, and adequately dynamic.

**Daring Adventures**

Polydor 829 728-2 (47:15)    [A + ]

The fact that this guy isn't a major star is eloquent testimony to the sickness in today's pop music industry. Although, in Thompson's case, lack of mass recognition may in large part be self-inflicted. He doesn't care enough to play the game. Instead, that energy goes into making some of the best music being played in the eighties. "Valerie" is the great rock single that no one ever heard. The rest of the material on this stellar 1986 release is as inventive, creative, and downright beautiful as anything you're likely to hear. Oh well, you can only lead a horse to water. The sound is all you can ask for, as well.

# Timbuk 3

**Greetings from Timbuk 3**

IRS 5739 (37:04)    [A–]

A guy (Pat McDonald) plus a gal (Barbara K nee Kooyman) plus a boombox equal Timbuk 3. And Timbuk 3 equals some of the wittiest, most attractive new pop product of the last few years. McDonald, whose prior classics include the unknown, but unforgettable "Assholes on Parade," writes some of the most perceptively entertaining lyrics you are likely to hear and it's all packaged in simple, basically guitar and rhythm sounds that provide a fitting setting for his jaundiced eye. The sound is impressive: clean, immaculately detailed, and dynamically precise. For a good time, try Timbuk 3.

# Pete Townshend

**White City**

Apco 90473-2 (38:42)    [D–]

"Almost as if he's learned how to avoid enjoying himself . . ." —*New Musical Express.* Aside from that, the sound is absolutely first-rate.

# UB40

**Labour of Love**

Dep CD5 (40:05)    [C]

The most successful American release for this black/white English reggae band, *Labour of Love* is a set of the group's updated cover versions of the earlier hits of many of reggae's original stars. If you don't take it too seriously, or are unfamiliar with the originals, it's a pleasant listen, but little more. The sound quality is fairly ordinary: slightly more dynamic and clean than the LP, but obviously compressed and a little muddy.

# U2

Formed 1978—Dublin, Ireland
Considered by many to be the finest rock & roll band in the world today (1987).

**War**

Island 90067-2 (42:21)    [A–]

It was with this release that U2's blend of punk, piety, sincerity, and heavy metal caught commercial fire. Fueled by wonderfully dramatic performance dynamics (à la Led Zeppelin), this anti-war protest release rings with the power of true commitment. U2 is a band that has captured its moment in time. The sound quality, while slightly compressed and occasionally a bit instrumentally muddy, still remains impressive.

**The Joshua Tree**

Island 90581-2 (50:16)    [A + ]

This is the fifth release since 1980 by an Irish band many consider to be the best in rock today. This record will do nothing to diminish that belief. U2 has a palpable vision and they don't sell out. They may get a little too strident or naive at times, but they don't sell out, and this time around, they avoid both the naivete and stridency as well: the best of a mature rock sound. The spirit of rebellion is still there, but tempered with the wisdom of age and experience. It's not that they want to change the world, just shift its course a little. *The Joshua Tree* is a powerful album filled with sadness, serenity, and hope. It is about the reality of faith. It is easily the strongest recording in an already brilliant career— probably because the band plays more within itself than on earlier work. In addition to Bono's compelling vocals and the searing minimalism of Edge's guitar, *The Joshua Tree* also showcases the potent bass work of Adam Clayton over Larry Mullen, Jr.'s, pulsing drums. This is music with sufficient depth to endure. This is also one of those rare recordings where there isn't any filler to be found; "Running to Stand Still" is one of the best songs in years. The sound is simply flawless.

## Stevie Ray Vaughn and Double Trouble

### Soul to Soul
Epic EK40036 (40:09)    [C + ]
Reheated Allman Brothers. Vaughn is a fine guitarist, but that's about it. The sound is above average, not real clean, but dynamic and fairly open.

## Suzanne Vega

### Suzanne Vega
A&M CD5072 (35:54)    [A–]
Sometimes labeled the savior of contemporary folk music, after this 1985 release remarkably received mass market acceptance. It's a fine debut, highlighted by, "Marlene on the Wall," "Undertow," and "Little Blue Thing." This is intelligent, contemporary folk material directly presented, that is ultimately affecting. The sound is marvelous.

### Solitude Standing
A&M CD5136 (44:24)    [B + ]
The material gets a little thinner and the arrangements a little thicker. Somehow that just doesn't balance out. The sound is even better than on her debut release: true demonstration quality.

# Tom Waits

### Rain Dogs
Island CID131 (54:08)    [A + ]
Waits is a true original with a voice out of *The Exorcist* and a vision out of Bukowski. He is also one of the most original and affecting artists working today. A reincarnation of the cool jazz, beat generation fifties, he's a breath of fresh air in the techno-eighties. This is one of his best efforts, but for a little too much filler, it might be his very best. The sound isn't as clean as it could be, but it's well-defined, detailed, and dynamic.

# Jennifer Warnes

### Famous Blue Raincoat
Cypress 661 111 2 (41:38)    [A + ]
Leonard Cohen wrote some of the most poetic and affecting material of any of the singer/ songwriters, but the monotonal delivery he utilized failed to attract much of an audience beyond sincere seventies college girls. Jennifer Warnes has been a fan as well as a musical contributor to Cohen's recent recordings and she has one of the finest pop voices around. Thus, this recording of Warnes doing essentially all Cohen material is a perfect match. Cohen, himself, joins in on "Joan of Ark," but the show belongs to Jennifer, the vocalist and coproducer with Roscoe Beck as well as to Van Dyke Parks and Bill Ginn for the perfect arrangements. This one is a sleeper. It's not rock & roll, but it's great pop/ folk product. The sound is absolutely awesome—this is the one to play to demonstrate what CD sound is capable of delivering.

# Stevie Wonder

### Musiquarium

Motown 6114TD (86:04—two discs)     [A + ]
An excellent compilation of the seventies and
early eighties work of one of the most influential artists of the times. All the goodies are
here: "Superstition," "Boogie on Reggae
Woman," "You Are the Sunshine of My Life,"
"Livin for the City," "You Haven't Done
Nothin," "Masterblaster," and ten others (four
of which are new to this release and digitally
recorded). They're all here in truly excellent
sound.

# X

### See How We Are

Elektra 60492-2 (37:46)     [A + ]
In the eighties, in the name of "classic" rock,
radio suppresses the spirit of rock itself with
its silent boycott of anything remotely con-
nected to the punk (translate: new rock & roll)
movement of the seventies. X, which was
born in L.A. in 1977, certainly traces its roots
to that city's second wave punk scene. However, a decade later, it is clear that this is one
of the great American rock bands of the
eighties, whether they get airplay or not. With
their incisive lyrics, haunting country-tinged
harmonies, and energetic drive, X is one of
the few current bands tending to the essential
spirit of the music. This is their first release
without founding lead guitarist Billy Zoom,
and the remaining trio (John Doe, Exene, and
Don Bonebrake) are here augmented by Dave
Alvin and Tony Gilkyson on guitars and
vocals. The result is one of the best recordings from a band whose musical standards
have always been exceedingly high. The
sound isn't clean, but it seems purposeful and
is thickly potent.

# EIGHTIES
# COLLECTIONS

"It's all music, no more, no less."

—Bob Dylan

**The Indestructable Beat of Soweto**

Shanachie SH43033 (45:54)  **[A + ]**
This compilation of South African township
jive leaves no doubt as to Paul Simon's acknowledged inspiration for his classic *Graceland.* A dozen cuts by the exuberant musicians who make some of the most joyously
compelling music being played anywhere. It's
irresistible. The sound, while a bit compressed, is still consistently first-rate.

# THE TOP

## ROCK COMPACT DISCS
## (by decade)

FIFTIES

| | |
|---|---|
| **Chuck Berry** | THE GREAT 28 |
| **Collections** | ATLANTIC RHYTHM AND BLUES VOL. 4 (1956–62) |
| | ROCK & ROLL THE EARLY DAYS |
| | THE SUN STORY |
| **Everly Brothers** | CADENCE CLASSICS (THEIR 20 GREATEST HITS) |
| **Buddy Holly** | BUDDY HOLLY FROM THE ORIGINAL MASTER TAPES |
| **Little Richard** | 18 GREATEST HITS |
| **Elvis Presley** | ELVIS |
| | ELVIS PRESLEY |
| | THE SUN SESSIONS |

SIXTIES

| | |
|---|---|
| **The Band** | THE BAND |
| **The Beach Boys** | ENDLESS SUMMER |
| **The Beatles** | ABBEY ROAD |
| | THE BEATLES (THE WHITE ALBUM) |
| | A HARD DAY'S NIGHT |
| | HELP! |
| | PLEASE, PLEASE ME |
| | REVOLVER |
| | RUBBER SOUL |

157

| | |
|---|---|
| **The Beatles** *(cont.)* | SGT. PEPPER'S LONELY HEARTS CLUB BAND |
| | WITH THE BEATLES |
| **James Brown** | THE CD OF JB (SEX MACHINE AND OTHER SOUL CLASSICS) |
| **Collections** | ATLANTIC RHYTHM AND BLUES (1947-74) VOL. 6 (1966-69) |
| | GREAT SONGS WRITTEN BY HOLLAND-DOZIER-HOLLAND |
| | THE SOUL OF NEW ORLEANS |
| | TOGA ROCK |
| **Sam Cooke** | THE MAN AND HIS MUSIC |
| **Creedence Clearwater Revival** | CHRONICLE (20 GREATEST HITS) |
| **The Doors** | THE BEST OF THE DOORS |
| **Bob Dylan** | BIOGRAPH |
| | BLONDE ON BLONDE |
| | BRINGING IT ALL BACK HOME |
| | HIGHWAY 61 REVISITED |
| | GREATEST HITS |
| | JOHN WESLEY HARDING |
| **Aretha Franklin** | 30 GREATEST HITS |
| **Marvin Gaye** | WHAT'S GOING ON/LET'S GET IT ON |
| **The Jimi Hendrix Experience** | ARE YOU EXPERIENCED? |
| | ELECTRIC LADYLAND |
| **Jimi Hendrix** | JIMI PLAYS MONTEREY |
| **Van Morrison** | ASTRAL WEEKS |
| | MOONDANCE |
| **Elvis Presley** | THE MEMPHIS RECORD |
| **The Rolling Stones** | AFTERMATH |
| | BEGGAR'S BANQUET |
| **Simon & Garfunkel** | BOOKENDS |
| **Diana Ross and the Supremes** | 20 GREATEST HITS |
| **The Velvet Underground** | THE VELVET UNDERGROUND & NICO |

SEVENTIES

| | |
|---|---|
| **Jackson Browne** | THE PRETENDER |
| | RUNNING ON EMPTY |

| | |
|---|---|
| The Clash | THE CLASH |
| Bob Dylan | BLOOD ON THE TRACKS |
| Bryan Ferry | THESE FOOLISH THINGS |
| Fleetwood Mac | FLEETWOOD MAC |
| Led Zeppelin | UNTITLED (IV) |
| Bob Marley and the Wailers | LEGEND (THE BEST OF BOB MARLEY AND THE WAILERS) |
| Joni Mitchell | COURT AND SPARK |
| Jonathan Richman and the Modern Lovers | THE BESERKLEY YEARS (THE BEST OF JONATHAN RICHMAN AND THE MODERN LOVERS) |
| Gram Parsons and the Fallen Angels Featuring Emmylou Harris | LIVE 1973 |
| Graham Parker & the Rumour | SQUEEZING OUT SPARKS |
| Pink Floyd | DARK SIDE OF THE MOON |
| The Pretenders | THE PRETENDERS |
| The Rolling Stones | EXILE ON MAIN STREET |
| Bob Seger and the Silver Bullet Band | NIGHT MOVES |
| The Sex Pistols | NEVER MIND THE BOLLOCKS HERE'S THE SEX PISTOLS |
| Paul Simon | GREATEST HITS, ETC. |
| Bruce Springsteen | BORN TO RUN |
| Sly and the Family Stone | GREATEST HITS |
| Rod Stewart | EVERY PICTURE TELLS A STORY |
| James Taylor | JT |
| Velvet Underground | LOADED |
| The Who | WHO'S NEXT |
| Stevie Wonder | INNERVISIONS |
| Neil Young | TONIGHT'S THE NIGHT |

EIGHTIES

| | |
|---|---|
| Collection | THE INDESTRUCTABLE BEAT OF SOWETO |
| Elvis Costello and the Attractions | IMPERIAL BEDROOM |
| John Hiatt | BRING THE FAMILY |
| Chris Isaak | CHRIS ISAAK |
| Van Morrison | NO GURU, NO METHOD, NO TEACHER |
| Prince | 1999 |

| Prince and the Revolution | PARADE |
| | PURPLE RAIN |
| R.E.M. | RECKONING |
| | DOCUMENT |
| Paul Simon | GRACELAND |
| Bruce Springsteen | BORN IN THE U.S.A. |
| | NEBRASKA |
| | THE RIVER |
| | TUNNEL OF LOVE |
| Bruce Springsteen and the E Street Band | LIVE/1975-85 |
| Talking Heads | SPEAKING IN TONGUES |
| | STOP MAKING SENSE |
| Richard Thompson | DARING ADVENTURES |
| | HAND OF KINDNESS |
| Richard and Linda Thompson | SHOOT OUT THE LIGHTS |
| U2 | THE JOSHUA TREE |
| Tom Waits | RAIN DOGS |
| Jennifer Warnes | FAMOUS BLUE RAINCOAT |
| Stevie Wonder | MUSIQUARIUM |
| X | SEE HOW WE ARE |

▶ The foregoing list was compiled as of October 10, 1987. Future releases will result in additions to and deletions from this compilation.

# BIBLIOGRAPHY

Aftell, Mandy. *Death of a Rolling Stone: The Bryan Jones Story.* New York: Delilah Books, 1982.

Anson, Robert Sam. *Gone Crazy and Back Again (The Rise and Fall of the Rolling Stone Generation).* New York: Doubleday, 1981.

Bacon, Tony, ed. *Rock Hardware: The Instruments, Equipment and Technology of Rock.* New York: Harmony Books, 1981.

Bane, Michael. *White Boys Singin' the Blues: The Black Roots of White Rock.* New York: Charles Scribner's Sons, 1982.

Baker, Glenn A., and Stuart Coups. *The New Music.* New York: Harmony Books, 1980.

Balfour, Victoria. *Rock Wives.* New York: William Morrow & Co., 1986.

Bangs, Lester. *Blondie.* New York: Delilah, 1963.

Bebey, Francis. *African Music: A Peoples Art.* Translated by Josephine Bennett. Westport, Conn.: Lawrence Hill & Co., 1975.

Belsito, Peter, and Bob Davis. *Hard Core California: A History of Punk and New Wave.* n.p.: Last Gasp, 1983.

Bockris, Victor, and Gerard Malanga. *Uptight: The Velvet Underground Story.* New York: Quill, 1983.

Boot, Adrian, and Michael Thomas. *Jamaica: Babylon on a Thin Wire.* New York: Schocken Books, Inc., 1977.

Bronson, Fred. *The Billboard Book of Number 1 Hits.* New
    York: Billboard Publications, Inc., 1985.
Brooks, Elston. *I've Heard Those Songs Before.* New York:
    Quill, 1981.
Brown, James, with Bruce Tucker. *James Brown: The
    Godfather of Soul.* New York: Macmillan Publishing Co.,
    1986.
Butler, Dougal, and others. *Full Moon: The Amazing Rock &
    Roll Life of Keith Moon.* New York: Quill, 1981.
Byrne, David. *True Stories.* New York: Penguin Books, 1986.

Castleman, Harry, and Walter Podrazik. *All Together Now (The
    First Complete Beatles Discography 1961-75).* New York:
    Ballantine Books, 1975.
Charone, Barbara. *Keith Richards Life as a Rolling Stone.* New
    York: Dolphin Books, 1982.
Christgau, Robert. *Any Old Way You Choose It (Rock and Other
    Pop Music, 1967-73).* New York: Penguin Books, 1973.
Christgau, Robert. *Christgau's Record Guide.* New York: Ticknor
    & Fields, 1981.
Clifford, Mike, consultant. *The Illustrated Encyclopedia of
    Black Music.* New York: Harmony Books, 1982.
Clifford, Mike. *The Harmony Illustrated Encyclopedia of Rock
    and Roll.* New York: Harmony Books, 1983.
Coleman, Stuart. *They Kept on Rockin'.* New York: Blandford
    Press Ltd., 1982.
Cott, Jonathan. *Dylan.* New York: Rolling Stone Press/
    Doubleday, 1984.
Coups, Stuart, and Glenn A. Baker. *The New Rock'N'Roll: The
    A-Z of Rock in the 80's.* New York: St. Martin's Press, 1983.

Dalton, David. *The Rolling Stones: The First 25 Years.* New
    York: Alfred A. Knopf Inc., 1981.
Davis, Stephen. *Bob Marley.* New York: Doubleday, 1985.
Davis, Stephen. *Hammer of the Gods: The Led Zeppelin Saga.*
    New York: William Morrow & Co., 1985.
Davis, Stephen, and Peter Simon. *Reggae Bloodlines: The
    Search of the Music and Culture of Jamaica.* New York:
    Anchor Books Press, 1977.
Davis, Stephen, and Peter Simon. *Reggae International.* n.p.,
    R&B, 1982.

Denisoff, R. Serge. *Solid Gold: The Popular Record Industry.* New Brunswick, N.J.: Transaction Books, 1975.

Doerschuk, Bob, ed. *Rock Keyboard.* New York: Quill, 1985.

Duncan, Robert. *The Noise (Notes From Rock'N'Roll Era).* New York: Ticknor & Fields, 1984.

Duncan, Robert. *Only the Good Die Young.* New York: Harmony Books, 1986.

Dylan, Bob. *Bob Dylan Writings and Drawings.* n.p.: Panther, 1974.

Dylan, Bob. *Bob Dylan Lyrics 1962-85.* New York: Alfred A. Knopf, Inc., 1985.

Dylan, Bob. *Tarantula.* n.p.: Panther, 1966.


Eisen, Jonathan, ed. *The Age of Rock (Sounds of the American Cultural Revolution).* New York: Vintage, 1969.

Eisen, Jonathan, ed. *The Age of Rock 2 (Sights and Sounds of the American Cultural Revolution).* New York: Vintage, 1970.

Elson, Howard, and John Burnton. *Whatever Happened To . . . ?* n.p.: Proteus, 1981.

Escott, Colin, and Martin Hawkins. *Sun Records.* n.p.: Quick Fox, 1975.


Fawcett, Anthony, *California Rock/California Sound.* n.p.: Reed Books, 1978.

Fawcett, Anthony. *John Lennon: One Day at a Time.* New York: Grove Press Inc., 1976.

Firth, Simon. *Sound Effects (Youth, Leisure and the Politics of Rock'N'Roll).* New York: Pantheon, 1981.

Flanagan, Bill. *Written in My Soul.* Chicago: Contemporary Books Inc., 1986.

Flippo, Chet. *On the Road with the Rolling Stones.* New York: Dolphin Books, 1985.

Fong-Torres, Ben, ed. *The Rolling Stone Rock'N'Roll Reader.* New York: Bantam, 1974.

Frame, Pete. *The Complete Rock Family Trees, Volumes 1 and 2.* Port Chester, N.Y.: Omnibus Press, 1980.

Friedman, Myra. *Buried Alive: The Biography of Janis Joplin.* New York: Bantam, 1974.

Gambaccini, Paul. *Critics Choice: The Top 100 Rock'N'Roll Albums of All Time.* New York: Harmony Books, 1987.

Gans, David. *Talking Heads.* New York: Avon, 1985.

George, Nelson. *Where Did Our Love Go? (The Rise and Fall of the Motown Sound).* New York: St. Martin's Press, 1985.

Gilbert, Bob, and Gary Therou. *The Top 10 1956-Present.* New York: Simon & Schuster, 1982.

Gillette, Charlie. *Making Tracks: Atlantic Records and the Growth of a Multi-Billion-Dollar Industry.* New York: E.P. Dutton, 1974.

Gillette, Charlie. *The Sound of the City (The Rise of Rock & Roll).* New York: Pantheon Books, 1970. Revised and updated, 1983.

Gleason, Ralph J. *The Jefferson Airplane and The San Francisco Sound.* New York: Ballantine Books, 1969.

Goldrosen, John. *The Buddy Holly Story.* n.p.: Quick Fox, 1975.

Goldrosen, John, and John Beecher. *Remembering Buddy.* New York: Penguin Books, 1987.

Greenberg, Allan. *Love In Vain (The Life and Legend of Robert Johnson).* New York: Doubleday & Co., 1983.

Greene, Bob. *Billion Dollar Baby.* New York: Signet, 1974.

Guralnick, Peter. *Feel Like Goin' Home: Portraits in Blues and Rock'N'Roll.* New York: Vintage Books, 1971.

Guralnick, Peter. *Lost Highway.* New York: Vintage Books, 1982.

Guralnick, Peter. *Sweet Soul Music (Rhythm & Blues and the Southern Dream of Freedom).* New York: Harper & Row, 1986.

Guthrie, Woody. *Bound for Glory.* New York: Plume, 1943. (Autobiography)


Hammond, John, with Irving Townsend. *John Hammond On Record.* New York: Penguin Books, 1977.

Haralambos, Michael. *Soul Music: The Birth of a Sound in Black America.* New York: Da Capo Press, 1974.

Heilbut, Anthony. *The Gospel Sound: Good News and Bad Times.* New York: Limelight Editions, 1985.

Helander, Brock. *The Rock Who's Who.* New York: Schirmer Books, 1982.

Henderson, David. *Jimi Hendrix: Voodoo Child of the Aquarian Age.* New York: Doubleday & Co., 1978.

Herman, Gary. *Rock'N'Roll Babylon.* New York: Perigee Books, 1982.

Hirshey, Gerri. *Nowhere to Run: The Story of Soul Music.* New York: Times Books, 1984.

Holliday, Billie, with William Duffy. *Lady Sings the Blues.* New York: Penguin Books, 1956.

Hopkins, Jerry. *Hit & Run—The Jimi Hendrix Story.* New York: Perigee Books, 1983.

Humphries, Patrick, and Chris Hunt. *Springsteen: Blinded by the Light.* New York: Henry Holt & Co., 1985.

Johnson, Howard, and Jim Pines. *Reggae: Deep Roots Music.* n.p.: Proteus Books, 1982.

Jones, LeRoy. *Blues People.* New York: William Morrow Co., Inc. 1963.

Kooper, Al, with Ben Edmonds. *Backstage Passes.* Briarcliff Manor, N.Y.: Stein & Day, 1977.

Landau, Jon. *It's Too Late to Stop Now: A Rock & Roll Journal.* n.p.: Straight Arrow Books, 1972.

Lewisohn, Mark. *The Beatles Lives.* New York: Henry Holt & Co., 1986.

Lydon, Michael. *Rock Folk.* New York: Dell Books, 1968.

Macken, Bob, and others. *The Rock Music Source Book.* New York: Anchor Press, 1980.

Marcus, Greil. *Mystery Train (Images of America in Rock'N'Roll Music.* New York: E.P. Dutton, 1975.

Marcus, Greil. *Stranded (Rock & Roll for a Desert Island).* New York: Alfred A. Knopf Inc., 1979.

Marre, Jeremy, and Hannah Charlton. *Beats of the Heart.* New York: Pantheon Books, 1985.

Marsh, Dave. *Before I Get Old: The Story of the Who.* New York: St. Martin's Press, 1983.

Marsh, Dave. *The Book of Rock Lists.* New York: Dell/Rolling Stone Press, 1981.

Marsh, Dave. *Born to Run The Bruce Springsteen Story.* New York: Delilah, 1979.

Marsh, Dave. *The First Rock & Roll Confidential Report.* New York: Pantheon Books, 1985.

Marsh, Dave. *Fortunate Son: The Best of Dave Marsh.* New
    York: Random House, 1985.

Marsh, Dave, and John Swenson. *The New Rolling Stone
    Record Guide.* New York: Random House/Rolling Stone
    Press, 1979, rev. 1983.

Marsh, Dave, and others. *Rock Topicon.* Chicago:
    Contemporary Books Inc., 1984.

Martin, George, with Jeremy Hornsby. *All You Need Is Ears.*
    New York: St. Martin's Press, 1979.

McDonough, Jack. *San Francisco Rock 1965/1985: The
    Illustrated History of San Francisco Rock Music.* San
    Francisco: Chronicle Books, 1985.

Meltzer, Richard. *The Aesthetics of Rock.* New York: Da Capo
    Press, 1970.

Mendelssohn, John. *Kinks Kronikles.* New York: Quill, 1985.

Miller, Jim, ed. *The Rolling Stone Illustrated History of Rock and
    Roll.* New York: Random House/Rolling Stone Press, 1976.

Millers, Wilfrid. *A Darker Shade of Pale (A Backdrop to Bob
    Dylan).* New York: Oxford University Press, 1985.

Morse, David. *Motown.* New York: Collier, 1971.

Morthland, John. *The Best of Country Music.* New York:
    Doubleday/Dolphin, 1984.

Muirhead, Bert. *The Record Producers File: A Directory of Rock
    Album Producers 1962/1984.* New York: Blandford Press
    Ltd., 1984.

Muirhead, Bert. *Stiff: The Story of a Record Label.* New York:
    Blandford Press Ltd., 1983.

Murrells, Joseph, compiled by. *The Book of Golden Discs: The
    Records That Sold a Million.* n.p.: Barrie & Jenkins, 1974.

Murrells, Joseph. *Million Selling Records from the 1900's to the
    1980's: An Illustrated Directory.* New York: Arco Publishing
    Co., 1984.


Naha, Ed, compiled by. *Lillian Roxson's Rock Encyclopedia.* New
    York: Grosset & Dunlap, 1978.

Nite, Norm N. *Rock On (The Illustrated Encyclopedia of Rock &
    Roll—The Solid Gold Years, Volume I).* New York: Thomas
    Y. Crowell, 1974.

Nite, Norm N. *Rock On (The Illustrated Encyclopedia of Rock &
    Roll—The Modern Years, 1964-Present Volume II).* New
    York: Thomas Y. Crowell, 1978.

Nite, Norm N. *Rock On Volume III (The Illustrated Encyclopedia of Rock & Roll—The Video Revolution 1978-Present)*. New York: Harper & Row, 1985.

Noble, Peter L. *Future Pop: Music for the 80's*. New York: Delilah, 1983.

Norman, Philip. *The Road Goes On Forever*. New York: Simon & Schuster, 1982.

Norman, Philip. *Shout! The Beatles and Their Generation*. New York: Simon & Schuster, 1981.

Norman, Philip. *Sympathy for the Devil: The Rolling Stones Story*. New York: Linden Press/Simon & Schuster, 1984.


Palmer, Robert. *Deep Blues*. New York: Penguin Books, 1981.

Palmer, Tony. *All You Need Is Love: The Story of Popular Music*. New York: Penguin Books, 1977.

Pareles, John, and Patricia Romanowski. *The Rolling Stones Encyclopedia of Rock & Roll*. New York: Rolling Stone Press/Summit Books, 1983.

Pattison, Robert. *The Triumph of Vulgarity*. New York: Oxford University Press, 1967.

Peellaert, Guy, and Nick Cohn. *Rock Dreams*. n.p.: R&B, 1982.

Pickering, Stephen. *Bob Dylan Approximately*. New York: David McKay Co. Inc., 1975.

Pleasants, Henry. *The Great American Popular Singers*. New York: Simon & Schuster, Inc., 1974.

Pollock, Bruce, *When Rock Was Young*. New York: Holt, Rinehart & Winston, 1981.

Pollock, Bruce. *When the Music Mattered: Rock in the Sixties*. New York: Holt, Rinehart & Winston, 1983.

Porter, Cole. *The Complete Lyrics of Cole Porter*. New York: Vintage Books, 1984.


Raker, Muck. *Rockbottom*. n.p.: Proteus, 1981.

Reese, Krista. *Chuck Berry Mr. Rock'N'Roll*. n.p.: Proteus, 1982.

Reese, Krista. *Elvis Costello*. n.p.: Proteus, 1981.

Reese, Krista. *The Name of This Book Is Talking Heads*. n.p.: Proteus, 1982.

Reich, Charles, and Jann Wenner with Jerry Garcia and others. "Garcia: A Signpost to New Space." *Rolling Stone* interview. Straight Arrow Books, 1972.

Rinzler, Allan. *Bob Dylan: The Illustrated Record.* New York: Harmony Books, 1978.

Rivelli, Pauline, and Robert Levin, eds. *Giants of Rock Music.* New York: Da Capo Press, 1978.

Robbins, Ira A. *The Trouser Press Guide to New Wave Records.* New York: Charles Scribner's Sons, 1983.

Rockwell, John. *Sinatra: An American Classic.* New York: Random House/Rolling Stone Press, 1984.

Rogan, Johnny. *Van Morrison.* n.p.: Proteus, 1984.

Rolling Stone eds. *The Rolling Stone Interviews Volume 2.* New York: Warner Books, 1973.

Rolling Stone eds. *The Rolling Stone Interviews 1967-80.* New York: St. Martin's Press/Rolling Stone Press, 1981.

Rolling Stone eds. *The Rolling Stone Record Review.* New York: Pocket Books, 1971.

Rolling Stone eds. *The Rolling Stone Record Review Volume 2.* New York: Pocket Books, 1974.

Russell, Ethan A. *Dear Mr. Fantasy.* Boston: Houghton Mifflin Co., 1985.

Sanchez, Tony. *Up and Down with the Rolling Stones.* New York: William Morrow & Co., Inc., 1979.

Saporita, Jay. *Pourin' It All Out.* Secaucus, N.J.: Citadel Press, 1980.

Sarlin, Bob. *Turn It Up (I Can't Hear the Words).* New York: Simon & Schuster, 1973.

Scaduto, Anthony. *Bob Dylan An Intimate Biography.* New York: Grosset & Dunlap, Inc., 1971.

Scaduto, Tony. *Mick Jagger: Everybody's Lucifer.* New York: Berkley Medallion, 1974.

Sculatti, Gene, and Davin Seay. *San Francisco Nights: The Psychedelic Music Trip 1965-68.* New York: St. Martin's Press, 1985.

Shaffner, Nicholas. *The British Invasion.* New York: McGraw-Hill Inc., 1982.

Shannon, Bob, and John Javna. *Behind the Hits: Inside Stories of Classic Pop and Rock & Roll.* New York: Warner Books, 1986.

Shaw, Arnold. *Honkers and Shouters: The Golden Years of Rhythm & Blues.* New York: Macmillan Publishing Co., 1978.

Shaw, Arnold. *Dictionary of American Pop/Rock.* New York: Schirmer Books, 1982.

Shelton, Robert. *No Direction Home . . . The Life and Music of Bob Dylan.* New York: Beech Tree Books, 1986.

Shepard, Sam. *Rolling Thunder Log Book.* New York: Penguin, 1977.

Shore, Michael, with Dick Clark. *The History of American Bandstand.* New York: Ballantine Books, 1985.

Sklar, Rick. *Rocking America.* New York: St. Martin's Press, 1984.

Stallings, Penny. *Rock'N'Roll Confidential.* New York: Little, Brown & Co., 1984.

Stambler, Irwin. *Encyclopedia of Pop, Rock & Soul.* New York: St. Martin's Press, 1974.

Stambler, Irwin, and Grelun Landon. *The Encyclopedia of Folk, Country & Western Music.* Revised and expanded. New York: St. Martin's Press, 1984.

Street, John. *Rebel Rock.* New York: Basil Blackwell Inc., 1986.

Stokes, Geoffrey. *Starmaking Machinery (Inside the Business of Rock & Roll).* New York: Vintage Books, 1976.

Swenson, John. *Bill Haley: The Daddy of Rock and Roll.* New York: Stein & Day, 1982.


Tabler, John, and Stuart Grundy. *The Record Producers.* New York: St. Martin's Press, 1983.

Taylor, Derek. *It Was Twenty Years Ago Today (An Anniversary Celebration of 1967).* New York: Simon & Schuster, Inc., 1987.

Tobler, John. *The Buddy Holly Story.* n.p.: Beaufort Books, 1979.

Tobler, John, and Andrew Doe. *The Doors.* n.p.: Proteus Books, 1984.

Tosches, Nick. *Country.* New York: Charles Scribner's Sons, 1977, revised 1985.

Tosches, Nick. *Hellfire: The Jerry Lee Lewis Story.* New York: Dell Books, 1982.

Tosches, Nick. *Unsung Heroes of Rock'N'Roll.* New York: Charles Scribner's Sons, 1984.


Ulsan, Michael, and Bruce Solomon. *Dick Clark's The First 25 Years of Rock and Roll.* New York: Dell Books, 1981.


Various authors. *New Women in Rock.* New York: Putnam, 1982.

Waller, Don. *The Motown Story.* New York: Charles Scribner's Sons, 1985.

Ward, Ed. *Michael Bloomfield: The Rise and Fall of an American Guitar Hero.* Port Chester, N.Y.: Cherry Lane Books, 1983.

Ward, Ed, and others. *Rock of Ages: The Rolling Stone History of Rock & Roll.* New York: Rolling Stone Press/Summit Books, 1986.

Weinberg, Max, with Robert Santelli. *The Big Beat.* Chicago: Contemporary Books Inc., 1984.

Wenner, Jann. *Groupies and Other Girls.* New York: Bantam Books, 1970.

West, Red, and others, as told to Steve Dunleavy. *Elvis What Happened?* New York: Ballantine Books, 1977.

Whitburn, Joel. *The Billboard Book of Top 40 Hits 1955 to Present.* New York: Billboard Publications, Inc., 1983.

Whitburn, Joel. *The Billboard Book of Top 40 Hits.* New York: Billboard Publications, Inc., 1985.

Whitburn, Joel. *Billboard's Music Yearbook 1986.* n.p.: Record Research, Inc., 1987.

Whitburn, Joel. *Billboard's Top 2,000 1955-85.* n.p.: Record Research, Inc., 1985.

Whitburn, Joel. *Pop Memories.* n.p.: Record Research, Inc., 1986.

Whitburn, Joel. *Top Pop 1955-82.* n.p.: Record Research, Inc., 1983.

Whitburn, Joel. *Top Pop Albums 1955-88.* n.p.: Record Research, Inc., 1985.

Whitcomb, Ian. *After the Ball.* New York: Simon & Schuster, Inc., 1973.

Whitcomb, Ian. *Rock Odyssey: A Musician's Chronicle of the 60's.* New York: Dolphin Books, 1983.

White, Charles. *The Life and Times of Little Richard (The Quasar of Rock).* New York: Harmony Books, 1984.

White, Timothy. *Catch a Fire: The Life of Bob Marley.* New York: Holt, Rinehart & Winston, 1983.

White, Timothy. *Rock Stars.* New York: Stewart, Tabori & Chang, 1984.

Wilder, Alec. *American Popular Song . . . The Great Innovators 1900-50.* New York: Oxford University Press, 1972.

Williams, Allan, and William Marshall. *The Man Who Gave the Beatles Away.* New York: Ballantine Books, 1975.

Williams, Don. *Bob Dylan: The Man, The Music, The Message.*
New York: Fleming H. Revell Co., 1985.

Williams, Paul. *Outlaw Blues (A Book of Rock Music).* New
York: E.P. Dutton, 1969.

Woliver, Robbie. *Bringing It All Back Home (25 Years of
American Music at Folk City).* New York: Pantheon Books,
1986.

York, William, ed. *Who's Who in Rock Music.* New York:
Charles Scribner's Sons, 1982.

# INDEX

| | |
|---|---|
| **Morrison, Van** *(cont.)* | A Sense of Wonder, 138 |
| | T.B. Sheets, 56 |
| **Nelson, Rick** | The Best of Rick Nelson, 27 |
| **Neville Brothers, The** | Fiyo on the Bayou, 139 |
| **New Riders of the Purple Sage** | The Best Of, 100 |
| **Nylons, The** | Happy Together, 140 |
| | One Size Fits All, 139 |
| | Seamless, 140 |
| **Parker, Graham, and the Rumour** | Squeezing Out Sparks, 100 |
| **Parsons, Gram, and the Fallen Angels** | Featuring Emmylou Harris Live 1973, 100 |
| **Pentangle, The** | Basket of Light, 101 |
| **Perkins, Carl** | Dixie Fried, 27 |
| **Persuasions, The** | No Frills, 140 |
| **Petty, Tom, and the Heartbreakers** | Damn the Torpedos, 101 |
| | Hard Promises, 140 |
| **Pickett, Wilson** | Greatest Hits, 56 |
| **Pink Floyd** | Dark Side of the Moon, 101 |
| | The Final Cut, 140 |
| | A Momentary Lapse of Reason, 141 |
| | The Piper at the Gates of Dawn, 57 |
| | The Wall, 101 |
| **Pitney, Gene** | Anthology (1961-1968), 57 |
| **Platters, The** | Greatest Hits, 28 |
| **Pogues, The** | Rum, Sodomy and the Lash, 141 |
| **Pointer Sisters, The** | Breakout, 141 |
| **Police, The** | Synchronicity, 141 |
| **Presley, Elvis** | Elvis, 28 |
| | Elvis Golden Records, 28 |
| | Elvis Presley, 28 |
| | The Memphis Record, 57 |
| | Reconsider Baby, 28 |
| | The Sun Sessions CD, 28 |